THE NORTHERN RAILROADS
IN THE CIVIL WAR, 1861-1865

THE NORTHERN RAILROADS
IN THE CIVIL WAR
1861–1865

Thomas Weber

INDIANA UNIVERSITY PRESS

Bloomington and Indianapolis

This book is a publication of

Indiana University Press
601 North Morton Street
Bloomington, IN 47404-3797 USA

http://www.indiana.edu/~iupress

Telephone orders 800-842-6796
Fax orders 812-855-7931
Orders by e-mail iuporder@indiana.edu

Originally published in 1952 by King's Crown Press, New York.
Reprinted in 1970 by Greenwood Press, Westport, Connecticut.
First reprinted by Indiana University Press in 1999. This
edition was photo-offset from the Greenwood Press edition.

The paper used in this publication meets the minimum
requirements of American National Standard for Information
Sciences—Permanence of Paper for Printed Library
Materials, ANSI Z39.48-1984.

Manufactured in the United States of America

Cataloging information is available from the Library of Congress.

ISBN 0-253-33549-3 (cl : alk. paper). — ISBN 0-253-21321-5
(pa : alk. paper)

1 2 3 4 5 04 03 02 01 00 99

The Highways of a people are one of the surest indices of their condition and character. Without them there can be neither commerce nor wealth; neither intelligence nor social order.

Henry V. Poor, *Railroad Manual of the United States*

FOREWORD

THE MANY GENERAL RAILROAD HISTORIES do not touch to any great extent on the Civil War; and only a few histories dealing with individual lines treat this period. This work is not, however, an attempt to write a general history of railroad transportation during this time of national crisis. Several events important for railroad historians, such as the founding in 1863 of the Brotherhood of Locomotive Engineers, have been omitted. Rather this book tries to establish a relationship between the railroads and the war, to note how the war affected railroad activities, and how in turn railroad experience affected the events of the war. It is therefore one phase of railroad history. Since the primary interest is railroads, not the Civil War itself, battles fought over railroad lines and junction points have also been omitted, except as they affected the function of the railroad in providing supplies and transportation of troops and other personnel in the various theaters of war. In general, it will be found that the period from 1861 to 1865 was an important one for the railroads, not because of any great expansion, but rather because of the general consolidation of gains made in the fifties, the experimenting with new and better methods of operation, the finding of new methods of economizing, and the growth in technical ability which enabled the railroads to handle the heavy wartime traffic. These factors once and for all established the railroads as an integral part of the American economy. On the other side, it will be found that the railroads, in their function of furnishing supplies and troops to the various theaters of war, materially affected the character of the war itself, and provided for the North a necessary element of victory.

ACKNOWLEDGMENTS

I OWE A DEBT OF GRATITUDE to Professor Allan Nevins, of Columbia University, whose helpful and stimulating criticism at various stages of this work has been a great encouragement in its completion. Miss Elizabeth O. Cullen kindly assisted in making available the library facilities of the Bureau of Railway Economics, Association of American Railroads, Washington, D. C. I would like to thank the Society of American Military Engineers for permission to quote from *The Military Engineer* the story on page 204, and other material on pages 135 and 156.

T. W.

CONTENTS

THE NORTHERN RAILROADS
IN THE CIVIL WAR, 1861-1865

Chapter I

THE NORTHERN RAILROADS AT
THE OUTBREAK OF THE CIVIL WAR

So far as breaking up the Union by force of arms was concerned, the attempt came fully a decade too late. It is not impossible that it might have succeeded in 1850, when over 40% of the nation's inhabitants formed a truly "solid South" and the opposition 60% was scattered from Skowhegan, Maine, to the Mississippi, with no completed means of transportation at either end. By 1860 the gaps in the north were bridged with steel.

Slason Thompson, *Short History of American Railways*

RAILROAD COMMERCE as we know it was really a creation of the 1850s. Previous to 1850 the only rail connection between the Eastern seaboard and the Great Lakes was the series of five short lines, not physically connected, which later were organized into the New York Central Railroad, and the only important railroad in the trans-Allegheny region was a line from Sandusky to Cincinnati.[1] The lines through New York state had to meet the competition of the Erie Canal, not an easy thing to do at first.

During the 1850s railroad construction underwent a tremendous advance. Lines were completed from Boston to Ogdensburg on Lake Ontario by way of Rouses Point; the New York and Erie touched Lake Erie at Dunkirk in 1851; the Pennsylvania Railroad was opened to Pittsburgh; and the Baltimore and Ohio to Wheeling. The Michigan Central and the Michigan Southern fought for entry into Chicago, and the Pittsburgh, Ft. Wayne, and Chicago provided an important route which was later to become part of the Pennsylvania Railroad. A similar but slower development took place in the South, as rails connected Georgia with the Tennessee River, and the Mississippi was touched at Memphis. By 1860 railroads radiating from Lake Erie and Lake Michigan tapped the Mississippi at ten points and the Ohio at eight.[2] The chief North-South routes were the Illinois Central from Dunleith and Chicago to Cairo, the Louisville, New Albany, and Chicago (now the Monon) in Indiana, the Cleveland, Columbus, and Cincinnati, and the Cleveland and Pittsburgh in Ohio. In the East it was possible, though with many changes and stopovers, to travel by rail from Boston to Washington.[3]

The Chicago and Rock Island Railroad had bridged the Father of Waters and connected with the Mississippi and Missouri Railroad to Des Moines.[4] The Chicago, Burlington, and Quincy connected at Burlington with the Burlington and Missouri to Ottumwa, Iowa, and at Quincy with the Hannibal and St. Joseph.[5] The Ohio and Mississippi Railroad did business with the Pacific Railroad of Missouri, which looked forward to a connection with the Kansas branch of the Union Pacific.[6] Of the approximately 30,000 miles of railroad in the United States in 1860, about 22,000 had been built in the last decade; of that 22,000 almost 15,000 was constructed in the North with Ohio, Indiana, and Illinois leading all other states.[7] Though numerous railroad connections existed between the Great Lakes and the seaboard, there was no connection between North-South railroads except by steamboat on the Ohio or ferry across the Potomac to Alexandria.[8]

By 1860, railroads were beginning to supplant canals, particularly in the carriage of through freight from Chicago and the West to tidewater ports along the Atlantic. In 1861, New York state railroads carried 3,390,850 tons, canals 2,980,144 tons; in Pennsylvania, railroads carried 6,921,354 tons, canals

5,349,513 tons.[9] From Cairo, Ill., it cost less to send goods via the Ohio River and the Pennsylvania Railroad to Philadelphia than to use the old route via the Great Lakes from Chicago to Buffalo—and Philadelphia was at tide water.[10] Likewise, the route directly east was cheaper and quicker than the route via the Mississippi to New Orleans. Cotton, shipped from Memphis to Cincinnati by water, thence by rail through Buffalo to Boston, cost $4.50 per bale for the entire journey. This was not only a great deal cheaper than the New Orleans route, but about thirty days quicker.[11]

In 1860 the railroads began to participate on a large scale in the carriage of Western grain to tidewater ports, where it was loaded on ships bound for Europe.[12] Besides participating in the Western grain trade, the railroads were developing an important trade in coal and in oil. The Philadelphia and Reading Railroad, the Delaware, Lackawanna, and Western, and the Lehigh Valley together shipped 3,000,000 tons of coal in 1861.[13] Oil was soon to become a major business for the Atlantic and Great Western Railway and the Philadelphia and Erie Railroad.

By 1860 the Northern railroads represented an investment of about $895,000,000.[14] Roads earning a gross income of $1,000,000 or more (the present definition of a Class I railroad) at the beginning of the war included such important lines as the Western Railroad of Massachusetts; the Philadelphia, Wilmington, and Baltimore Railroad; the Northern Central; the New Jersey Railroad; the Central Railroad of New Jersey; the Philadelphia and Reading; the Pennsylvania Railroad; the New York and Erie; the New York Central; the Baltimore and Ohio; the Illinois Central; the Little Miami and Columbus and Xenia Railroad; the Louisville, New Albany, and Chicago Railroad; the Cleveland and Toledo Railroad; the Cleveland, Painesville, and Ashtabula Railroad; the Cleveland and Pittsburgh

Railroad; the Michigan Southern and Northen Indiana Railroad; the Michigan Central Railroad; the Pittsburgh, Ft. Wayne, and Chicago Railroad; the Milwaukee and Prairie du Chien Railway; the Chicago and Rock Island Railroad; and the Chicago, Burlington, and Quincy Railroad. During the course of the war years this roll call was expanded to include the Boston and Maine Railroad, the Boston and Worcester, the Atlantic and Great Western, the Lehigh Valley, and the Chicago and North Western.[15]

A good part of railroad capital was invested in track and roadbed. Railroads were almost universally of single track. By 1861, the original strap rail, or U-rail as it was called, had been discarded by most Class I roads for T-rail, varying somewhat in weight on different roads. The Boston and Worcester Railroad in 1861 had 59, 60, 63, and 66-pound rail; during the course of the war some of this was taken up and 80-pound rail was substituted.[16] The Pennsylvania Railroad used 67-pound rail, substituting some 83-pound rail during the war.[17] An 1862 law in New York state required at least 50-pound rail for reasons of safety.[18] The ties were usually unseasoned, therefore necessitating frequent changes because of rapid disintegration from exposure to the weather.[19] A few progressive railroads were trying to find means of lengthening the life of ties, and hence cut down on maintenance cost. The Michigan Central found that with a cyanizing treatment the life of the tie could be prolonged to eight years.[20] The Philadelphia, Wilmington, and Baltimore Railroad used a process known as "burnetizing," or injecting forcibly into ties zinc chloride diluted with water, which was supposed to double the life of a tie.[21] Generally speaking, the kind of rails, ties, and ballast in use varied widely from one railroad to another. Rail iron was of poor grade, ties were unseasoned, and ballast was poorly laid.[22] The railroads could hardly be said to be fit for the task they were about to attempt in time of war.

Nor was all track the standard width of 4 feet, 8½ inches. Though this was the most commonly used, the gauge varied enough to present difficulty in accommodating the growing amount of through freight and passenger traffic. New England roads generally used the 4-foot, 8½-inch gauge.[23] Of the four routes between the trans-Allegheny region and the Atlantic seaboard, the Baltimore and Ohio and the Pennsylvania Railroads used 4 feet, 8½ inches, though the latter's Pittsburgh connection to Chicago was of 4 feet, 10 inches, hence necessitating a change of cars at Pittsburgh.[24] During the war the New York Central shifted to the 4-foot, 8½-inch gauge; the Erie stuck to its broad 6-foot gauge throughout.[25] The much used route between New York and Washington came in for a great deal of criticism from Congress and from newspapers during the war years, and the route was handicapped from the beginning in that the New Jersey portion was 4 feet, 10 inches wide while that south of Philadelphia was 4 feet, 8½ inches.[26] Other important Eastern roads such as the Philadelphia and Reading, Central Railroad of New Jersey, Lehigh Valley, and Northern Central were of the common variety.[27] In the West, the main lines centering in Chicago, such as the Chicago, Burlington, and Quincy, Chicago and North Western, Chicago and Rock Island, Illinois Central, Michigan Central, and Michigan Southern and Northern Indiana were all 4 feet, 8½ inches,[28] but beyond that there was a great deal of variation. Ohio railroads seemed to favor 4 feet, 10 inches, while 5 feet, 6 inches was used in Canada and by the Pacific Railroad of Missouri.[29] In the South 5 feet was favored, a fact which was to hamper somewhat the operations of the United States Military Railroads.[30]

To some extent the differences in gauge were overcome by using adjustable axles which enabled cars to run on roads of slightly different gauge. Such "compromise cars" ran between Buffalo and Chicago.[31] These expedients were of course dangerous, and accounted for many accidents. To accommodate wide differences in gauge, a third rail was sometimes laid. The 4-foot, 10-inch Cincinnati, Hamilton, and Dayton Railroad laid a third rail in order to do interchange business with the Atlantic and Great Western and to form its link with the Ohio and Mississippi Railroad. A third expedient was to make wheel treads extra broad.[32] Cars equipped with these wheels were organized into "fast freight lines" to handle interchange freight traffic.[33] The gradual movement toward the establishment of a standard gauge, the only really effective remedy for the proper accommodation of through traffic, had been opposed by cities which saw advantages to their own business if passengers and freight had to change cars and stations; but the war period, with its high percentage of through traffic, was to accelerate the change toward standardization.[34]

As an additional handicap to through traffic, few railroads had adequate terminal facilities to handle an expanding business. Most large cities lacked a union station. In Baltimore, for instance, each of the three railroads serving the city—the Northern Central, the Philadelphia, Wilmington, and Baltimore, and the Baltimore and Ohio—had its own separate depot, and there was no rail connection between depots.[35] Philadelphia had four main depots—those of the Pennsylvania Railroad, Philadelphia and Reading, Philadelphia, Wilmington, and Baltimore, and Philadelphia and Trenton—and three minor ones.[36] One of the few union stations in operation in 1861 was that at Toledo, used by six railroads.[37] The Jersey City ferry depot, operated by the New Jersey Railroad and Transportation Company, accommodated 112 trains daily, belonging to six different railroads.[38]

Loading facilities and interchange yards varied considerably in size and capacity. The *American Railroad Journal* of September 7, 1861, praised the large and efficient grain storage facilities of the Toledo and Wabash Railroad at Toledo, but the mounting pressure of eastward grain movements quickly swamped all available storage space. At one time 1,400 cars waiting to be unloaded at Toledo were simply used as warehouses to supplement normal capacity.[39] In the West, the Milwaukee and Prairie du Chien Railway had no capacity to handle peak grain shipments and the Chicago, Burlington, and Quincy, with an 800,000-bushel grain elevator in 1861, found it necessary to purchase additional land in 1862 along the south branch of the Chicago River for a freight house and transfer shed. At eastern tidewater the Pennsylvania Railroad was obliged to build a 475,000-bushel grain elevator in connection with its railroad extension to the Delaware River for foreign shipments.[40] The New York Central had facilities at Buffalo which could load and dispatch 250 to 300 cars daily, amounting to 25,000 to 30,000 barrels of flour.[41]

Likewise, there was considerable variation in necessary buildings such as machine shops and engine houses. The Michigan Southern and Northern Indiana Railroad was generally considered to be well equipped in this respect.[42] On the other hand, roads bearing the brunt of the Civil War traffic very soon found their facilities inadequate. In 1862 the Philadelphia, Wilmington, and Baltimore was already citing the need for a new freight house at Philadelphia and a new machine shop at Wilmington.[43] Similarly, the Northern Central pointed to the need for new and larger shops and engine houses.[44]

Variations among the railroads were not limited to track

gauge and terminal facilities. Rolling stock and motive power, depending on track gauge for its size, was not standardized at all. The most commonly used type of engine was that with two leading wheels and two drivers on each side. This 4-4-0 wheel arrangement was called the American type. Other distinguishing marks were a tall stack, more often a balloon type than a straight one, a large cowcatcher, an oversize decorative headlight, a square cab, and a proportionally small boiler.[45] Some locomotives had three leading wheels and only one driver.[46] The first of the Mogul type of 2-6-0 wheel arrangement was built in 1863 for the New Jersey Railroad.[47] Weights and dimensions of locomotives varied considerably, even on one railroad. A typical locomotive weighed between 20 and 30 tons, the diameter of the driving wheels usually ranging from $4\frac{1}{2}$ to $5\frac{1}{2}$ feet.[48] The fuel most commonly used to fire the engines was wood, though a number of railroads, such as the Philadelphia, Wilmington, and Baltimore, the Pennsylvania, the Central of New Jersey, and the Illinois Central, were experimenting with the use of coal, a development which the Civil War was greatly to accelerate.[49] Many locomotives could use either fuel interchangeably. Generally speaking, a ton of coal and a cord of wood were about equivalent in the distance they would drive a locomotive.[50] Whatever they burned usually produced a great deal of smoke, most of which descended on the passengers. A traveler on the Philadelphia, Wilmington, and Baltimore Railroad reported that between Havre de Grace and Philadelphia, "passengers were almost suffocated by smoke."[51]

Passenger cars and freight cars used similar four-wheel trucks (some of the lighter cars two-wheel trucks), except that those for passenger cars were equipped with springs.[52] Passenger cars, usually made of wood, were characterized by open vestibules at either end, making it impossible to go from one car to another except at the risk of one's life. They usually seated from 50 to 60 passengers on seats which were straight-backed, austere, and lacking in any ornamentation.[53] Raised roofs, improved fan ventilation, and gas illumination replacing greasy and smoky oil lamps were innovations being introduced by the more progressive railroads.[54] The Cleveland and Toledo and the Cleveland and Erie were enclosing the ends of their cars to reduce dust.[55] The Chicago and North Western heated cars by small stoves at either end, with hot air being passed under the car and through registers into the interior.[56] This system was usually more effective than placing the stove in the center of the car, which resulted in an uneven distribution of heat.[57] New passenger cars on the Michigan Southern and Northern Indiana Railroad were 52 feet long, 10 feet wide, and 10 feet high, two feet higher than usual. Ventilators were placed in alternation with stained glass windows.[58] Link and pin couplers were used everywhere, and since the air brake was unknown, the locomotive had to carry the entire burden of braking a train and bringing it to a halt.[59] Experiments were being made on iron passenger cars. One constructed for the Hackensack and New York Railroad had walls and roof of sheet iron, and was lined with felt.[60] Another such car, three tons lighter than a wooden coach, was running on the Chicago and St. Louis Railroad in 1865.[61] Dining cars were unknown, but a few railroads had sleeping cars. In 1862, the Michigan Central had nine, of which six were first class.[62] During the war, sleeping accommodations were built into ordinary day coaches to meet the demand.[63] Sleeping cars operated from New York to Boston, New York and Philadelphia to Pittsburgh, Cleveland to Chicago, and from Chicago to Madison, Prairie du Chien, and St. Paul.[64] These cars were not exactly models of luxury. Dirty bed clothing, ill-smelling mattresses, and bad ventilation seem to have been characteristic.[65]

Most railroads had a great many more freight cars than

passenger cars, and each railroad classified them differently so that detailed comparisons are difficult. Box cars, stock cars, coal cars, merchandise cars, flat cars, gravel cars, and gondolas were listed in the annual reports. Confusion in terminology sometimes resulted in embarrassment when the government requisitioned cars from the companies.[66] Most of these cars were wooden, though the New York Central was constructing iron freight cars at its West Albany shops.[67] Coal trains, then as now, were the heaviest trains the railroads hauled, those on the Philadelphia and Reading weighing an average of 754 tons.[68] On the other hand, freight trains in New York state, where not much coal was carried, averaged only 83 tons in 1861.[69] More usual, an average New York and New Haven freight train of 17 cars weighed 225 tons.[70] The average tonnage per car usually ranged between 5 and 10 tons.[71] Freight trains, usually less than 20 cars in length, ran at an average speed of 11 to 20 miles per hour. Passenger trains of 5 to 10 cars averaged about 30 to 33 miles per hour for express, 25 miles per hour for locals.[72]

It would be difficult to determine the maximum capacity of the railroads in handling either troops or general freight. Capacity would be determined not by rolling stock alone, but also by availability of rolling stock (much of it was constantly in repair shops), condition of track, ruling grades, and capacity of terminal facilities. The New Jersey Railroad claimed it could handle a maximum of 10,000 men daily, or up to 50,000 daily in cooperation with other roads.[73] Samuel Felton said the Philadelphia, Wilmington, and Baltimore Railroad had a "capacity" of 2,000 cars, but the road's total rolling stock was 32 locomotives and 674 cars.[74] The three main East-West trunk lines (not including the Baltimore and Ohio which was out of operation during much of the time) had a combined rolling stock in 1861 of over 650 locomotives, over 400 passenger cars, and about 8,700 freight cars of various types.[75] According to the *American Railway Review*, February 14, 1861, this rolling stock plus the Erie Canal would have been almost enough to haul the entire cotton crop to the Eastern seaboard.

The long distance traveler, then as now, had at his disposal a choice of routes. From New York to Chicago, one could go by way of the Hudson River Railroad to Albany, the New York Central to Suspension Bridge (Niagara Falls), the Great Western of Canada to Detroit, and the Michigan Central to Chicago. Two trains daily ran over this route, taking between 37 and 39 hours.[76] A second route ran via the Central Railroad of New Jersey to Harrisburg, the Pennsylvania Railroad to Pittsburgh, and the Pittsburgh, Ft. Wayne, and Chicago beyond. Third, travelers could go via the Erie Railroad to Buffalo, the Lake Shore Railroad to Toledo, and the Michigan Southern and Northern Indiana Railroad to Chicago. These routes both required about 36 hours.[77]

One reached St. Louis from the East via the Ohio and Mississippi Railroad from Cincinnati, a 340-mile line which one railroad man called "one of the pleasantest Roads in the Western country."[78] Other routes to St. Louis were the Bellefontaine Railroad via Indianapolis and Terre Haute, a combination of lines via Pittsburgh, Galion, and Indianapolis, and the long way around via Chicago.[79] Other typical routes and times were: Chicago to St. Louis via the Chicago and St. Louis Railroad, 13 hours; Chicago to Cincinnati via Logansport, 12 hours; and New York to Washington, 11 to 12 hours.[80]

In general, long distance travel was a minor business for the railroads. Most roads were primarily local in character, acting as feeders to cities rather than as connecting links between them.[81] Keen rivalry existed between cities for commercial supremacy. Building more railroads was a good way for one city to assert its superiority over its neighbors.[82] The increasing urban population of the Middle West dramatized this commercial rivalry. In the sixties, Cleveland, Toledo, and Indianapolis each more than doubled its population, and Chicago almost tripled in size.[83] One result of these conditions was little interchange of traffic and wide diversity in construction of roadbed and equipment.[84] The local character of the railroads was emphasized by the fact that each railroad scheduled its. trains according to the clock in its principal depot, a practice valid for short hauls, but chaotic with the growth of through traffic.[85]

By 1861, the railroads were playing an important economic role in local areas serving large cities. The long distance routes of travel created in the 1850s between the Middle West and the East were only just beginning to be developed. It was significant that such physical connections existed. They had first been used on a large scale in 1860 in the transportation of Western grain to the Eastern seaboard. The war, with its unprecedented demands on the railroads for transportation of personnel and equipment over long distances, was to emphasize this still largely potential aspect of railroading, rather than its already developed local activities. By so doing, the war was to accelerate the transformation of railroads into enterprises national in scope, and just at the very time when the railroad itself was helping to bind together the interests of the East and Middle West.

Chapter II

RAILROAD EXPANSION
DURING THE WAR

The Pacific railroad . . . is an overwhelming military necessity.
Congressional Globe, 37th Cong., 2d Sess., Part 2,
April 19, 1862 (Representative Sargent of California)

THE WAR PERIOD, as we shall demonstrate, brought many
changes in railroading. Contrary to practice in the preceding
decade, energies were now turned less to expansion, than to
better methods of operating existing facilities. But the sixties
did not witness a complete cessation of building. In 1860
Northern railroads had a mileage of 21,276;[1] in 1865, the
figure was 25,372, over 4,000 miles more.[2]

Perhaps the most ambitious private project undertaken during the war years was the building of the 6-foot gauge Atlantic
and Great Western Railway, to form a connecting link between
the Ohio and Mississippi Railroad and the Erie Railroad, and,
unforeseen by the founders, destined to do a tremendous business
in coal, oil, and iron.[3] Three separate companies had been
formed before the war, the Atlantic and Great Western in Ohio
in 1851, another company in Pennsylvania in 1857, and one in
New York in 1859.[4] Work begun in the early fifties was suspended during the pre-war depression. When Henry Doolittle,
the first backer of the project, died, he was succeeded in March,
1861 by James McHenry, a wealthy Pennsylvanian living in
London,[5] who managed the financial part of the enterprise, and
T. W. Kennard, who served as engineer-in-chief. Construction
was begun in earnest in May, 1860. Starting from Salamanca,

N. Y., where a connection with the New York and Erie could be made, Jamestown was reached in September, and by May, 1861, the road was open 60 miles to Corry, Pa.[6] The uncertainty of acquiring labor and materials under war conditions forced suspension of construction on May 27, 1861.[7] In September, Kennard, Henry A. Kent, and William Reynolds went to Europe to seek capital with which to resume construction.[8] McHenry entered into correspondence with M. de Salamanca, a Madrid capitalist, who responded favorably and brought along with him the Duke de Rianzares, husband of the Dowager Queen of Spain.[9] English backers included Sir Samuel Morton Peto, chairman of the London Board of Control of the Atlantic and Great Western, Edward Betts, and Hayward, Kennards & Co. of London.[10] Having tapped these new sources of capital, McHenry proceeded to send 5,000 laborers from England to work on the railroad under Kennard.[11] Though the opinion was expressed that the projected line would get no farther than Akron,[12] McHenry and Kennard expected to complete construction through to Dayton, Ohio, and a connection there with the Ohio River valley. Resuming construction in the spring of 1862, the railroad reached Meadville, Pa., on November 10, and Warren, Ohio, on January 1, 1863.[13] At Corry, the line connected with the Oil Creek Railroad to Titusville, tapping the rich oil region of Pennsylvania. Between the termini of the two railroads, iron pipe was laid to carry petroleum from one road to the other.[14] Akron was reached January 12, 1863, nine months and 140 miles from Corry.[15] The year 1863 was to be a memorable one in Atlantic and Great Western history. The road was already doing a heavy local business even before its through connections were established.[16] In its first full year of operation, it was already a Class I road, carrying 216,000 passengers, and hauling 469,000 tons of freight.[17] This freight haulage included 533,487 barrels of petroleum, most of it east-bound, and the line was already complaining that its Eastern connection could not handle all the business which the new line offered.[18] The connection to Cleveland, leased in October, 1863, and joining the main line at Leavittsburg, brought more inter-change business from that prosperous lake port.[19] The line to Cleveland from Youngstown was known as the Mahoning Division, and it ran through an excellent coal region. The 1863 report of the railroad said that with adequate rolling stock the railroad could supply 1,700 tons of coal a day. The value and extent of this traffic was limited only by the means of transpor-tation, but a profitable and increasing traffic was certain for generations.[20] McHenry himself advanced $300,000 for improv-ing and equipping this division.[21]

Gradually the line kept building westward, crossing the Pitts-burg, Ft. Wayne, and Chicago at Mansfield, and on the last day of the year reaching Galion on the Bellefontaine Railroad.[22] Originally, the railroad expected to reach Dayton before the win-ter of 1863-64 set in.[23] But progress was delayed by the un-certainties of importing iron rail from England, bad weather, and a strike. In April, 1864, only one and a half miles of track were being laid daily.[24] Finally, on June 21, 1864, Dayton was reached. Kennard was present to drive the last spike connecting the Atlantic and Great Western with the Cincinnati, Hamilton, and Dayton Railroad, which had meanwhile laid an extra rail outside its normal 4-foot, 10-inch gauge to accommodate the 6-foot cars of the Atlantic and Great Western.[25] The first through train from New York to St. Louis via the Erie, Atlantic and Great Western, the Cincinnati, Hamilton, and Dayton, and the Ohio and Mississippi Railroad arrived at St. Louis August 26, 1864, with a trainload of officials who had left New York 44 hours earlier.[26]

The completed road was almost too prosperous. The oil trade alone accounted for all its rolling stock, and left begging a potential trade in coal and livestock.[27] This intensive trade, with heavy trains and high speeds, prompted the *United States Railroad and Mining Register* to forecast an early depreciation of the light 56-pound rail and insubstantial ballast with which the road was constructed.[28]

Laying the track was only part of the work of building this railroad. Permanent stations were erected at Salamanca, Meadville, and Mill Village, and railroad shops were set up in Meadville and Franklin Mills.[29] In 1863 the line had a rolling stock of 74 locomotives, 19 passenger cars, 14 baggage and mail cars, and 1,370 freight cars. The wartime difficulty in contracting for engines and cars forced the railroad to lease the Jersey City Locomotive Works to build 100 engines by the close of 1864.[30] Also, the Railway Car Works of Ramapo were leased and it was hoped that four freight cars plus some passenger cars could be turned out daily.[31] Outside contracts were let for 800 more freight cars.

The Western connection proved to be something of an anticlimax. It did no good to expect business from Cincinnati or Indianapolis if the rolling stock was all engaged in carrying oil and coal on the Eastern districts of the line. The second annual report showed that the gross earnings for the first six months of 1864 were $50,000 more than the earnings of the entire year 1863. Even so, "a large amount of business has been rejected for want of sufficient equipment to do it."[32] Even with the leases of the locomotive and car works, the line found in July, 1864, that there was more rolling stock under contract than actually on the road.[33]

In view of this record, it was hardly any wonder that the backers of the Atlantic and Great Western were so optimistic about their line. But others pointed out possible difficulties, especially in the West. Several rival East-West routes were already well established. The broad gauge connection at Dayton was not so advantageous as it might have been, because through passengers from the Ohio and Mississippi had to change cars at Cincinnati.[34] Interchange traffic in Ohio seemed to be something for the future to decide. Cleveland was at this time not so active a lake port as Toledo or Buffalo; the hostile Pittsburgh, Ft. Wayne, and Chicago offered no interchange at Mansfield; and at Dayton, the Cincinnati, Hamilton, and Dayton already had an outlet via the Cincinnati, Dayton, and Toledo, the Lake Shore Railroad, and the New York Central.[35] The 388-mile Atlantic and Great Western Railway was a monument to the energy of Kennard and the faith of McHenry in pouring more and more money into the enterprise. Certainly, as the directors conceived it, the whole project might easily have been a colossal failure, because the great business and large profits of the Atlantic and Great Western came from the oil fields of Pennsylvania and the coal fields of Ohio, neither of which had been envisioned in the original plans.

This oil and coal region was tapped by another railroad during the Civil War period, the Philadelphia and Erie. This line began at Sunbury where it joined the Northern Central Railroad, and continued in a westerly direction toward Erie, Pa. In 1860 and 1861 the road was already doing a heavy oil business, carrying in the latter year 134,927 barrels of oil, a 600 per cent increase over its 1860 business.[36] This business, on a still uncompleted road, prompted the *American Railroad Journal* to predict an annual trade of 400,000 barrels when the road was completed, plus 100,000 tons of bituminous and anthracite coal.[37]

The war brought a large passenger trade to the Philadelphia

and Erie. In 1861 the line had a heavy interchange traffic in troops with the Northern Central, and in 1862 the Philadelphia and Erie delivered 15,829 troops to the Northern Central at Sunbury, more than any other railroad.[38] Heavy trade was not, however, confined to passenger traffic. The two railroads entered into an agreement in 1862 to furnish jointly 200 house cars, 200 gondolas, and 200 stock cars to take care of this interchange freight traffic.[39] The Philadelphia and Erie was leased by the Pennsylvania Railroad February 1, 1862,[40] and since there was a close tie between the Northern Central and the Pennsylvania, a through route was created from the new road to Philadelphia via Sunbury, Williamsport, and Harrisburg. By early 1863, only 47 miles were completed, but the line boasted a rolling stock of 30 locomotives and 549 freight cars, and was carrying 378,000 tons of freight, and 362,500 passengers.[41]

It was first expected that the line would be finished to Erie by November 1, 1863, then by January 1, 1864, but scarcity of labor postponed completion until July 2, 1864.[42] The first through train ran from Williamsport to Erie on August 13, 1864, and regular service began October 17 from Philadelphia.[43] When the Pennsylvania Railroad leased the road it transferred 50 cars to the line, and in 1864 put over $1,000,000 in earnings into the road, transferring 19 locomotives, and 400 new cars.[44] But even though the line grossed over $1,000,000 in 1864, it experienced a net loss, chiefly because of inadequate equipment and the lack of a through connection until late in the year.[45] In the last year of the war, the earnings almost doubled, but the expenses went up even more, the road showing a net loss of over $270,000, in spite of the fact that business was nearly twice the original estimate.[46]

Thus in traffic the Philadelphia and Erie Railroad had an experience somewhat similar to that of the Atlantic and Great

Western. Financially, the continued losses of the former line could easily be absorbed by the Pennsylvania Railroad, thus overcoming the chief disadvantage of this road. The city of Philadelphia, however, was to find its rail connections with Columbus, Cincinnati, and Chicago more profitable than the line to Erie.[47]

New construction was not confined to the eastern part of the country. In the spring of 1864 the Chicago Great Eastern Railroad was rapidly building to La Crosse, Ind., and a connection with the Cincinnati and Chicago Air Line, the latter running to Richmond, Ind., where the Little Miami Railroad afforded a connection to Columbus. At the latter city, one route led via the Central Ohio Railroad to Bellaire and the Baltimore and Ohio, and another via the Pittsburgh and Steubenville Railroad to the Pennsylvania.[48] Thus another route would be opened between the Northwest with its agricultural produce and the Atlantic cities with their access to large markets. With the grain trade booming as it was, it would have been strange if there had been no new construction in this area. The expected opening of the railroad in the fall of 1864 was delayed until March, 1865. The Chicago Great Eastern then combined with the Cincinnati and Chicago Air Line, opening a new direct route from Chicago to Richmond, Ind.[49]

Likewise in the West, the war years found the Chicago and North Western Railway building westward to Fulton on the Mississippi, and in the Lake Superior Region organizing the Peninsula Railroad from Escanaba to Marquette, Mich., giving the road access to valuable iron ore deposits.[50] In the East, the Raritan and Delaware Bay Railroad was offering competition to the Camden and Amboy monopoly.[51] Plans were also made to complete a railroad link which would connect several of the

East-West lines in Connecticut and Massachusetts to the Erie Railroad on the Hudson. Under the name of the Boston, Hartford, and Erie Railway, organized in 1863, this proposed line found the obstacles of high prices and scarce labor too great to overcome.[52]

Finally, the Civil War gave impetus to the project of a railroad between the Missouri River and the Pacific Ocean. Though very little construction of the Union Pacific Railroad actually took place before 1865, nevertheless the war, by stressing the necesity of binding the state of California to the Union, added the argument of military defense in favor of the project. The argument, however, was not new in the sixties. In 1851, the year after California became a state, Matthew Maury of the Navy Department had recommended the construction of a Pacific Railroad as a defense measure for California.[53] The reopening of the question of slavery in territories by Stephen Douglas and the resulting Kansas-Nebraska Act of 1854 were partially motivated by the possibility of rail communication with the Far West.[54] Both political platforms of 1856 favored a Pacific Railroad and in 1857 President Buchanan supported the idea as a method of holding the Pacific coast to the Union.[55] The arguments for Union were strong in the 36th Congress, and, under the leadership of Samuel R. Curtis of Iowa, the House of Representatives passed a Pacific Railroad bill in December, 1860, but though Lincoln favored it, the bill never passed the Senate.[56] In the second session of the 36th Congress many references were made to the military importance of the proposed railroad. Representative Polk of Missouri thought that one of the great objects of the bill was to facilitate the transportation of troops, supplies, and munitions of war.[57] Representative Foot of Vermont said that a rail connection between the Atlantic and Pacific coasts was demanded "by the interests of commerce, by the necessitites of our postal intercommunication, and by the necessities of our national defense."[58] Representative Latham of California stressed national defense, pointing out that in case of a foreign war, the railroad would be the only reliable means of communication and reinforcement.[59] In the debates on the 1862 bill, Representative Phelps of California said that the railroad was necessary for defense against a foreign war, that otherwise California was an isolated and tempting prize: "We must have a railroad across the continent by which troops and munitions of war can be rapidly transported to that coast."[60] This view was supported by Representative Kelly, who quoted the report of Jefferson Davis as Secretary of War showing the inadequacy of existing means of transportation. Representative Campbell remarked that if a rebellion had broken out on the West coast, the railroad would have helped to crush it.[61] The argument was well summed up by Representative Sargent of California:

The Pacific railroad . . . is an overwhelming military necessity, necessary for the integrity of the country, the preservation of its honor, and called for by considerations of patriotism and safety. . . . That it is a work of this character . . . has been shown by the events of this war, where railroads have been used to an extent never before seen in the history of the world in precipitating armies into the field. . . . In case of a foreign war you cannot hold this continent together without rapid communication across it.[62]

Under pressure of these arguments, and with the elimination of the consideration of Southern routes because of the withdrawal of Southern Congressmen,[63] the House passed the bill in May, 1862. In the Senate, the leadership of Senator James Harlan of Iowa carried the legislation through on June 20, and the bill became law with the President's signature on July 2, 1862.[64]

In spite of all the urgent arguments about national defense, very little in the way of actual construction was accomplished until after the war. The company was organized in September, 1862, with Henry B. Ogden as president (later replaced by John A. Dix), but it was not until the spring of 1863 that Lincoln had decided on a definite eastern terminus at Council Bluffs, Iowa, and a standard gauge of 4 feet, 8½ inches.[65] Ground was finally broken at Omaha, Neb., on December 1, 1863, and when the original act was modified in 1864 about $500,000 was spent in surveying and grading the line. The first rail was finally laid in July, 1865, and by the end of that year, the road was completed 40 miles to Fremont.[66] The Kansas branch west from Kansas City fared better as to actual construction. It was complete to Lawrence by the end of 1864, and in the spring of 1865 was ready to run trains to Independence, Kansas.[67]

By comparison with the explosive decade of the fifties the Civil War period was not one characterized by railroad expansion. Yet neither did the war suddenly bring a halt to all construction. Railroading was a dynamic business, and it was natural that the prosperity engendered by the war years should once again give rise to plans for building new lines and tapping undeveloped regions after the temporary blight of 1858-60. As the events of the war demonstrated the importance of railroads, the argument of military necessity provided added impetus for expansion. But this new enthusiasm and this new optimism were to be tempered by high prices of materials, scarcity of labor, and by the necessity of carrying on the tremendous job of transportation that the war demanded.

Chapter III

EMERGENCY PROBLEMS IN 1861

The construction of railroads has introduced a new and very important element into the war.

> General McClellan, Aug. 4, 1861, quoted in
> Carl R. Fish, *The American Civil War.*

"Mr. Quincy, I haven't met a man on your road that's worth a damn but your Superintendent of Construction, and he's a damned rebel."

> General Landers to Baltimore and Ohio Railroad agent,
> quoted in *Book of the Royal Blue.*

IN A MILITARY SENSE, railroads are important as lines of communication and lines of supply. They distribute troops, arms and ammunition, food and equipment to areas where they are needed; they return wounded and furloughed soldiers, prisoners of war, surplus and worn out equipment to rear areas. In addition, like rivers, they may be avenues of invasion into hostile country. In serving these functions, railroads, particularly at junction points, become legitimate military objectives—to establish a supply depot and to secure a particular line of communication, to prevent a similar use of the railroad by hostile forces, or to advance a step further into enemy territory. Hence the possession of Manassas, Va., Bowling Green, Ky., and Corinth, Miss., was important for the Union armies. The American Civil War was the first important war in which railroads played a leading role, a role which was somewhat foreshadowed by the restricted use of railroads in the Italian campaign against Austria in 1859.[1]

Before 1861, the possible military use of railroads in war had been foretold by only a few men. This fact should not be surprising. Railroads were comparatively new, having grown from nothing within the memory of most living men. Americans, not being a militaristic people, were not prone to think first of the military aspect of a new development. Finally, the forties and fifties were decades of expansion and manifest destiny, when men thought only reluctantly of the possibility of sectional conflict over slavery. Thus before 1861 there were but few suggestions as to the military importance that railroads might assume in wartime.

In 1839, Major General Gaines had reported to Congress that railroads should be thought of merely as an aid to coast defense.[2] In 1851, Matthew Maury, noted for his pioneering work in oceanography, was almost alone in forecasting the use of railroads in quick transportation to facilitate the concentration of large masses of troops at desired points.[3]

By the time hostilities broke out in 1861, leaders on both sides had begun to cite the importance of railroads in the military scene. General George B. McClellan thought they would prove important in the concentration of troops and in creating lines of operation.[4] In 1861, he asked Edwin M. Stanton if any plans existed relative to a rail-water movement of troops to Kentucky: "My mind is turning more and more in that direction."[5] In 1862, Lincoln himself objected to the use of steamboats for McClellan's Peninsular campaign. He wanted the troops transported via railroad to a point southwest of Manassas.[6] Perhaps an intimation of the importance railroads were to have in the coming conflict could be discerned in the secret journey made by Lincoln from Harrisburg to Philadelphia and Washington on February 22 and 23, 1861, to begin his presidential administration. Rumors of a conspiracy against Lincoln's life had spread rapidly among officials of the Philadelphia, Wilmington, and Baltimore Railroad. A mysterious man appeared to the bridgekeeper at Back River Bridge, five miles east of Baltimore, and said conspirators would attack Lincoln's train or any troop train and burn the bridge.[7] Railroad president Samuel Felton's fears were scoffed at by Marshall Kane of the Baltimore police, but Felton proceeded to arm 200 men and assign them as bridge guards.[8] These men then coated the bridge with a whitewash saturated with salt and alum to make it fireproof.[9] When Felton heard that the conspiracy had been transferred to the Northern Central Railway, he arranged Lincoln's secret journey via Philadelphia and Baltimore.[10] On the President-elect's special train east from Harrisburg rode the Division Superintendent, Mr. Franciscus, and the General Superintendent, Enoch Lewis.[11] At Philadelphia, the general superintendent of the Philadelphia, Wilmington, and Baltimore took over, and two officials of the road stood constant guard during the night. At 3:30 A.M. the car was drawn through the silent streets of Baltimore to Camden station, and at six in the morning the President arrived safely at the capital.[12]

It was not long before the national government was to learn even more dramatically how dependent it was for its very security on the railroad connection it had with the North. The city of Washington found itself almost isolated in April, 1861. Confronted with a hostile Virginia and a threatening Maryland, Lincoln had to tread warily lest a misstep bring disaster at the very outset. Washington was connected with Baltimore only by the 40-mile Washington Branch of the Baltimore and Ohio Railroad. Near Baltimore, the Baltimore and Ohio turned westward through Harper's Ferry and Cumberland to its connection with the Ohio River near Wheeling. Two other lines ran north from Baltimore: the Northern Central to Harrisburg, where it met the Pennsylvania Railroad; and the Philadelphia, Wilmington, and Baltimore Railroad, connecting with the Pennsylvania at Philadelphia. It was mainly over these lines that troops mustered under Lincoln's call for volunteers would have access to Washington and eventually to Virginia. The Washington Branch was a particularly heavy carrier of troops and munitions. An historian of Baltimore city pointed out that "the earnings of the 30 miles of track between the Relay House (9 miles from Baltimore) and Washington exceeded anything ever known in the history of railroads."[13]

Presiding over this booming trade was John W. Garrett, president of the Baltimore and Ohio Railroad. Born and reared in Baltimore, Garrett worked as an apprentice in his father's commission house.[14] He became adept at figures, and once prepared a financial report for a subcommittee of the Board of Directors of the Baltimore and Ohio. Garrett maintained so well the contact thus made, that in 1858, on the motion of Johns Hopkins, the largest individual stockholder, he became president of the road. He was then only 38 years old. Garrett immediately instituted measures of economy which gave the Baltimore and Ohio a net income during the depression years of 1859 and 1860. In spite of the fact that Garrett had referred to his railroad as a "Southern line,"[15] he realized that his main source of revenue was in Western merchandise. Early in 1861, the B & O was losing its Western business, because Westerners, particularly Ohioans, feared that Maryland would secede. Garrett undertook to guarantee safety for their freight on his line, and trade partially revived until April.[16] Garrett's views were constantly governed by whatever would bring the most income to his road.

In his Civil War career John Garrett proved himself loyal to two things. One was his railroad. The Baltimore and Ohio suffered extensive damage in the war from both Union and Confederate troops. Always the first job after any destruction was inflicted was to restore the line. To accomplish this as quickly as possible, Garrett sometimes even went out to work with the reconstruction gangs himself. His second loyalty stemmed from his first. Since the B & O connected Washington with the West and with the North, loyalty to the railroad made him of necessity loyal to the Union. Leading Confederates in Maryland held Garrett responsible for their inability to seize the city of Washington. Thus Garrett's loyalty to the Union was the result of business interests rather than personal conviction. This was also true of James Guthrie, the elderly president of the Louisville and Nashville Railroad. In neither case, however, was the loyalty less effective than it might have been if based on other than economic considerations. Garrett's energy and enthusiasm for doing everything possible to protect and develop his railroad gradually won him the admiration and support of some of the leading figures in Congress and in the Cabinet, and undoubtedly helped him a great deal in the fight to save his road from government seizure. A less able man could not have hoped to deal successfully with the tremendous problems faced by the B & O during the war period.

When Lincoln called for 75,000 volunteers on April 15, 1861, Garrett first arranged with Governor William Dennison of Ohio to transport 800 volunteers from Parkersburg and Wheeling to Washington.[17] Garrett was then notified of 2,500 troops coming from the North to Baltimore and Washington, so he withdrew his arrangement with Dennison because he would need all available rolling stock to move Northern troops. Governor Dennison, however, misconstrued Garrett's action as one of a Southern sympathizer. He wired Secretary of War Cameron on April 18:

We had made arrangements with Baltimore and Ohio Road to transport troops, and Mr. Garrett was anxious to take them until late last night, when he declined on the alleged ground that the

Washington Branch will employ all his empty cars in transportation of troops. We hope Harpers Ferry is safe.[18]

Harper's Ferry was far from being safe, however. Even as Dennison telegraphed his message, Confederate troops occupied the arsenal and railroad bridge, and from then on Baltimore and Ohio trains operated westward only with the sufferance of the Confederate commanders. The news of the destruction of the Harper's Ferry arsenal created an intense excitement among the people of Baltimore. Sympathetic with the South, though hardly secessionist, the majority of Baltimoreans were determined to show their opposition to the passage of Federal troops through the city for the purpose of invading the South. Proclamations were issued by the mayor and the governor that no troops would be furnished by Maryland except for the purpose of defending Washington.[19] Six hundred regulars of the Pennsylvania militia had passed through the city April 18, with an excited but not violent crowd watching them. But the news of Harper's Ferry, coupled with the arrival on the nineteenth of volunteers from Massachusetts, inflamed the mob to the point of violence.[20] That Massachusetts troops were the first to arrive on that fateful morning of April 19 was due to the foresight and energy of John Murray Forbes, a railroad builder and financier. Forbes had been involved in completing the Michigan Central Railroad to Chicago, and in building several railroads west of Chicago which were later to combine into the Chicago, Burlington, and Quincy Railroad. During the Civil War, Forbes aided Governor John A. Andrew of Massachusetts in putting the state on a war footing as quickly as possible.[21]

At 11 A.M., 35 cars with 2,000 troops of the 6th Massachusetts, 1st and 4th Pennsylvania, and the Washington Brigade of Philadelphia arrived at the President Street Station of the Philadelphia, Wilmington, and Baltimore Railroad.[22] It was necessary to go about a mile crosstown to the Camden station of the B & O in order to continue the trip to Washington. On regular trains this was done by hauling the cars themselves individually by horsepower on tracks along Pratt Street. At Camden station travelers would change cars. The Massachusetts regiment, under the command of Colonel Edward F. Jones, had left Boston on the 17th and arrived at Philadelphia on the 18th. There Colonel Jones, warned that his reception in Baltimore would be quite different from that in Philadelphia and New York, distributed live ammunition to his troops, and gave orders that the regiment was to march between the stations without paying attention to anyone and without firing unless attacked or fired on.[23] In spite of that order, however, when the troops arrived at Baltimore, the cars were detached and started crosstown individually in the regular manner before the troops were able to unload. A strong police force under Marshall Kane was stationed at the Camden Street terminal, though apparently the police had not known of the coming of the troops until within an hour of their arrival.[24] Nine cars, containing seven companies of Massachusetts troops, were drawn by horses along Pratt Street to the accompaniment of a yelling, ever-growing, but still not violent, crowd. The last car, because of defective brakes, broke down. Almost immediately the crowd began piling obstructions on the track in front of the car: rocks, a load of sand, even a ship's anchor. Attempts were made to pull up the rails. Confronted with these obstacles, the driver finally managed to return his car to the original station, and the crowd immediately gathered to prevent the troops from marching crosstown. Led by the police, four companies of troops were able to organize and make their way along Pratt Street to the accompaniment of a shower of stones and bricks. At the Pratt Street bridge, where a pile of timber formed a temporary blockade, Mayor Brown joined the troops, and for a time marched at their head in an effort to keep order. Rioters rushed the soldiers, and on two occasions grabbed muskets from their hands. At Commerce Street the troops fired into a dense crowd blocking the way and in the resulting confusion several civilians and soldiers were killed. Undoubtedly some of those civilians killed were innocent bystanders, because the chief rioters were in the rear following the troops, and hence difficult to shoot at. Who fired first, civilians or soldiers, is a question which cannot accurately be answered. Marching double quick now, the troops, aided by Kane and about 50 police who lined the route, finally arrived at Camden Street station, where the crowd "pressed up to the car windows, presenting knives and revolvers, and cursed up into the faces of the soldiers."[25] Quickly joining their buddies on the train, the troops, loaded in a 13-car train with the blinds drawn, left for Washington at 12:45 P.M. The death toll was 4 soldiers and 12 civilians, with 36 soldiers and several civilians injured.[26] That the civil authorities of Baltimore did everything in their power to secure safe passage to the troops and to prevent bloodshed, was borne out by Captain Dike, one of the subordinate officers of the 6th Massachusetts, who wrote to the Boston *Courier:* "The mayor and the city authorities should be exonerated from blame or censure, as they did all in their power to quell the riot."[27] Colonel Jones himself thanked Marshall Kane in these words: "Many, many thanks for the Christian conduct of the authorities of Baltimore in this truly unfortunate affair."[28]

Mayor Brown immediately sent word to President Lincoln describing conditions in the city and saying that it was impossible to send any more troops through Baltimore, a sentiment in which Governor Hicks concurred.[29] J. Edgar Thomson and Samuel Felton, presidents respectively of the Pennsylvania

Railroad and the Philadelphia, Wilmington, and Baltimore, with headquarters at Philadelphia, wired Secretary of War Cameron that they could not transfer troops to the Baltimore and Ohio at Baltimore. The Adjutant General replied immediately to send the troops anyway, prepared to fight their way through if necessary.[30]

President Garrett was thus placed on the horns of a dilemma. With his railroad menaced by a Baltimore mob, he himself was threatened with treason by Cameron if the B & O carried Southern troops, and threatened with confiscation of his railroad by Governor Letcher of Virginia if he transported Federal troops.[31] On the evening of April 19, Governor Hicks, Mayor Brown, Marshall Kane, and ex-Governor Lowe met in consultation. Determined to protect the city from mob violence and unwarranted property destruction, they decided to burn the railroad bridges of the Northern Central Railway, and the Philadelphia, Wilmington, and Baltimore in the vicinity of Baltimore, thus isolating the city from rail communication with the North.[32] At 2:30 A.M. on the 20th, the orders were carried out, under direction of Lieutenant Colonel Johnson and First Lieutenant Hubbell of the Purnell Legion of Maryland,[33] each of two parties destroying three bridges on each railroad, along with the telegraph lines.[34] Baltimore was thus cut off from communication with Philadelphia, Harrisburg, and New York. The danger in which this "official" action placed the city of Washington was far too great to justify the action taken. When Marshall Kane and the Board of Police were later arrested by General Nathaniel P. Banks in June, 1861, the extent of their action was made clearer. The Police Board inspected all communications via telegraph between Baltimore and Washington. On April 22, the Board refused permission to the Northern Central Railway to rebuild the destroyed bridges, and on April

26 refused a similar request from the Philadelphia, Wilmington, and Baltimore. The position of the Police Board was that the railroad should not be used to transport troops for the use of the government.[35] The railroad, on the other hand, claimed it could not prevent the destruction, and asked the legislature to reimburse the companies for damages amounting to $117,609.63. Said the Northern Central:

The protection to property and reparation for its injury, are eminently due where the wrong had been perpetrated by officials of the highest position. Rights hardly merit the name where there is neither security for their preservation nor compensation for their destruction.[36]

The Northern Central Railway was closed from Hanover Junction to Baltimore, 46 miles, until May 21, and this was the most productive part of the line for passenger and freight revenue.[37] The Philadelphia, Wilmington, and Baltimore was disabled for 40 miles, and not reopened to Baltimore until May 14.[38]

Meanwhile, faced with the necessity of getting troops to Washington, Cameron was forced to take immediate action. The 7th New York regiment arrived at Philadelphia on the twentieth and was ordered by Cameron to proceed to Havre de Grace by rail, thence by ferry to Annapolis.[39] Troops were also converging on Baltimore from the West. News that 5,000 Northern troops were marching toward Baltimore from Cockeysville on the Northern Central had the electric effect of arousing the populace of Baltimore to arms, as a result of which the troops were temporarily ordered back to Harrisburg.[40] Both General Winfield Scott and Secretary Cameron favored using the Northen Central with the troops fighting their way through Baltimore if necessary (though Scott would have preferred that they march around the city, not through it), but Major-

General Patterson, commanding the Department of Pennsylvania, influenced by Thomson and Felton, convinced his superiors that the rail-water route by way of Annapolis was best.[41]

These two railroad men urged the government to take possession of the Annapolis and Elk Ridge Railroad, and that part of the Baltimore and Ohio from Annapolis Junction to Washington. They offered their services to Cameron to supervise the transportation of troops and to furnish locomotives, cars, and men from their own roads.[42] Brown, Hicks, and Garrett interceded with Lincoln to get a reversal of the order to send troops through Baltimore.[43] Cameron, favoring the Northern Central route to the last, finally yielded to the views of the majority, and on April 27, 1861, appointed Thomas A. Scott, vice-president of the Pennsylvania Railroad, to be in charge of the railways and telegraph between Washington and Annapolis. His chief assistant was 26-year-old Andrew Carnegie.[44]

Scott, a Pennsylvanian by birth, had his first job with the Pennsylvania Railroad in 1850 at the age of 27. He rose rapidly to third assistant superintendent of the Pittsburgh Division, then general superintendent, and finally vice-president in March, 1860.[45] At the outbreak of war, Scott was summoned to Governor Curtin's office to assist in the transportation of Pennsylvania troops, and there, "with a relay magnet and key placed on a window sill,"[46] opened the first military telegraph office in the country. Scott called in four expert railroad telegraphers and sent them to Washington to become the first operators employed in what was soon to become the Military Telegraph Corps.

Scott, with the aid of John Tucker,[47] organized the route by way of Perryville, where the Philadelphia, Wilmington, and Baltimore reached the Susquehanna River, thence by the steamer "Maryland" to Annapolis, then the Annapolis and Elk Ridge to the B & O and on to Washington. Locomotives and cars were ordered from other railroads to supplement what B & O rolling stock the government had been able to appropriate.[48] Under Carnegie's direction, the railroad was repaired in three days, and by April 29 the route was open between Washington and Annapolis.[49] Carnegie had the able assistance of General Benjamin F. Butler, who had stationed guards along the Annapolis road and then advanced up the B & O to seize the important junction at Relay House, where the Washington Branch joined the main line from the west. By the middle of May, 1861, Baltimore was occupied by General Butler,[50] among whose troops were some of the same 6th Massachusetts regiment which had been attacked the previous month on their passage through the city. With the occupation of the city and the repair of the railroad bridge, direct communication between Washington, Baltimore, Harrisburg, and Philadelphia was again possible. Carnegie himself rode in the cab of the first train into Washington.[51]

Andrew Carnegie and Tom Scott had already experienced many years of close association before the outbreak of war. As an alert and talented operator in the Pittsburgh telegraph office, the 16-year-old lad from Scotland had attracted Scott's attention, and soon became the railroad executive's private secretary and telegrapher.[52] Carnegie remained with the Pennsylvania Railroad until 1865, eventually becoming superintendent of the Pittsburgh Division. In Washington, he was Scott's right hand man. It was Carnegie who recruited the four telegraphers from Pittsburgh, Greensburg, Altoona, and Mifflin to start the Military Telegraph Corps. In the summer of 1861, Carnegie personally supervised the transportation of the defeated Federal troops after Bull Run; in November he moved to Pittsburgh to help see the Pennsylvania Railroad through the war.[53]

Scott was commissioned a Colonel of District of Columbia Volunteers in May, 1861, and that same month his jurisdiction was extended to all railways and telegraphs appropriated for government use.[54] His powers were merely advisory, however, and very little in the way of coordination was accomplished. There was some conflict of authority. John Tucker, under the Quartermaster General, made contracts for rail transportation, but his office had no title and he received no compensation.[55] In August, Scott became Assistant Secretary of War to supervise government railways and transportation,[56] and his former position was filled in September by R. N. Morley, captain in the Quartermaster Corps. Scott accepted his position on the understanding that he could retire October 1 and return to his job with the Pennsylvania Railroad, but the war emergency kept him in office until June 1, 1862.[57] Of Scott's accomplishments as assistant secretary, Cameron, twenty years later, said that soon after Scott came to the War Department, he

had his office placed in telegraphic communication with all the army stations that could be reached, with every telegraph station in every loyal state of the north. . . . He built a line of railway through the streets of Washington to the Long Bridge, so as to make a direct connection with the Orange and Alexandria Railroad. . . . In less than a month . . . he could tell the capacity for transportation toward every division of the army.[58]

It was unfortunate that the first year of the war should bring Scott into conflict with Garrett. Both were young (Garrett 41 in 1861, Scott 38) ; both were energetic ; both had ability. Their mutual hostility had developed out of a pre-war competition between the Baltimore and Ohio and the Pennsylvania for control of the Northern Central Railway.[59] The Pennsylvania, with both J. Edgar Thomson and Scott, was the stronger road, and had the advantage in this battle. When Lincoln became President, Scott found an ally in the Cabinet

in Secretary of War Cameron, one of the directors of the
Northern Central. In the differences of opinion that arose
between Cameron and Scott on the one hand, and Garrett on
the other, the tensions of war almost inevitably introduced the
question of disloyalty, and it was Garrett who suffered most
from the charge. The replacement of Cameron by Stanton not
only deprived Scott of a voice in high places, but also brought
in a man more sympathetic to Garrett; a fast friendship soon
developed between the new secretary and the B & O president.
The growing realization that all railroads had a cooperative
job to do in the war and could ill afford to quarrel was another
factor which helped to dispel the earlier hostility. By 1863,
Scott and Garrett were cooperating enthusiastically in arranging the transfer of Hooker's corps from Virginia to Tennessee.

During 1861 the government expanded its transportation
facilities in Virginia. Morley's report of November, 1861,
showed that the army in Virginia was operating nine miles of
the Orange and Alexandria Railroad, and eleven miles of the
Hampshire and Loudoun Railroad, both roads originating at
Alexandria, and supplying troops stationed along their routes.
A machine shop was in operation in Alexandria to repair rolling
stock and to fabricate ironwork for bridge construction. The
small amount of rolling stock not destroyed or carried off by
the enemy was supplemented by three engines borrowed from the
Philadelphia and Reading, and twelve passenger cars and one
baggage car from the Pennsylvania. Sidings were built both
in Alexandria and in Washington to connect with wharves and
to facilitate operations around warehouses.[60] These facilities
provided the groundwork on which the United States Military
Railroads later built an elaborate organization. Morley, whose
official title was General Manager of United States Military
Railroads, was replaced in February, 1862, by Daniel C. Mc-
Callum.[61]

This rather haphazard development of an organization responsible for transportation in Virginia was duplicated to some extent in the West. There, too, the United States Military Railroads had small beginnings, and these were for the most part simply expedient solutions to whatever transportation problems happened to arise at the particular time. It was not until November, 1861, that Captain Lewis B. Parsons, a former director and treasurer of the Ohio and Mississippi Railroad, was assigned to take charge of rail and river transportation at St. Louis, working on the Quartermaster staff under Major Robert Allen. The next month his jurisdiction was extended by Allen to include the whole Department of the Mississippi.[62] Lewis Baldwin Parsons was a Yale graduate of 1840, and took his LL. B. degree at Harvard in 1844, after which he practiced law in Alton, Ill., and in St. Louis. In the decade before the war, Parsons had been an attorney for the Ohio and Mississippi Railroad, and during his service with that line he formed a firm friendship with its vice-president, George B. McClellan. In the fall of 1861 Parsons joined McClellan's staff as captain, and soon after was transferred to his western position, where he distinguished himself throughout the war.[63] Parsons found that General Fremont had instituted a system of chartering river boats over a long period of time, with payment given on a per diem basis. Finding the system extravagant and unnecessary, especially because the river was controlled by the Union only to Cairo, Parsons abolished the charter system in favor of temporary contracts for specific work by the river boats, a method which gave better service at less cost to the government.[64]

Turning to rail transportation, Parsons found a good deal of confusion. Railroad passes were being issued by almost any government officer, and many unauthorized persons were traveling at government expense. Railroads, not knowing which trans-

portation orders were good and which were not, honored all of
them and in so doing lost a great deal of money. After Parsons'
chief, Fremont, was replaced by General Halleck, Parsons established rules regulating the procedure of issuing passes, and
provided for periodic reports. The railroads cooperated enthusiastically, and almost immediately order appeared where
there had previously been only confusion.[65] Another practice
frequently abused, resulting in unnecessary cost to the government, concerned the procurement of railroad tickets. Tickets
might be bought for 40 men, and only 30 would actually make
the trip, the other tickets being unused or given away. Sometimes the route was changed, or the troops traveled only part of
the distance, yet the government paid the railroads for the
entire number the entire distance. Parsons corrected this abuse
by requiring separate passes on each railroad, and certification
by the railroad for only the actual number of men carried.[66]
Thus by regulating the issuance of travel orders, Parsons provided the railroads with a more certain source of income from
the government, and by correcting other abuses saved the
government much wasteful expense.

The capital city of Washington was located in a very strategic
geographical position. Though the nerve center of the Union, it
was situated almost as a forward outpost, uncomfortably close
to enemy lines. Transportation and communication were therefore of primary concern to the government. It took the Baltimore riot and the subsequent severing of rail communication
with the North to demonstrate the vital necessity of a secure line
of railroad between the capital and the industrial areas of the
North. In a similar way, this beachhead into the Confederacy
early had to develop some semblance of organization looking to
the use of its location as a base for an attack upon the heart of
the Confederacy which of necessity had to be made by rail. The

solutions to the problems created by the events of 1861 emphasized the tremendous importance of railway transportation in
maintaining communication between the loyal states, and resulted in the passage of a comprehensive law to bring the railroads into the war economy, only nine months after the war
started.[67] The Confederate government, meanwhile, was not regarding the development of its railroad system as desirable from
a military point of view, though railroad transportation of
troops had been used to its advantage in the first Battle of
Bull Run. Southern railroads were poorly equipped, and the
constitutional emphasis on state authority prevented any comprehensive development over the Confederacy as a whole.[68]
Before the miracles of railway transportation of 1863 and 1864
could be accomplished, other obstacles had to be overcome, but
none was to be so severe as those of 1861.[69] By the end of that
year, the immediate problems had been met. Washington felt
secure in its supply lines to the North; Scott was doing herculean work for which he had no precedents to guide him; and
Parsons was bringing order out of chaos in the West. Founda-
tions were thus being laid for the dramatic accomplishments of
the railroads in war. Before relating them, however, it is necessary to consider first what effect the war was having on the ordinary business of the railroads.

Chapter IV

EFFECT OF THE WAR UPON RAILROAD
BUSINESS: THE NORTHEAST

Keeping the B & O in repair in war time was a task for Hercules.
W. E. Porter, superintendent of construction,
in *Book of the Royal Blue*

The past year has been . . . the most prosperous ever known to the
American Railways.
American Railroad Journal, Jan. 2, 1864

IN MAY, 1861, the *Railroad Record* predicted that most Northern railroads would be unaffected by the war. Railroads in
Maryland would be injured because of proximity to military
operations, and North-South railroads such as the Mobile and
Ohio and the Louisville and Nashville would be benefited as
Southern commerce, deprived of its normal seaboard outlet because of the blockade, sought new channels to its markets. But
the *Record* thought the war would leave other railroads unaffected.[1] It was a bad guess. The war was to have a profound
influence on all the Northern railroads, and those effects were
not slow in revealing themselves.

The immediate impact was one of pessimism, tempered by that
native optimistic outlook so characteristic of the decade of the
fifties. Some railroads, such as the Illinois Central, complained
that government business brought on by the war was ruining
their ordinary traffic and they were fearful that the war would
bring a permanent dislocation of the economy on which they had
been based. This pessimism was reflected by the decline in advertisements in the *American Railroad Journal* during the sum-

mer of 1861, and by the *American Railway Review's* change from a weekly to a semi-monthly in July.[2]

This gloomy reaction to the impact of civil war was only temporary. It was soon lost in the jump in earnings and in the increasing business which came to the railroads. For the Civil War brought them prosperity. Increasing business, whether directly in the form of transporting troops and supplies, or indirectly from private manufacturers with government contracts, or for other reasons, was something all the railroads pointed to with pride.[3] No longer were the railroads overexpanded or suffering from the ill effects of depression.[4] Each year gross income increased and profits went up almost as fast. The *American Railroad Journal*, January 2, 1864, called 1863 "the most prosperous ever known to the American Railways." Railroads which had suffered a decline in freight and passenger revenues in the three years immediately preceding the outbreak of war, soon found themselves swamped with business, and vied with each other in placing orders for more locomotives and more cars. As we shall see, the business of some roads increased so much that part of it had to be turned away for lack of rolling stock.[5] Increased profits were partly passed on to the stockholders as higher dividends. The Erie Railroad, which paid nothing until 1863, paid 8 per cent beginning in that year. From 1860 to 1864, New York Central dividends rose from 6 per cent to 9 per cent, Cincinnati, Hamilton, and Dayton from 7 per cent to 19 per cent; Cleveland, Painesville, and Ashtabula 15 per cent to 26 per cent; and Cleveland and Toledo from zero to 10 per cent.[6]

But the picture had a dark side, too. As the war progressed, the railroads found themselves faced with a shortage of labor and with increasing prices of materials. The Civil War, as do all wars, drained away skilled manpower and led to attempts on the part of the railroads to have their skilled workers exempted from the draft. Failure to do so meant that the price of labor went higher as its skill deteriorated. Rising prices in materials was the most important factor pointed to as limiting the possible profits from increasing business. Fuel and iron were the chief culprits here. The rising price of wood as locomotive fuel hastened change-overs to coal, though of course the latter, too, rose in price during the war. Likewise the price of iron went so high as to be nearly prohibitive, and was an important factor in leading several railroads to experiment with steel rails as a substitute.

Finally, one other common characteristic resulted directly from the others. As the war dragged on, the railroad plant began to deteriorate. The railroads had so much business they could not shop their rolling stock for any but the most essential repairs, and maintenance of track and of motive power was likewise neglected. Rising prices of materials and labor led many railroads to postpone major repairs until better times. One result of this situation was an increase in the number of railroad accidents. In 1861, 63 accidents killed 101 and injured 459; by 1864 there were 140 accidents, killing 404, injuring 1,846.[7]

The railroads of New England, far removed from the seat of war, less expansive, and less concerned with through business than other railroads, nevertheless experienced the same effects that other roads did in these critical years. The war years were prosperous years, though sometimes this increase in income did not show up until the war was half over, and was usually preceded by a definite recession. The Boston and Maine Railroad, for instance, suffered a sharp decline its its gross revenue from $930,000 in 1861 to $732,000 in 1862.[8] The railroad attributed this setback to the decline in local business because of the uncertainty among businessmen, and pointed out that the war was proving unfavorable for New England railroads, but favorable to railroads to Washington.[9] Officers and employees of the line took a 10 per cent cut in wages and salaries.[10]

The next year, however, the effects of the war began to be felt. Gross receipts hit $945,000, net $450,000 both figures the largest in the company's history.[11] Troop transportation and military business were the chief factors in the increased earnings; even its subsidiary, the Portland, Saco, and Portsmouth, profited.[12] This trend continued in 1864 and 1865 with gross receipts topping $1,000,000 in each case.[13] But the net of 1864 ($482,000) proved to be the high water mark of the war period. By that time, expenses were cutting severely into receipts. In the fiscal year ending May 31, 1862, the road spent $16,500 for coal; in 1863, $27,000; in 1864, $53,000; in 1865, $65,000, all without great changes in motive power or conversion from wood to coal.[14] Taxes almost tripled in 1864 over 1863, due partly to the government tax on gross passenger receipts.[15] Because of the increasing expenses, the line raised its rates, but not enough to prevent a sharp drop in net revenue in 1865. With record gross receipts of $1,200,000, the expenses had risen to $928,000, and the net of $367,000 was the lowest of the war period except 1862.[16] High prices, said the railroad, were responsible. New iron rails, costing $57.50 a ton as of November 30, 1860, rose to $120 a ton by November 30, 1865.[17] Hard wood went up from $4.25 a cord to $6.75. Soft coal, costing $5.50 in 1860, sold for $14 a ton in 1865. Spikes had jumped 200 per cent from 3½ cents to 9½ cents per pound, and coach varnish went up from $2.75 to $7 a gallon. Not only materials, but labor costs were up, too. Enginemen's wages had risen from $2.50 to $3 a day, machinists from $1.59 to $2.25, and others comparably. Thus though the Boston and Maine was enjoying record business, hauling 2,600,000 passengers, and carrying

275,000 tons of freight in 1865,[18] net revenue showed a sharp drop in the closing years of the war.

One of the important New England routes was that from Boston to Albany. During the Civil War, the route consisted of two railroads, the Boston and Worcester between those points, and the Western Railroad from Worcester to Albany. The experiences of these railroads proved to be no exception to the general war trends, except that, as with the Boston and Maine, the effects were felt somewhat later. The receipts of the Boston and Worcester for the year ending November 30, 1861, were less than those of the preceding year. As a result, the labor force was reduced, and the working day cut down from ten hours to nine hours.[19] The next year brought a moderate increase in gross receipts from $929,000 to $1,000,000, and in net from $408,500 to $490,000.[20] In that year the line carried about 1,500,000 passengers, and about 382,000 tons of freight.[21] By 1864 it was carrying more than 2,000,000 passengers, and more than 450,-000 tons of freight. Although its track, rolling stock, and storage facilities were being used to capacity, its net revenue suffered a slight decline in both 1863 and 1864.[22] The answer to this paradox was increasing expenses, which almost exactly doubled from $515,000 in 1862 to $1,100,000 in 1865.[23] Prices of labor, fuel, and materials all contributed to this increase in expenses. In 1863-64 the cost of fuel per mile increased from 14.23 cents to 20.96 cents; the cost of transportation rose from 1.564 cents to 1.705 cents.[24] Additions to rolling stock and laying new rail in the main line added to these costs.[25] As a result of these expenses, the Boston and Worcester did not experience a substantial rise in net revenue until 1865, when its gross was $1,700,000 ($1,000,000 from passengers alone) and its net $537,000.[26]

The 117-mile Western Railroad from Worcester to Albany

profited in 1861 from an increased western trade in flour. Its gross receipts of $1,900,000 were higher than any year since 1857, but so were its expenses of $1,000,000.[27] This line had more motive power than the Boston and Worcester, more freight cars, and generally did a greater business.[28] Receipts and expenses both continued to mount through 1862 and 1863, but the railroad pointed with pride to the fact that it was the income which was going up faster.[29] In 1863 its net for the first time exceeded $1,000,000, and included a small profit from the Pittsfield and North Adams Railroad.[30] High prices and scarcity of labor forced abandonment of a double track on the main line with only 40 miles to finish, but the road did not suffer so much from these factors as the Boston and Worcester because its passenger traffic was becoming better distributed both as to direction and kind, and it had a large amount of supplies on hand which had been purchased at the beginning of the year while prices were still reasonable.[31] From 1863 till the end of the war, net receipts remained fairly constant, though both gross income and expenses increased considerably.[32]

The New York and New Haven Railroad, like so many other New England lines, was primarily a passenger carrier. Travelers between New York and Boston rode to New Haven whence they took the New Haven, Hartford and Springfield, and the Boston and Worcester. This interior route, now the long way to Boston, was the chief rail route between Boston and New York.[33] The war experience of the New York and New Haven was typical in that the first year of the war brought a decline in business. Gross receipts of $808,000 were the lowest since 1853.[34] The decline had begun noticeably in June, 1861, and the road blamed the absence of its normally high summer tourist business, of which a great part was southern, and was now cut off by the war.[35] To meet declining revenue, the railroad cut the number of its employees 20 per cent and reduced the pay of others by one third.[36] But the war shortly began to have its cumulative effect. An improvement in business began in early 1862, and picked up especially after July 1. For the rest of the year the company did the largest business in its history, carrying 1,100,-000 passengers and grossing $1,000,000.[37] The jump in one year from the lowest receipts in nine years to the highest in its history was dramatic evidence of the economic effect of the war. But costs were rising too. The rise in fuel prices, plus heavier trains, brought the fuel cost per mile from 12.53 cents in 1861 to 14.43 cents in 1862. The line warned its patrons that with increasing costs in labor and materials and increasing taxes, higher rates were in the offing.[38] The next year an even greater business was experienced. An increase of 300,000 passengers brought gross receipts to $1,400,000, net $720,000.[39] In May, 1863, an additional regularly scheduled passenger train was put on the line. Heavy traffic, however, was beginning to wear out the locomotives just at a time when it was difficult to get new ones. The average passenger train was now six cars long instead of five, and the additional weight meant wear on both motive power and track.[40] In November, 1863, the road had contracted for three locomotives from Danforth, Cook and Co. of Paterson, N. J., but in March, 1864, the government found it necessary to requisition these engines for use on the military railroads in the West.[41] Similar difficulty was experienced in getting new cars, and new iron for rail; fuel cost rose to 20.5 cents per mile.[42] In 1864, expenses went far beyond any previous experience, rising from $704,000 to $1,200,000. Hence the record gross receipts of $1,800,000 produced a net of only $622,500, less than that of the previous year.[43] The costs incurred were unavoidable. Four new locomotives added to the line were essential to carry on its business. Another large expenditure was in the line's share of six new passenger cars, three railway post office cars, and three smoking and baggage cars purchased for the New York-Boston run.[44] In addition, fuel cost had risen to 27.3 cents per mile, and the large number of heavy trains made necessary a higher expenditure than usual on track repair.

The New York and New Haven Railroad thus showed with particular clarity the characteristics trends of the period. A jump in one year, 1861-1862, from the lowest receipts in nine years to the highest in the road's history brought a new prosperity after the uncertainty of the opening years of the war. When expenses soared in 1864 to well over $1,000,000, they showed that the high wartime profits were limited by the highest expenses in the line's experience. On the whole, therefore, the New England railroads encountered record profits and record expenses, though not always in the same proportion which lines elsewhere experienced. Prosperity came late, 1862 or 1863, but it did come. Heavy expenses were noted early in the war because of the generally local character of much of the roads' business.

Because railroads in the eastern region south of New England were closer to the theater of war, their location placed upon them a greater burden in meeting the emergency demands of this time of national crisis. The experiences of the Northern Central Railway proved typical of lines in this region. Connecting Sunbury and Harrisburg with Baltimore via York,[45] the Northern Central provided an important link through the Pennsylvania Railroad and the Philadelphia and Erie Railroad with other parts of the East. The railroad found its traffic suddenly increasing in the summer of 1861 to a new high which was to remain fairly stable throughout the war. Its gross earnings increased 44½ per cent over 1860, reaching a total of $1,417,-977.06, of which $360,874.83 was the income from carrying troops and munitions.[46] Forty-one engines, 30 passenger cars, and 1,400 freight cars (including 744 for coal) handled this business. The line had contracted with the Baldwin Locomotive Company for seven more locomotives, and the 1862 report listed 51 engines.[47] By 1862 the Northern Central was receiving a great deal of trade from the Philadelphia and Erie, much of it in oil, and in order to take care of this trade, 100 house cars, 100 gondolas, and 100 stock cars were ordered.[48] Of necessity, the business of the government was almost entirely one way, south. In the year 1861, 67,094 troops were carried from Harrisburg to Baltimore, and 14,053 from Sunbury to Baltimore—a total of 81,147 troops southbound. Those carried north totaled only 27,205.[49] It was the same with freight; here too most of the business was through freight south, transported in conjunction with the Pennsylvania Railroad from Pittsburgh and the West. The 1861 report pointed out that its *local* freight had *decreased* during the year, not because of less business, but because all the rolling stock of the company was required to handle the business of the government.[50] Of 458,724 tons of freight transported in 1861, 107,892 came from the Pennsylvania Railroad.[51] A glance at the products carried from Pittsburgh to Baltimore would probably have led a stranger unacquainted with the fact of a civil war to guess that an army was encamped somewhere south of Baltimore. The tonnage figures showed that 30,247 tons of livestock, 13,854 tons of flour, 9,842 tons of salt meat and fish, 6,402 tons of tobacco, and 3,251 tons of whisky and alcohol traveled the rails from Pittsburgh to Baltimore in 1861.[52] By 1862 the troop traffic had declined somewhat, bringing in a revenue of $318,522.91, but the net earnings of the road had jumped from $734,144.86 to $927,341.09.[53] The road's total freight earnings had passed the million mark.[54] Even with its slight decline in troop revenue in 1862, the road reported so great a demand for its 28 passenger cars that it was "impossible to take the cars from the trade long enough to renew the painting."[55] Passenger locomotives were piling up an average of 25,000 to 30,000 miles per year, the highest being 43,947 miles.[56] Troop transportation, no less in 1861 than in 1941, meant wear and tear on car seats and cushions; even in 1861 the road estimated that it would require $10,000 just to put the cars in first class condition.[57] Carrying troops brought also a good deal of interchange traffic, particularly with the Pennsylvania, the Philadelphia and Reading, and the Philadelphia and Erie.[58] Two years of prosperity brought deterioration not only to rolling stock, but to rails as well. The 1862 report estimated that 3,000 tons of iron would be needed for new rails in 1863.[59] The report of 1863 showed an increase of 10.1 per cent in the operating ratio (ratio of operating expenses to income) to a high of 61.8 per cent, the road offering as the reason for this increase the advance in the price of labor and materials while rates remained constant in order not to endanger the Baltimore trade.[60] The tremendous increase in expenses meant that, though gross receipts topped two million dollars, net revenue was only $435,-216.78, considerably less than the two previous war years. From the government $185,364.11 was due but not yet paid.[61] Some of the increased business came from the lease of the Shamokin Valley and Pottsville Railroad (tapping the anthracite coal region), and the Elmira and Williamsport Railroad. By means of traffic agreements with the Erie, the Northern Central could tap trade as far north as Buffalo and Rochester.[62] But the amount of business accepted was limited by the inability of the railroad to move more over a single track; and because officials were taxing the road beyond capacity in order to meet the requirements of the government, delays did occur.[63] Double tracking was in progress to meet the difficulty, and a train was put on to handle local on-line traffic because of delay to through trains.[64] The line made valiant efforts to increase its rolling stock. In 1863 it had a contract with Baldwin for two passenger engines, and with the New Jersey Locomotive Works at Paterson for ten ten-wheel freight engines. Besides these, 266 new freight cars and gondolas were added and contracts let for an additional 225 freight cars, 200 coal cars, and 215 gondolas.[65]

Damage inflicted by Lee's army in the Gettysburg campaign of June and July of 1863 caused considerable dislocation to the railroad.[66] From June 7, when Lee's intentions began to be clear, the line concentrated on military transportation and in preparing blockhouses for soldiers guarding the line. A week later, operations were partially suspended and most of the rolling stock moved north. Only troop trains and local freights moving property continued to run. Then on the 25th all shipments stopped. When communications with the Hanover Branch were interrupted, engines were fired to move rolling stock concentrated at York north to Columbia. York fell to the rebels a day later. The enemy destroyed all twelve bridges between Hanover Junction and Goldsboro, and all nineteen on the Wrightsville Branch. Repairs commenced July 5 after Lee's retreat from Gettysburg, and ten days later all bridges were restored. The general superintendent of the railroad made the following estimate of damage:

Loss of trade	$109,000
Cars destroyed at York	12,000
Cars destroyed at Gettysburg	5,600
Scale and fixtures at York	1,800
Ironclad car #319	800

When labor and materials necessary to construct the blockhouses and to repair the damage were added, the estimated loss totaled $234,900.

After that interruption, business boomed again, up to 63 per

cent over 1861, the vast bulk of it south. In all, 483,036 tons
were transported south in 1863, only 69,646 north.[67] The year
1864 was even better. Gross receipts topped three million dollars, and though expenses edged toward two million, net revenue
of $1,085,326.63 was the highest yet, and was recorded in spite
of a net loss on the Elmira Division.[68] Actually, though its operating ratio went up to 64.75 per cent, the road was earning
about 18 per cent on its capital stock, until the latter was
doubled to provide funds for the second main line track.[69]
Though the line did a large amount of government business, this
latter was actually only about one sixth of the gross receipts,
totaling $586,907.36. Except for the necessity of transporting
government troops and supplies at rates one third less than
1861, the coal business might have increased 100 per cent, and
coal receipts alone would, in that case, have met expenditures.
The railroad thus considered itself handicapped in reference to
roads not used for military purposes.[70] Fifteen miles of double
track between Baltimore and Cockeysville were completed and
in use, and the road purchased 12 passenger engines and 10
freight in 1864 to handle traffic and to replace worn out equipment.[71] But of the 85 locomotives now on the roster, only 41 were
in first class condition, while 21 more could run.[72] In the course
of the year, 619 cars were added to the rolling stock, making a
total of over 3,500 cars to handle a record business of 602,380
tons of freight south, and 142,295 north.[73] By this time both
motive power and rolling stock were more than twice as large
as in 1861.

Though the year 1865 brought for many lines a definite re-
ceding from the peak, the Northern Central made more money
than in any previous year. Here are the figures: receipts $4,-
242,388.18 (double 1863); expenses $2,765,498.50; net earn-
ings $1,476,889.68. The double track was completed to York,

and the road had eight passenger trains daily leaving Baltimore, three of which ran through to Sunbury.[74] The months after the war were used to make extensive repairs to engines and cars, plus repairing the damage done on the Elmira Division by the Susquehanna flood of March, 1865.[75]

Thus the war brought prosperity to the Northern Central Railway. Its net earnings increased every year except 1863, the year of Lee's invasion of Maryland and Pennsylvania. It is interesting to note that the *net* earnings of 1865 ($1,476,889.68) were actually more than the *gross* earnings of 1861 ($1,417,977.06). This great increase came in spite of the handicap of being a North-South line with most of its business one way, with the result that many empty trains had to be run north. One should also note that the transportation of troops and military supplies, an important source of income, was only partly responsible for greater revenue (the higher demand for coal and other products being equally important), and indeed was even listed as a handicap in the 1864 report. Finally, the tremendous expansion of the railroad through leases and traffic agreements, through additions to rolling stock, and construction of double track was partly responsible for the ability of the road to tap new sources of income.

Samuel Felton and the Philadelphia, Wilmington and Baltimore encountered experiences similar to the Northern Central. Connecting the cities named, the 105-mile road (now the Pennsylvania Railroad) was an essential link in the all-important supply line from New England and New York to Baltimore and Washington. As we shall note, much of Felton's time and energy were taken up defending the policies of his road and helping to defeat the authorization of a government railroad between New York and Washington. His position is, in large measure, justified by the statistics contained in his annual reports.

With a rolling stock of 32 locomotives and 674 cars, the PW & B transported 154,303 troops from April 18, 1861, to the end of the fiscal year October 31.[76] A large number of sick and disabled troops were also carried, "for whose transportation we have not received any pay."[77] The annual reports did not keep separate figures on troop earnings as distinct from ordinary passenger traffic. Passenger receipts for 1861 were $1,067,275.42, an increase over 1860 of about $236,000.[78] The next year its rolling stock had increased to 37 locomotives and 801 cars, its passenger receipts jumped to $1,645,024.83, and its net earnings were above $1,000,000.[79] Thus the road had less rolling stock than the Northern Central, but carried on more business. Passenger receipts alone of the PW & B were more than the total receipts of the other road. In November, 1862, men furloughed from the Army of the Potomac crowded stations and trains all along the line.[80] Much of the surplus was still on paper, however. As Felton put it, "A considerable portion of the surplus is due from the United States government."[81] The increased earnings of the road occurred in spite of the fact that a large business in Western produce from the Baltimore and Ohio had been cut off by the war.[82]

The PW & B was one of a number of railroads making experiments with coal as fuel and finding that the change-over from wood to coal would prove profitable in the long run. As far back as 1857 Felton took the initiative in inaugurating coal burning passenger locomotives on his line.[83] But at first the innovation did not work too well. Felton presented an engaging picture of some of the difficulties encountered.

A want of practical knowledge among enginemen, and a natural prejudice against a change from old habits, for some time stood in the way of entire success. We were often mortified by the spectacle of a train coming to a standstill between two stations for want of steam, and comments of the passengers were in no way flattering to ourselves or to the task in which we were engaged.[84]

But the difference in cost was important. Coal burners averaged about 6 cents per mile for fuel cost, against 14 cents for wood burners.[85] With a gradual increase in practical knowledge, coal was found to be more economical and wood was gradually abandoned. We shall note this change in the operation of other railroads. It was not caused by the war itself, but a combination of circumstances during the war—increasing business, scarcity of wood and its rising price, opening up of coal fields on the lines of the Pennsylvania, Philadelphia and Reading, Lackawanna, and Lehigh Valley railroads—accelerated the change that had begun before the war.

Like the Northern Central, the PW & B did not find that a large amount of government business was necessarily an advantage to the railroad. Normal freight business was greatly interfered with because the government detained cars in Washington, and frequently sent them loaded into Virginia. Some of them never did return.[86] In spite of these inconveniences, however, Felton thought in 1862 that the road had passed its period of uncertainty and doubt, and assured the stockholders of steady dividends in the future.[87]

The year 1863 saw a general increase in the prosperity of the road. With net revenue $1,042,266.42, the company declared a 10 per cent dividend, built 16½ miles of second track and additional track, and sank the first pier for the bridge over the Susquehanna River in 42 feet of water.[88] This last project was Felton's favorite. The fact that the railroad broke in two at the Susquehanna River, forcing the use of ferries, was something Felton desired to correct: "Ferries are justified only by necessity, and where they can be avoided it is the duty of all railroads to avoid them as soon as they have the means to do so."[89] The

railroad's chief engineer, George A. Parker, was in charge of
the project, and the company employed Benjamin H. Latrobe
as consulting engineer. The bridge was to be completed in
1865.[90]

Economic difficulties began to make themselves felt in 1863.
The new engines acquired during the year were constructed of
poor materials with inferior workmanship, and needed repairs
more often than usual. Iron and lumber were scarce and high
priced, making it difficult to renew or repair sections of track,
or to construct new sections.[91] At the same time, the railroad
was offered enough business to work the rolling stock to its full
capacity, this factor setting the practical limit on freight business.[92] Local freight traffic, however, frequently had to give
way to requirements of the government, and through freight
was costly because PW & B cars frequently traveled over the
B & O, and that line was constantly in danger of rebel attacks.[93]

Finally, like the Northern Central with its unprofitable Elmira Division, the PW & B had an unprofitable branch in Delaware. It had an important peach trade, however, and Felton said
that only the inability of the company to furnish it more rolling
stock kept it from showing a profit.[94] Thus while earnings, both
freight and passenger, were rising, so were expenses. While
prosperity was there, so were difficulties, delays, and exaspera-
tions. The results were all that could be expected, but "to accomplish these results has required unremitting labor, judgment,
and patience, far more so than in ordinary times."[95] This was
Felton's last year as head of the railroad. The strain of his wartime presidency, plus the necessity of defending his line against
government regulation, deprived him of the health necessary to
carry on. Sam Felton was, as much as any soldier, a casualty
of the war.

Profits soared again in 1864, the peak year for the PW & B.

The road double tracked 26 miles of line, bought eight new
locomotives (at $12,500 each), 13 new passenger cars (at
$5,000 each), and 230 new freight cars (at $700 each). Five
more piers of the Susquehanna bridge were built, a 10 per cent
dividend declared, and a record net revenue of $1,343,431.93
listed. Even the Delaware branch showed a profit.[96] The next
year brought larger gross earnings, but expenses increased by
almost 50 per cent,[97] and the net earnings decreased slightly. Ten
of the thirteen bridge piers were completed in 1865, and work
on the superstructure begun. Passenger earnings reached the
highest figure in the history of the road, just short of $3,000,-
000, chiefly due to the large number of demobilized troops using
the road just after the war.[98] Troops bound from Virginia to
the north and east were marched to Baltimore (the Washington
Branch of the B & O being occupied with carrying westbound
troops), and then used the PW & B in their homeward journey.[99]
Thus the PW & B found its business and its earnings increasing
throughout the war, but operations were confronted with difficulties, and rolling stock began to deteriorate under pressure
of heavy business. These wartime features were characteristic
of the railroads as a whole, whether they had a high percentage
of government business or none at all.

Chapter V

EFFECT OF THE WAR UPON RAILROAD BUSINESS: THE EAST-WEST TRUNK LINES

[In view of the increasing prices of materials,] how then can [the New York Central] be asked to carry passengers at a limited rate? It will carry them. Oh, yes! Restrict the price of razors to ten cents each, and razors will continue to be sold still. But what kind of razors? And what kind of traveling do we get for two cents a mile?

Merchants' Magazine and Commercial Review, LII, Jan.-June 1865

THE FOUR IMPORTANT EAST-WEST RAIL ROUTES in 1861 were the New York Central, the Erie, the Pennsylvania, and the Baltimore and Ohio. All except the B & O experienced increased business and increased profits during the war years, largely because of two important circumstances. First, the war had closed the Mississippi River as an avenue of travel. It is true that this route had not been used so much since 1855 as it had been before the trans-Allegheny railroads had been built. These railroads had been draining the valley of its commerce for some years before the war came, and by so doing had helped to tie the West economically to the North. The closing of the Mississippi River in 1861 made certain, however, that the agricultural produce of the vast western area of the United States would find its way to eastern markets by railroad.[1] Even after the Mississippi River was opened again in July, 1863, with the capture of Vicksburg, trade showed no inclination to use the southern route.[2]

The second important circumstance was that the early years

of the war coincided with poor crops in Europe, particularly England, with the result that there was an important European demand for American wheat and flour, a demand which meant much business for the railroads hauling produce to the eastern seaboard, chiefly New York, where the transatlantic steamship companies had their headquarters.[3] Fortunately for the railroads, the foreign demand coincided with the closure of the Mississippi as a trade route. The coincidence of these two factors with the occasional closing of the B & O due to war conditions provided the East-West lines with a land office business. While Europe was having crop failures, the states of Indiana, Illinois, Wisconsin, and Iowa were harvesting bumper crops. Each year of the war Chicago shipped 20,000,000 bushels of wheat and wheat flour; never before 1860 had similar shipments been as high as 10,000,000 bushels.[4] Record shipments were received and forwarded by Milwaukee, Detroit, Toledo, Cincinnati, and Buffalo. Much of this eastbound freight, of course, traveled by water via the Great Lakes and the Erie Canal. But increasing amounts of it went also by rail.[5]

The Pennsylvania Railroad participated profitably in this traffic. This line extended from Philadelphia to Pittsburgh. At the latter city it connected with the Pittsburgh, Ft. Wayne, and Chicago Railroad to serve the Middle West. The Pennsylvania's period of expansion in New Jersey and Maryland was still in the future. Net earnings of the road in 1861 were $3,646,938.19, an increase of one and one-third million over 1860, most of the increase being in the freight business. Freight revenues alone were $5,400,000:[6] "Nearly the whole of the increase in the revenues of the company, during the past year, was derived from the transportation of eastward bound freight, to meet the European demand for breadstuffs."[7]

It is interesting to note that the directors regarded this in-

crease as only temporary, to last until the Mississippi River
was reopened.[8] The trade was mostly a one-way business. Of
over 1,000,000 tons of freight moved by the railroad in 1861,
863,000 were eastbound. Of the through freight from west of
Pittsburgh, flour (87,500 tons), grain (46,000 tons), and livestock (45,500 tons) were the largest items carried, others being
coal, oil, lard and tallow, salt meats and fish, whisky and alcohol, tobacco, cotton, butter and eggs.[9] Though the railroad
regarded the trade as temporary, steps were taken to provide
adequate facilities for it. A grain elevator of 475,000-bushel
capacity was erected in connection with the railroad extension
from West Philadelphia to the Delaware River for shipment of
grain abroad.[10] Rolling stock was increased, though much of this
extra was to be used on the Philadelphia and Erie, acquired by
lease February 1, 1862.[11]

The grain trade, however, was not carried on to the exclusion
of other business. The Pennsylvania Railroad did a large business on government account. Its large movement of livestock
was accounted for by government orders. The railroad added
100 stock cars during 1861 to take care of this trade, but more
were needed.[12] In April, the railroad notified the public that
troops and munitions would have preference over its lines.[13]
Since the outbreak of war, 85,991 troops had been carried mostly
by special train, and as a result passenger cars began to show
distinct signs of wear.[14] Even this early, by the end of 1861, the
single-track main line was difficult to keep in repair because of
the large number of trains in operation. For this situation, the
early completion of a second track was the only possible
remedy.[15]

Business skyrocketed in 1862. The income from transporting
108,524 troops was $379,393.21, about 14 per cent of the en-
tire passenger revenue (to 1861's 10 per cent). Total earnings

passed $10,000,000, with freight at $7,600,000, and net earnings reached a record $4,800,000.[16] The coal tonnage alone increased so much that the railroad contracted for 200 coal cars, to be used along with 200 built by the Philadelphia and Reading, for the coal trade in the Allegheny and Broad Top regions.[17] Thirty-seven new engines were acquired (31 of them freight), and 930 new freight cars.[18] A second track was being laid between Harrisburg and Pittsburgh, with about 33 miles left to go, and President J. Edgar Thomson remarked that some busy sections of the road would soon require a third track.[19] The report of Superintendent Enoch Lewis attributed the road's prosperity to bumper crops, the closing of the Mississippi River, and government transportation. The only limiting factor in the traffic picture was the inadequate equipment of the road.[20] The equipment at this time consisted of 255 locomotives, 158 passenger, baggage and express cars, and 4,016 freight cars.[21] Valiant efforts were made to keep the equipment in good order. All the freight engines, and 10 passenger locomotives were burning coal as fuel, and many locomotives were using improved steel fire boxes. The cost of fuel per mile was reduced to $5.98 in 1862 from $6.41 in 1861.[22] All rebuilt passenger cars had raised roofs, improved ventilation, and were lighted with gas. But cars were seeing so much service that it was difficult to find time to keep them in first class condition.[23] The large amount of transportation increased considerably the expense for maintenance of way. The chief engineer also reported that the high labor demand coupled with the scarcity of workers because of the war, had interfered with the prosecution of ordinary repairs.[24]

The year 1863 brought, again, more business but also higher expenses. Gross earnings totaled $11,800,000, with net $5,100,-000. About 4,500,000 tons of freight were moved, over one third of which was coal; troop earnings increased to over $500,000.[25]

Maintenance of road alone cost $1,500,000, and new locomotives, new cars, and second track, $1,600,000.[26] Earnings were also put into the Philadelphia and Erie Railroad, and in the extension of the main line across Virginia from Pittsburgh to Steubenville, Ohio.[27] Scarcity of labor had forced a six months postponement in the opening of the Philadelphia and Erie. Scarcity of labor also accounted for the fact that the construction of the last 21 miles of second track between Lewistown and Mill Creek was suspended.[28] It was the military draft which accounted for much of this labor scarcity. Almost all the railroads complained that when they needed workers badly to handle the increasing business, these workers were being drained away into the armed forces. The Pennsylvania Railroad found that one of its greatest war time difficulties was that of maintaining an efficient labor force. Facilities had been stretched so tightly that "For a time it was impossible to procure a sufficient number of raw recruits even to run trains."[29] The draft affected the railroads indirectly also. Locomotives, cars, and rails all were of inferior quality because so much skilled labor had been drafted into the army.[30]

Higher train speeds and heavier locomotives than had previously been built were playing havoc with iron rails, already of inferior manufacture. Scarcity of labor and interruption of work in rolling mills meant even less replacement of worn rail than was expected, with the consequent rough and increasingly dangerous track.[31] Heavy traffic sometimes caused the iron to peel off in flakes, and occasionally rail ends would curl up and plow into the cars.[32] President Thomson, concerned with this state of affairs, noted that the tendency on European railroads was to substitute steel rails, or iron capped with steel.[33] In spite of the higher initial cost of steel, Thomson felt justified in procuring 150 tons of cast steel rails to test in termini and stations, where heavy use tended to wear out iron rail in as little as six months.[34] We shall note similar beginnings of the use of steel rails on other lines. The conditions imposed by the war were here working to bring about an important change in railroad operation. Undoubtedly the change would have eventually come without the war, but the war helped to bring about the adoption of steel rails more quickly than otherwise would have happened.

Lee's invasion of Pennsylvania in June, 1863, forced the adoption of protective measures by the railroad. Regular work was suspended at Columbia, Harrisburg, Mifflin, and Altoona, and attention turned to the protection of property.[35] Through freight traffic was suspended, and passenger business curtailed. For a time, a large amount of rolling stock was removed from the Midde Division (between Harrisburg and Altoona), but the company's property escaped unharmed.[36] The railroad posted scouts along the telegraph line south of the road along the state border. These scouts kept the railroad informed of Lee's movements, and they were one source of government information as to the whereabouts of the enemy. One author (a scout himself) says that the first information on the concentration at Gettysburg came from a railroad scout who carried it from Chambersburg to Port Royal, where it was wired to Harrisburg.[37]

The year 1863 saw the tremendous business of the railroad accompanied by a 40 per cent rise in labor cost, and inferior workmanship and materials in all classes of railroad supplies. The line increased its rolling stock and motive power, and made a separate branch of the car department to inspect and look after running repairs to the rolling stock.[38] It is interesting to note that, in contrast to 1861, the railroad now felt that wartime tonnage gains would be maintained, because of branch line extension and heavy demand for the products of the state.[39]

The next year brought even more business, the gross earnings being $14,700,000, but accelerating depreciation of the railroad plant caused a jump in expenses to over $10,600,000, leaving a net revenue of $4,100,000, considerably under 1863.[40] Troop earnings declined slightly, while freight tonnage and passenger business increased.[41] President Thomson's analysis of expenditures showed that in 1864 three dollars bought what one dollar would in 1861. As far as labor was concerned, the general principle seemed to be that as its price went up, its productivity decreased. Inferior workmanship coupled with great demand for locomotives and cars brought an increase in accidents. One result was that the railroad made no improvements that were not absolutely necessary.[42] The need to find better rails, however, resulted in continued experiments with steel rails. The steel rails purchased in 1863 were installed in sidings at Altoona and Pittsburgh. Though they appeared too brittle for main line work, at the end of the first year of use none were broken and none showed signs of wear. The chief engineer was, therefore, confident that the experiment would be successful. Thomson thought their high cost, however, would preclude their general introduction. Meanwhile new iron rails were increased $4\frac{1}{2}$ inches in depth to provide 30 per cent additional vertical strength.[43] Steel began to be used in other parts of the railroad plant, also. A number of engines were fitted with steel tires, which promised greater durability. Passenger cars were constructed with steel axles to give greater safety.[44]

The end of the war brought heavy troop transportation to the Pennsylvania Railroad as the Army of the Potomac was demobilized. About 18 per cent of the 1865 earnings came from troop transportation, contrasting with about $3\frac{1}{2}$ per cent in 1864.[45] The months after the war showed a gradual decline in quantity of freight hauled. Rolling stock was not fully employed, and existing lines were somewhat in excess of requirements. Competition became stiffer and forced the railroad to lease some of its freight business to private companies, as the New York trunk lines had already done.[46] Thus the Pennsylvania Railroad, one of the important East-West trunk lines, exhibited the typical characteristics of the war era—prosperity, tempered with rising prices, scarcity of labor, and deterioration of equipment.

At Pittsburgh, the Pennsylvania received the bulk of its Western traffic from a line soon to be completely absorbed within its system, the Pittsburgh, Ft. Wayne, and Chicago Railroad, characterized as the "cheapest, quickest, and safest" freight route from West to East.[47] Like many other lines, this one had been forced into receivership in the depression years succeeding the panic of 1857. It was in 1861 that the railroad emerged from the red for the first time, with net earnings of $1,299,-721.05.[48] Freight traffic in that year passed 500,000 tons, and earnings in this category showed an increase of 75 per cent, chiefly in livestock (hogs and sheep) and in flour and grain, which provided the greatest amount of business for the railroad.[49] Almost all of this additional tonnage was through traffic eastbound, that is, destined for points east of Pittsburgh. Freight earnings were highest in the winter months when the Great Lakes route was closed and all tonnage had to go by rail. Troop travel was estimated to be 25 per cent of the increase in total passenger travel. Since the latter was about 124,-000, the number of troops carried by this railroad in the first year of the war totaled about 31,000.[50]

In 1862 the railroad was reorganized as the Pittsburgh, Ft. Wayne, and Chicago Railway Company. George W. Cass became president, and J. Edgar Thomson of the Pennsylvania, and Samuel J. Tilden, the New York Democrat whose legal practice had concerned the reorganization of several railroads, were directors of the road. Business, stimulated by war demands, boomed in 1862. Net earnings reached almost $2,000,000, with both eastbound and westbound tonnage (the latter being mostly coal, lumber, and general merchandise) gaining over 1861.[51] The expected decrease in traffic in the summer because of Great Lakes shipping failed to materialize, and already necessary maintenance work on track was being postponed in order to care for the heavy traffic.[52] Available motive power was decreased when the government requisitioned three engines from the railroad in July.[53] The directors felt that the concentration of the meat packing industry at Chicago and the increasing produce of the Northwest would assure the road of a constant source of revenue; the fact that the road had substantial traffic in 1860 seemed to suggest that the reopening of the Mississippi River would not dry up the traffic being built up during the war years.[54] An ominous note was sounded, however, in the fact that increases in operating expenses were greater than increases in earnings.[55]

In 1863 the road fared even better. Net earnings topped $2,100,000, freight providing 65 per cent of the gross income of the line. The annual report stated that the company was unable to handle all the freight offered to it because of lack of necessary rolling stock.[56] Earnings surpassed all expectations in 1864, with gross income at $7,120,465.76, and net just over $3,000,000. From troop transportation the company earned $510,023.75, and from hauling military supplies $196,217.09. Thus the total earnings from military transportation, $706,-240.81, were less than 10 per cent of the gross earnings.[57] The prosperity of this railroad was not due to military transportation but to eastbound tonnage in livestock and grain, most of it headed to points east of Pittsburgh. Cattle, sheep, beef, manufactures, coal, and lumber were carried in increasing quantities, while army supplies such as horses, hogs, and liquor showed a large falling off in tonnage.[58] Passenger traffic increased over 100 per cent, a phenomenon which the report attributed to the large amount of paper money in circulation, giving more people the means to travel, and to the fact that the war had withdrawn from the Ohio Valley, giving the eastern division of the road (between Crestline and Pittsburgh) more passenger traffic.[59] As a result, passenger car equipment proved inadequate to handle the traffic. More than half the coaches, baggage, and mail cars in service needed repair, "yet the pressure of travel is so great that they cannot be spared from the track long enough to go into the shops."[60] Neither did the road have the necessary freight cars. Company shops for building new cars remained uncompleted, and at the same time the road had to build 40 box cars for the government—for $1,071 each, a rate less than that prevailing in the industry.[61] Inadequate rolling stock was accompanied by deterioration of track and roadbed. High-priced railroad iron was inferior in quality, and the defective track resulted in casualties that impaired the efficiency of the road.[62] Scarcity and high price of labor also plagued the line. Special work done on the railroad in 1864 was estimated to be worth $1,900,000, but actually cost $2,700,000. Grading projects at Alliance and Crestline were suspended because the price of labor was higher than the contractors were able to pay.[63]

The increase in through traffic experienced during the war years by railroads which connected points not far distant from each other served to make the railroads interdependent on one another, and to provide an economic basis for the consolidation of short lines into great systems which came about in the postwar years. Many railroads carried much freight which originated on a different line and was destined for a third road. The business of most railroads was not entirely localized on their own lines, so that inevitably a community of interest began to grow up among groups of lines. Of course this trend had been active to some extent in the fifties—witness the consolidation of the New York Central from several smaller links—but the war, with its increasing amount of through traffic, both freight and passenger, accelerated the trend. The railroads were losing their primarily local character, and becoming more truly national or at least sectional in scope. This trend toward cooperation was most dramatically evident in the long-distance mass troop movements which took place during the war, but it also was present in the day to day small-scale movements, military and otherwise. An illustration can be cited by listing the different lines which owed accounts to the Pittsburgh, Ft. Wayne, and Chicago Railway in 1864. Amounts were due from 73 other railroads, the following list giving military accounts only:[64]

Bellefontaine
Ohio Central
Chicago and Rock Island
Chicago and North Western
Cincinnati, Hamilton & Dayton
Cleveland, Columbus &
    Cincinnati
Chicago, Burlington and Quincy
Illinois Central
Jeffersonville
Little Miami, & Columbus
    & Xenia
Michigan Southern and
    Northern Indiana

Atlantic and Great Western
Milwaukee and Prairie du Chien
Northern Central
Great Western
Cleveland and Pittsburgh
Lafayette and Indianapolis
Steubenville & Indiana
Illinois & Southern Iowa
Chicago and Milwaukee
Indianapolis & Madison
Cleveland & Toledo
Milwaukee and St. Paul
Indianapolis, Peru, and Chicago
Ohio and Mississippi

At the same time, the Pittsburgh, Ft. Wayne, and Chicago owed military accounts to the following railroads:[65]

Hannibal and St. Joseph
Pennsylvania
Sandusky, Dayton, and
    Cincinnati
St. Louis, Alton, and Terre
    Haute
Terre Haute and Richmond
Western
Sandusky, Mansfield, and
    Newark
Evansville & Crawfordsville

Oswego and Syracuse
Cleveland, Zanesville, &
    Cincinnati
Toledo and Wabash
Chicago and Alton
Ohio and Mississippi
Quincy and Toledo
New Castle and Beaver Valley
Great Central
Erie and Pittsburgh

The year 1865 saw increases in passenger earnings, expenses, and in net earnings, with about 6½ per cent of the business being military transportation.[66] Freight tonnage was down, especially in the eastbound through traffic.[67] Though a good deal of main track was relaid, the company considered inferior railroad iron at $135 a ton an unsatisfactory investment, and decided to experiment with steel rails imported from Europe in 1866.[68] Like the Pennsylvania Railroad, the Pittsburgh, Ft. Wayne, and Chicago contracted with two private transportation companies for carriage of merchandise. Though opposing such a system at first, the competition of other lines forced the move.[69]

Together, the Pittsburgh, Ft. Wayne, and Chicago and the Pennsylvania Railroad formed one of the important East-West routes between the Midwest and the Eastern seaboard. Another of these trans-Allegheny lines was the Erie Railroad, with a 460-mile main line from Jersey City to Dunkirk, and an important 60-mile branch to Buffalo. The Erie Railway Company was organized in 1862, taking over the old New York and Erie Railroad from receivership. The Civil War Period of the Erie was one of good management, under President Nathaniel Marsh and Superintendent Charles Minot.[70] Numbered among the directors were Daniel Drew and Commodore Vanderbilt, but the chief machinations of these gentlemen were reserved for later years. The Erie was safely remote from the theater of military conflict, and did not receive any considerably amount of business from the government. The line attributed its increased earnings in 1862 to a general increase in business, inflation, and the foreign demand for wheat.[71] For a railroad just emerging from receivership, the line was showing immense profits. Its net earnings in 1862 exceeded $3,500,000, and its surplus amounted to $1,636,350.77. Of the earnings, 71 per cent came from eastbound freight, which amounted to 972,332 tons, an increase of more than 150,000 tons over the previous year.[72] Rolling stock and equipment was being maintained to care for the record business. The railroad was fenced and stone ballast replaced the lighter gravel.[73] Fifteen locomotives and 100 freight cars had been ordered, and company shops were busy repairing and reconditioning rolling stock, and converting locomotives to burning coal, a step which the railroad found quite economical.[74] It should be noted that this excellent financial condition of the Erie had developed *before* any substantial traffic was being received from the Atlantic and Great Western, or from the Pennsylvania oil fields. But the road was anticipating this business. Its new terminus at Long Dock (Jersey City) was capable of handling more business than the railroad could transport to it.[75] The new connection at Cleveland was expected to take some revenue from the Lake Shore Railroad; in addition, the line already had arrangements for through passenger travel from Buffalo via the leased Buffalo, New York, and Erie to Corning, hence via the Elmira and Williamsport to Philadelphia and Baltimore, with a change only at Elmira.[76]

Dunkirk was the western terminus of the Erie, and it was from there that the company calculated its business. Eastbound tonnage in 1862 totaled 308,000 tons. Of this total, 138,000 (including 180,000 barrels of flour, and over 6,500,000 dressed hogs) was from the Buffalo and Erie Railroad, 81,500 tons from Toledo (including 479,500 barrels of flour), and 15,500 tons from Sandusky (including 110,000 barrels of flour). All of these figures were substantial increases over 1861. More cattle, hogs, and horses were transported than in the previous year, only sheep showing a slight decline.[77] In 1863 the line, in spite of increasing expenses brought on by high prices and high wages, increased its net earnings to over $4,000,000, and its surplus to over $2,000,000.[78] The character of its business was changing, however. Eastbound through tonnage decreased by 18,500 tons, but was more than offset by the revenue derived from way freight, particularly the carrying of coal from the Pennsylvania fields.[79] More branches were being constructed to tap bituminous coal fields from the Buffalo, Bradford and Pittsburgh Railroad.[80]

Beneath the prosperity, however, there were adverse factors which were affecting the general condition of the line. The railroad was being worked to capacity, and there were delays because the track was constantly filled with trains. The difficulty of procuring iron limited the construction of double track.[81] Though the line had 271 locomotives, and about 3,500 freight cars, its rolling stock was inadequate to handle the business offered, a condition which was calculated to have deprived the road of $1,000,000 in income. Finally, the government had requisitioned some of the rolling stock for use south of Elmira, lessening the revenue from that source.[82] In spite of these adverse factors, however, "the condition of the company was never more prosperous than it is now, and the prospects of a successful year never more flattering."[83]

The optimistic outlook was justified when the net earnings

in 1864 reached $4,594,725.10. Expenses had increased to 65.7 per cent of the total earnings.[84] Increasing expenses resulted partly from the higher price of coal which increased the operating cost of locomotives, and partly from the higher price of iron rail and the increasing amounts of it laid. Railroad iron cost the Erie $105 a ton in 1864, only $58.66 in 1863.[85] Coal was one third cheaper than wood, the latter being extremely scarce.[86] Rolling stock was inadequate and most of it badly in need of repair. Engines worked 24 hours a day for periods far too long for the most economical maintenance; nor were there enough shops to do all repairs necessary.[87] Most railroads followed the policy of postponing permanent improvements until the postwar period when they expected there would be some recession from the high prices, but the Erie justified such expenses at this time because of the high demand for its services. The Atlantic and Great Western Railway, still lacking its expected connection with Cincinnati, was already complaining that the Erie could not handle its eastbound freight.[88]

In 1865, the railroad began to see some reversals of the trend that seemed to bring a constant deterioration of rolling stock and equipment. Its net earnings passed $5,000,000 with freight business up 10 per cent, passenger business 34 per cent. Most of the latter was in way traffic, probably troops returning to towns along the line.[89] Expenses passed one million dollars, the increase being chiefly in repairs to rolling stock and in fuel cost. Generally speaking, the cost of railroad materials was going down. Railroad iron was down to $90 a ton, but even this was so high that the line was substituting cast steel in renewals of axles and tires.[90] Once again the railroad was able to handle all business offered to it.[91]

The New York Central Railroad, 298 miles from Albany to Buffalo, was even farther removed from the scene of conflict than the Erie. As an important East-West carrier, however, it found its business increasing during the war years, carrying east the livestock and agricultural produce of the Middle West in return for merchandise freight. By 1861 the road already had a history of growth and prosperity. Earnings had increased every year since 1853 except for the depression years of 1858 and 1859.[92] The closing of the Baltimore and Ohio Railroad because of military action increased the tonnage of the New York Central as well as that of other East-West roads. Noting that the railroad sent 20,000 bushels of wheat east by rail in a recent 10-day period, the Rochester *Democrat* stated: "The obstruction of the Baltimore and Ohio Railroad will make one less competitor to the Central for some time, and will no doubt contribute materially to the increase of traffic this way."[93] In May, 150 cars a day were being sent east from Buffalo, with as many more from way stations.[94] By November, business had increased to the point where 400 to 450 freight cars (16 to 18 trains), plus 12 passenger trains, were arriving at Albany daily.[95] Flour was the big factor here. In one week, 19 ships with an average of 4,000 barrels of flour each, cleared Toledo for the New York Central at Buffalo, and about 5,000 barrels of flour daily came from the Michigan Southern and Northern Indiana at Toledo.[96]

In the year ending September 30, 1862, the road handled 1,064,128 tons of freight eastbound, an increase of almost 200,000 over the previous year. Westbound tonnage also increased to 323,305.[97] While passenger earnings remained constant, freight earnings jumped from $4,664,000 to $6,607,000.[98] In 1863, the upward spiral continued. With 239 engines and 4,006 freight cars, the road's freight earnings totaled $7,499,000, though the actual tonnage was about 20,000 less than the previous year, higher rates accounting for the

difference.[99] Monthly earnings had passed $1,000,000 in October
and December, 1862, and quite commonly after September,
1863.[100] In 1864, income from passengers showed a substantial
increase, bringing in $3,923,000, and accompanied by a 20
per cent increase in the number of passengers carried. Freight
tonnage again resumed its upward trend, totaling over 1,500,-
000 tons, and bringing in $8,543,000 in spite of the 2½ per
cent government tax on earnings, collection of which began
in July, 1864.[101] For the New York Central, the peak earnings
of the Civil War period came in the fiscal year ending September
30, 1865. Though freight tonnage had shown a small decrease,
total freight earnings increased slightly. Passenger business,
heavy in July, August, and September, carrying home demobilized troops, jumped to over 3,750,000 passengers carried, an
income of about $4,500,000, with total earnings just under
$14,000,000. The earnings of 3.26 cents per ton mile were
the highest since the organization of the railroad in 1853.[102]
As with other railroads these earnings came in spite of higher
prices for materials. During 1864-65 alone, rerolled iron rail
rose from $22 to $52 a ton, wood from $2.25 to $6 a cord, and
car wheels from $16 to $25.[103]

It remains to speak of the carrier most affected by the war
itself. The Baltimore and Ohio Railroad was the southern-
most of the four East-West lines, and exposed along its whole
flank to attack and destruction by both sides because of its
geographic location on the border between North and South.
The Washington Branch, the feeder from the North to the
Virginia military railroads, suffered less war damage than the
main stem of the B & O. Although the passenger revenue of the
former declined from $42,000 in March, 1861, to $8,000 in
April, then climbed again to $11,000 in May, and $25,000 in
June, the road was open except for the short interval in April

and May, and in October the entire branch was returned to the company for operation.[104] The main stem of the B & O, westward from Relay House through Harper's Ferry and Cumberland to Wheeling, was a constant objective of the Confederate forces, and was throughout the war subject to destructive raids.[105] On May 28, 1861, Confederates occupied over 100 miles of line, mostly between Point of Rocks to the east of Harper's Ferry and Cumberland to the west.[106] This occupation was a severe blow to East-West communication, because the main stem was an important outlet for Western produce. Governor Dennison of Ohio expressed to Garrett the hope that the route from Cincinnati to Baltimore might be reopened so that livestock could be sent east.[107] Besides livestock, the road carried coal, lumber, and flour eastward. The road was important enough to be the main objective of McClellan's northwestern Virginia campaign in the spring of 1861, which succeeded in keeping the line west of Cumberland free of enemy occupation.[108] The Confederate commander whose headquarters were at Harper's Ferry was Thomas J. "Stonewall" Jackson. For some time after May 28, Jackson allowed all trains to run back and forth, probably because he was trying to win as many Confederate sympathizers in the area as he could, and hence did not want to indulge in too much property destruction. For more than two weeks, B & O East-West trains were literally run through the lines of both armies.[109] Because the Confederacy sorely needed locomotives and rolling stock, Jackson soon contrived a ruse to capture some from the railroad. On the pretext that the long, noisy coal trains rattling through Harper's Ferry at all hours of the night were disturbing the sleep of his men, he sent a message to Garrett proposing to concentrate the traffic in daylight hours. Garrett, his railroad leading a precarious day-to-day existence, was only too glad to comply. The plan was to set up an area extending 27 miles east and west of Harper's Ferry, with Point of Rocks the eastern boundary and Martinsburg the western. All eastbound trains were to enter this area between 11 A.M. and 1 P.M. daily, and at no other time.[110] Jackson then extended the restriction to westbound trains, using the same hours. Watching his plan work out in practice, the crafty Confederate leader soon realized what a perfect trap he had. When it became necessary for Jackson to retreat from Harper's Ferry in June, 1861, he decided to spring the trap. One morning he stationed guards at either end of the 54-mile area, ordering them to allow trains to enter the area between the hours of 11 and 1, but not to leave. It worked perfectly. Caught in the trap and destroyed were 42 locomotives and 386 cars; 23 bridges were burned, 102 miles of telegraph line torn down, and two water stations destroyed. Because of his own transportation difficulties, Jackson could carry with him only 14 locomotives, and undetermined number of cars, and 36½ miles of rail which his men had torn up.[111] Wreaking damage on the machine shops and engine houses at Martinsburg, and blowing up the bridge at Harper's Ferry, Jackson disappeared south. His work had been done well. From June 14, 1861, until March 28, 1862, no trains ran between Baltimore and Wheeling.[112] As a result of these events, the earnings of the main stem westward (distinct from the Washington Branch) declined over $700,000 from the previous fiscal year, though passenger revenue alone was up because of troop transportation in the area between the Ohio River and Cumberland.[113] Freight tonnage naturally fell off. Shippers did not care to risk the B & O route as long as other routes farther north were available. Besides periodic interruption of the line by military events, rolling stock was frequently absorbed in military usage, further hampering normal operations.[114] The wartime reports of the

B & O include a diary kept by W. P. Smith, master of transportation. Citing some of these entries will reveal the problems with which this line had to cope. On June 2, 1861, the destruction of a bridge hurled more than 50 loaded coal cars into a chasm, where they burned for two months, the intense heat melting axles and wheels.[115]

In 1862 the main stem was open only from March 29 to May 5, and June 15 to September 5. But reduced rates and heavy eastbound tonnage enabled the road to show a million dollar increase in net earnings over the previous year.[116] The extensive military service performed by the road was usually done on short notice, and as a result deranged the normal freight business.[117] Passenger income showed an increase of over $800,000, though it was noted that government accounts were frequently left unsettled for a long time.[118] One important element in the increased business of the road in spite of its precarious location was the growth of the city of Washington. From a pre-war population of 60,000, the city was swollen with war workers and government clerks; an army of 200,000 was encamped in the vicinity. In addition, another mode of transportation to the city, by water via the Potomac River, was cut off by hostile batteries on the southern shore. The chief result of this situation was that, while pre-war needs of the city could be filled by eight freight cars per day, now "the number of cars delivered at Washington frequently exceeded four hundred daily, loaded with the greatest possible variety of supplies for the army and citizens."[119] Track repairs continued at a somewhat slower pace during this year because long periods of occupation by the enemy prevented any work whatsoever. Nevertheless 49.9 miles of track were relaid, and a direct connection made at Relay House between the Washington Branch and the main stem.[120]

A glance at the diary of this year showed that not all destruction to the line was done by the Confederates. January 31, 1862, "U. S. troops burned 6 pens for loading cattle at Patterson's Creek"; February 7, "U. S. forces, under Col. Geary . . . [at Harper's Ferry] burned the Company's hotel, warehouse, ticket office and water station."[121] In March, cold and swift currents hampered the rebuilding of Harper's Ferry bridge. It was completed on March 30, but high water in April took out one span with 14 loaded coal cars on it, and a few days later three more spans collapsed.[122] In September, during Lee's invasion of Maryland, the enemy blew up the suspension bridge at Monocacy, forcing the workmen to bury dead men, horses, and cattle before reconstruction could be commenced.[123] The battle of Antietam was fought eight miles north of the B & O's Kearneysville station.[124]

The fiscal year ending September 30, 1863, brought continued destruction of track, bridges, rolling stock, and other property of the company. In November, 1862, 25 miles of track was destroyed from three miles west of Harper's Ferry to 10 miles west of Martinsburg. Shops and buildings at the latter place were also destroyed.[125] The raid of Jones and Imboden in April, 1863, resulted in the capture of a stock train and the destruction of several bridges, including the three 205-foot iron spans over the Monongahela River, the largest iron bridge on the road.[126] By May 14, the line was reopened, but not for long. On June 5, Lee was reported crossing the railroad at Point of Rocks. Ten days later the report was confirmed, and all rolling stock and motive power was sent east of Martinsburg. On June 17, Cumberland was occupied, and for the next three weeks, bridges, stations, and rolling stock were destroyed in wholesale manner. On July 5, with the tide of battle surging in the opposite direction, Union troops burned trestle work at

Harper's Ferry and over the Chesapeake and Ohio Canal. It was July 14 before repairs east of Cumberland could be commenced. July 23 an ironclad train ran from Harper's Ferry to Opequon, but it was August 10 before the line was officially open again.[127] In this entire fiscal year, the road was in possession of the company only six months and six days, but even that was more than the four and a half months of the previous fiscal year. As a consequence of this improvement, plus higher freight rates, the main stem showed net earnings of $4,500,000.[128] In spite of these conditions, the railroad shops at Mount Clare were busy rebuilding 180 cars of various types, and constructing 263 new freight cars.[129]

Though the railroad was free from prolonged occupation in 1864, the year did produce more than its share of alarms and difficulties. Here are two typical entries in the diary:

Jan. 4, 1864: Attack threatened upon Martinsburg and Cumberland by a large force of cavalry and infantry. Engines and cars were sent from Martinsburg to Sandy Hook. Express train west was held at Monocacy until the 5th, and the passengers sent forward on mail train. . . . Mail train east was held at Cumberland. Troop trains were run to Cumberland, and on the 6th all trains ran regularly.[130]

Sometimes the threatened attacks never materialized, but the threat itself was enough to dislocate traffic.

Oct. 13, 1864: The enemy were reported by military authority to be advancing on Martinsburg. Engines and cars were all sent east from that station. Express trains and Tonnage trains west did not leave Baltimore. Express train east was held at Cumberland.

Oct. 14, 1864: The alarm at Martinsburg was premature, and business was fully resumed.[131]

Probably the most serious raid was that of Jubal Early in the summer of 1864. The attack began on July 2 when troops in an ironclad train drove off an attacking party at Great Cacapon

River.[132] Frederick was evacuated July 8, and the next day the railroad had to send several trains to transport wounded from the battlefield at Monocacy. By July 11, Early had pushed beyond the B & O and was destroying bridges on the Philadelphia, Wilmington, and Baltimore, the Northern Central, and harassing men constructing a second track on the Washington Branch at Beltsville, Maryland. After capturing a work train and burning clothing and provisions, the raiding force moved south on the 13th. That afternoon a hand car from Bladenburg and Engine 19 from Washington got through to Baltimore with the first news of the enemy's retreat.[133] Early was gone, but the main line was not opened through until after Sheridan had defeated Early at Winchester in September.[134]

The 1864 report first spoke of manpower difficulties on the railroad. Repeated conscriptions plus bounties for volunteers caused the company to lose many of its best men. Others left because of the dangerous conditions of work. Still others were lost through disease, capture, or accident.[135] Practically no mention is made of troops defending the railroad. Occasionally military protection was furnished to workers restoring the railroad,[136] and in July, 1864, 100-day volunteers from Ohio were defending bridges along the line.[137] Apparently the destruction and protection of the railroad was only a means to get at opposing armies, not an end in itself, and no systematic military defense was ever undertaken by the government.

The collapse of the Confederacy in the fall and winter of 1864-65 was reflected in the now only occasional small-scale attacks at isolated points along the railroad. These were mere pin pricks compared to the full-scale attacks of other years. The heaviest railroad operation of the year came with the disbanding of the armies of Grant and Sherman after the national reviews at the end of the war. In this operation, the Baltimore and

Ohio Railroad sent a daily average of 4,245 men north and west from Washington. Highs were achieved on June 5, 1865, with 13,943 men shipped out, June 7 with 13,935, and June 9 with 10,259. In 49 days, 208,037 troops traveled over the Baltimore and Ohio.[138]

So the nightmare ended. As a conclusion one might well cite the report of the master of machinery in 1865 that of the 14 engines taken by Jackson in the first raid in 1861, 12 engines, 11 tenders, and a boiler of a 13th engine were ultimately recovered, but in very bad condition.[139] Military events had caused untold amounts of damage, most of which had to be made up by the railroad itself. In December, 1868, John W Garrett told his Board of Directors that for all the property destroyed by the Confederates, "amounting to many mililons of dollars, no payment had been made by the government, nor has any compensation yet been made for large amounts of property destroyed by our Federal forces for strategic purposes."[140]

Prosperity had come to these trunk lines during the Civil War, whether or not they had government patronage. Greater demand for goods at higher prices both at home and abroad brought large profits, growing larger with each succeeding year of conflict.[141] But with larger earnings, came larger expenses. Lack of manpower made materials scarce and of inferior quality, and labor expensive. The demand for transportation kept trains running, cutting down on time for repair and maintenance, and contributed to progressive deterioration of rolling stock and equipment. The demands of the government could not wait, nor could the military. It was a time of troubles that no railroad official cared to experience more than once.

Chapter VI

EFFECT OF THE WAR UPON RAILROAD
BUSINESS: THE CHICAGO RAILROADS

As labor and material advanced in price, the quality of both depreciated. The high bounties paid for enlistment, and the several drafts, took or scattered the better of our laborers, leaving us, as a general thing, for laborers, those physically disabled for military service.

> *4th Annual Report of the Milwaukee and*
> *Prairie du Chien Railway Co, ... 1864.*

RAILROADS terminating in Chicago went through experiences similar to those in other sections of the North. Booming prosperity, based here largely on the grain trade, was again hampered by lack of rolling stock, mounting expenses, and increasing depreciation of equipment. The experience of the Michigan Central Railroad clearly showed these changes during the war years. The opening of the Civil War found the Michigan Central recovering slowly from earlier depression years. This progressive road, under the direction of John W. Brooks, lay in the rich territory connecting Detroit and Chicago. Since about 90 per cent of its tonnage was grain, flour, and lumber, all eastbound, business fluctuated considerably; and many cars were run westward empty for lack of tonnage to transport.[1] Passenger business declined sharply in late 1860 and early 1861. The road was accustomed to heavy business in that field, having experienced a boom the previous year in carrying passengers to the Republican National Convention in Chicago. Four sleeping cars were built to handle passenger traffic on the line.[2] The general superintendent, R. N. Rice, blamed the war for the decline in passenger business.

It is quite evident that the Passenger business of the road is injured to some extent by the war. . . . the Passenger traffic of some of the lines south and east of us are not affected in like manner, they being to a greater or less extent participants in the transportation of troops, munitions of war, and other business incidental to the war, in which this line, from its geographical position, does not participate. Our natural business from the south has been almost entirely cut off by the present state of non-intercourse with that region.[3]

Troop transportation, of course, was an uncertain source of income, and the uncertainty, making necessary the holding of cars in readiness for any sudden demand for this type of transportation, probably deprived this source of income of much of its attractiveness. For instance, troop transportation accounted for 3½ per cent of the Pennsylvania Railroad's earnings in 1864, 18 per cent in 1865. Resulting wear and tear on cars must certainly have been a factor in overloading the repair facilities of the railroads. Both the Pennsylvania and the Northern Central complained of this fact. Many railroads such as the New York Central, and Erie, which must have transported some troops, did not bother to keep these statistics separate from ordinary passenger traffic, apparently not regarding troop transportation as an important or continuing source of income. Nevertheless the Michigan Central continued to be envious of roads favored with a large amount of government business. The 1862 report said, "The injury caused to our business by the state of the country has been but in very small degree made up by the patronage of the government." Again, ". . . the transportation of troops and munitions of war has been almost exclusively of a local nature, and quite limited in amount."[4] Financially speaking, the road was well off. Its net earnings in 1862 amounted to $1,212,088.48, an increase of almost $300,000. Its operating ratio was only 45.1 per cent.[5] With freight earnings up 28 per cent, the railroad arranged with the Louisville,

New Albany, and Chicago to operate between Michigan City
and Lafayette, Indiana, running through cars to the latter
town. The Michigan Central also furnished cars for two through
trains between Cincinnati and Chicago.[6] In 1863, the road reported a 23 per cent increase in passenger receipts, the first
increase in five years. Local freight was up 20 per cent, and
the road was already looking forward to permanent prosperity.[7]
Freight tonnage reached the highest point of the war period,
564,827 tons, and the road increased its dividend from 3 per
cent to 8 per cent.[8]

The gain in passenger receipts continued in 1864, the rise of
41.8 per cent to over $1,000,000 being attributed to the im-
proved financial condition of the Western states.[9] It was pointed
out that the increased earnings came without the aid of any
significant amount of government patronage, though the passenger business to some extent comprised local troop movement.[10]
The Michigan Central was handicapped for through troop
movements, because its eastward connections ran through
Canada, and the government would not allow the use of the
route for eastward movements.[11] If the road lacked government patronage, it was not because Washington ignored it. The
War Department requisitioned both cars and engines, and in
1864 the government bought 75 box cars, 4 second-class cars,
and one engine, the "Stranger."[12]

The prohibition of the use of Canada for eastward troop
movements arose from the fact that the north shore of Lake
Erie was a favorite haunt of Confederate sympathizers, who
conducted raids across the border and on Great Lakes shipping.
In the winter of 1864-65, a government order required all
through passengers traveling via Canada to have passports.
The inconvenience of obtaining them diverted many passengers
to the Michigan Southern and other lines, and by cutting off

through passenger business on the Michigan Central for the three months the order was in effect, cost the railroad a large revenue.[13] In addition, the company had to maintain an expensive organization to protect its river-front premises from threatened raids from Canada, the government providing no military force for this purpose.[14] More revenue was lost because Eastern connections could not handle all the freight offered, and because much more Western produce was going to the armies in Tennessee.[15]

In spite of these handicaps, however, the fiscal year 1864-65 saw net earnings rise to a new high of $1,739,269.94, a figure which would have been much higher but for increasing prices of labor and materials. These latter advanced more quickly than transportation rates, even though freight rates were up 26 per cent over the previous year. The operating ratio had risen to 55.8 per cent.[16] Grain and livestock were the chief interests of the Michigan Central. In 1864 the railroad built a 700,000-bushel elevator at Detroit to give adequate storage space to its grain shipments.[17] In 1865, the line, along with several other railroads centering in Chicago, formed the Union Stock Yards Company to handle the increasing livestock business.[18] Thus in spite of severe obstacles to overcome, and lack of government patronage, the road continued to increase its net earnings each year of the war, and its dividends rose to 12 per cent in 1864, and 18 per cent in 1865, the peak year of its prosperity.[19]

One of the most important lines radiating from Chicago was the Illinois Central Railroad, running south from Dunleith to Cairo, Ill., with a branch from Chicago joining the main line at Centralia.[20] Pre-war traffic on this railroad lay chiefly in connections with railroads south of the Ohio River. Merchandise, coal, wheat, corn, lumber, hides, and dressed pork were the chief products carried. The war suddenly disrupted this traffic. In April, 1861, a military force of 8,000 to 9,000 troops was concentrated at Cairo, and the railroad for 253 miles south of the Terre Haute and Alton was used chiefly for transportation of troops and stores.[21] The directors of the road did not regard government patronage as of any advantage whatsoever in 1861. Perhaps if the Michigan Central officials had read the Illinois Central report, they would not have been so envious of railroads which were favored (or handicapped) with government business. Financially, the Illinois Central performed only $207,000 worth of government service in 1861, when total receipts of the road were $2,899,612.64, and net $1,315,268.55.[22] But this small segment had important effects on the general business of the line, because troops and munition trains had preference over other traffic. Only short notice was given for troop movements, and the amount of time spent in concentrating the rolling stock was twice that required for ordinary business.[23] In addition, the railroad could not charge the same rate for government business as most other lines. Land-grant roads, of which the Illinois Central was one, were obliged to charge only one and one-third cents per troop mile, instead of the two cents established as a general rate in 1862. For munitions, the line was forced to give a one-third cut below the regular 10 per cent reduction other roads gave to government business. Thus the government paid cheap rates in return for the land grants originally made to aid in the building of the railroad. Since the actual cost of operating the troop trains was 1.8 cents a mile, the return of 1.3 cents made the business a losing proposition and took away potential profits from local traffic by tying up rolling stock.[24] The passenger cars of the Illinois Central were not in first class condition in 1861, and troops proved to be a severe hardship on the passenger cars.

Large masses of men, with guns and accoutrements, crowded into cars, without the restraints of ordinary passengers, has resulted in extraordinary destruction to this class of property. With a probability of considerable service of this kind before us, we have merely endeavored to keep the passenger cars in a safe condition.[25]

The year 1862 found the Illinois Central voicing the now familiar complaint of insufficient rolling stock to transport the freight offered. The road noted a steady tide of immigration into Illinois from adjoining states, families who bought land from the railroad and paid for it in grain. At this time the city of Chicago and the state of Illinois were rapidly expanding in population. Chicago almost tripled its population in the ten years between 1860 (about 112,000) and 1870 (about 299,000). The state population increased by 800,000, far more than any other state.[26] The railroad found itself unable to provide cars to handle the record grain crop offered.[27] Net earnings rose to $1,830,570.84, including $475,313.97 from army transportation, mostly in carrying 151,967 troops.[28] This was still, however, not a business which the road looked upon with pleasure. The average amount earned per mile of troop transportation in 1862 was $580.31, the comparable figure for ordinary passenger travel being $1,300.55.[29] In the last six months of 1862, the price of labor rose by 15 to 20 per cent, that of materials by 10 to 50 per cent, this too a familiar experience to the wartime railroads.[30]

The next year brought prosperity. Total earnings surpassed $4,500,000, net amounting to $2,419,241.71, the increase being attributed to greater variety of products carried (such as lead, tobacco, and cotton), and the opening of the Mississippi River in July after the victory at Vicksburg.[31] Costs were rising sharply. In 1862, the cost per mile run by each locomotive was 17.4 cents; in 1863 it was 22.3 cents, most of the increase being due to the 72 per cent rise in the cost of coal, used as fuel by 82 of the road's 123 engines.[32] Though fewer troops were carried, the disadvantage of this type of traffic to the Illinois Central was even more dramatically illustrated: it yielded only $421.69 per mile, as against $2,121.41,[33] for ordinary passenger traffic. By 1864, the road was less impressed with its record net earnings of $2,868,707.81, than the fact that the 18 per cent rise in net earnings had come with a booming traffic increase of 38 per cent. There was great dissatisfaction over the disruption of normal traffic due to the necessity of shipping large amounts of forage to the armies in the Southwest.[34] The scarcity of skilled machinists meant overtime and night work which doubled the cost of this type of work. In addition, the cost of locomotives per mile run soared to 33.5 cents.[35] The last year of the war brought a continuation of these trends. Expenses remained so high that net earnings decreased in spite of record gross earnings. Once again, prosperity was limited, the railroad thought partially because of, rather than in spite of government patronage.

The Chicago and North Western Railway, carrying chiefly wheat, flour, and lumber, experienced increasing traffic in 1861 that overtaxed its motive power and exceeded the capacity of its cars.[36] Running from Chicago to Oshkosh and Appleton, Wis., the road expected to complete its Green Bay branch by August, 1862, and open that port for grain shipments via the Great Lakes to Buffalo and the East.[37] Though the road hoped to reach $1,000,000 gross earnings by 1864, it actually passed that mark in 1863, when net earnings increased 20 per cent over 1862 to $513,272.52. Increasing development of the area northwest of Chicago, the Green Bay extension (its completion delayed until November, 1862, because of scarcity of labor), and arrangements for wheat parity prices between Milwaukee and Chicago were the factors accounting for this prosperity.[38]

There was not rolling stock to handle the lumber business from Oshkosh and Fond du Lac to Green Bay, nor was there enough to handle all the grain offered for transport.[39] The road planned to add 200 cars to its rolling stock, and organized the Peninsula Railroad from Escanaba to Marquette, Mich., to tap the copper and iron trade of the Lake Superior region.[40] The line was opened to Marquette and the iron mines in December, 1864. The quarter-mile ore dock at Escanaba could handle 20,000 to 30,000 tons of ore in pockets, shunting the ore directly into the holds of ships.[41]

The railroad was developing at a fast pace during the war years. Presided over by William B. Ogden, who was first mayor of Chicago in 1837 and was judged by one contemporary to be of the same stamp as B & O's Garrett,[42] the railroad ran west to Fulton on the Mississippi, where it connected with lines leading to Cedar Rapids and Boonesboro; an extension to Council Bluffs on the Missouri was proposed. The line to Fulton was completed in the summer of 1862. A bridge over the Mississippi was started immediately and completed in 1864. It was the second railroad bridge over the Mississippi below St. Paul, the Rock Island being first. Consolidating with the Galena and Chicago Union Railroad in 1864, the road leased its western connections, looking eventually to a connection with the Union Pacific at Omaha. Its Freeport line had connections to Racine, as well as westward via Illinois Central to Dunleith and Dubuque. A branch ran to Madison, connecting there with the Milwaukee and Prairie du Chien. The Green Bay Line crossed the Milwaukee and St. Paul at Watertown. Thus the railroad had comprehensive coverage of the area north and west of Chicago.[43]

The road was growing faster than rolling stock could be acquired to service it. The 1865 report expressed the need for

500 additional cars, and predicted that earnings would surpass $1,000,000 per month during the fall harvest season if the necessary rolling stock could be had.[44] Net earnings for the year ending May 31, 1865, amounted to $2,199,387.91, a 46 per cent increase over the previous year alone, and more than 500 per cent over the first year of the war.[45] The 32 locomotives of 1862 had increased to 123, the 19 passenger cars to 79, and the 630 freight cars to 2,773, excluding 214 iron ore cars on the Peninsula Division.[46] Of course, expenses had skyrocketed. The *total* expenses in 1862 (about $435,000) were less than *each* of five highest categories of expenses in 1865.[47]

Like so many of the Western roads, the Milwaukee and Prairie du Chien Railway depended on grain for its existence. The trade was seasonal in character, and at its peak the railroad was swamped with business it could not take care of. Working its rolling stock to capacity to get the Wisconsin grain to market, the line still had 75,000 to 100,000 bushels of wheat awaiting transportation at Prairie du Chien.[48] More than 3,000,000 bushels of wheat were shipped east over the road, bringing in over $1,000,000 gross revenue, with a net of $436,039.41.[49] To the same markets, 26 freight locomotives and 632 freight cars carried hides, dressed hogs, and butter and eggs. Westward went smaller loads of merchandise, lumber, and agricultural implements.[50] The road saw two alternatives to meet the seasonal trade problem: by increasing the rolling stock with the attendant risk that much of it would be idle most of the year, or by building a grain elevator at Prairie du Chien.[51] The elevator, the more economical solution, was built, though smaller crops in 1862, combined with shortage of manpower because of the draft, hampered its effective use.[52] Crop failure plus reduced passenger business, because many on-line residents had joined the army, brought a decline in net revenue in 1862 to $414,740.81.[53] The road did considerably more military business that year, however, taking in $62,688.56 from troop transportation, almost double the amount in 1861.[54]

In 1863 and 1864, the road's business increased in all categories. Tonnage, gross revenue, and net revenue all mounted. The latter year was especially profitable, with an increase of almost $500,000 in gross revenue and a record net of $564,330.21.[55] At the same time expenses were climbing, surpassing $1,200,000 in 1864, and forcing a steady increase in the operating ratio to a high of 70.53 per cent in 1864.[56] The railroad sought a better solution to its seasonal trade problem by building branch lines to act as feeders tapping new territory. One of these, the McGregor Western Railway, tapped agricultural areas in Iowa. This new trade was desirable because constant crop failures in Wisconsin diminished local trade; moreover, through traffic was more desirable because it lessened the dependence of the road on one crop and one area.[57] Passenger traffic in these years revived considerably, over one third of the increase being accounted for by military traffic. The establishment of camps and of hospitals at Milwaukee, Madison, and Prairie du Chien helped to bring in a military revenue of $115,274.92.[58]

The 50 per cent increase in expenditures in 1864 over 1863 was largely accounted for by inflationary prices. Rerolled iron rail increased from about $35.40 a ton in 1863 to about $48.60 in 1864. Other typical increases were: fish-plate splices, about 92 cents each in 1863 to about $1.40 in 1864; spikes, 4 cents a pound to 7 cents.[59] Expenses on locomotive repairs almost doubled; those on car repairs more than doubled.[60] Fuel cost almost doubled, not only from higher prices, but from the necessity of burning green wood in the locomotives, with consequent loss of efficiency.[61] Because of these almost prohibitive expenses, rolling stock and motive power could not be expanded very much. In 1864, there were 27 freight engines and about 680 freight cars. With this equipment the railroad carried east 4,100,000 bushels of wheat, 14,200,000 pounds of dressed hogs, 1,600,000 pounds of butter, 911,000 pounds of wool, 2,600,000 pounds of hides, 1,500,000 pounds of hay, and 3,500,000 pounds of general merchandise.[62] The increasing passenger business was actually carried with *less* rolling stock than in 1861.[63]

Net earnings reached a record $647,631.45 in 1865, and though expenses increased also, the proportionate increase was considerably less than in the previous year.[64] The chief factors in the brighter outlook in 1865 were a steady and important through business in conjunction with the McGregor Western Railway, a record high military account, better crops, and a welcome decline in prices.[65]

So it was that the impact of the war upon the railroad business brought changing reactions from railroad presidents everywhere. At first, they were wary and uncertain whether or not the war would be of advantage to them; then came relief and satisfaction at mounting profits and increased tonnage; finally misgivings at rising costs which bit deeply into income and brought severe depreciation to equipment. Visions of new expansion disappeared when every ounce of energy was needed for the daily job of transportation. No one had time to think of the future. Every change in operating methods and every addition to equipment was aimed at increased efficiency. Doing the daily job as efficiently as possible became even more important and more urgent as the move toward regulatory legislation on the part of the government gradually gained momentum.

Chapter VII

THE MOVEMENT FOR REGULATORY
LEGISLATION

The purpose of the Government in wishing to have this power [of seizure] over the railways of the country, is to be enabled to move the armies of the United States during the next few months in all portions of the country. . . . I think the object a good one.

> *Congressional Globe,* 37th Congress, 2d Session,
> Jan. 28, 1862 (Senator Wilson of Massachusetts)

THE RELATIONSHIP between the railroads and the national government is a complex and interesting subject. The necessities of sudden conflict and the gathering of armies forced cooperation from the reluctant companies at the same time as the business of the government was bringing prosperity in its wake. But though government business was carried out as required, the railroads took care to point out its disadvantages, particularly in the early months of the war. Prosperity accentuated the individualism and laissez-faire that were so characteristic of the period, and railroad presidents early resented the necessity of subordinating their own plans to the business of the government, particularly because a large percentage of it was on an almost emergency basis, and hence unpredictable as far as building up a stable business was concerned. The conflict naturally aroused when a state based on free enterprise finds itself confronted with the necessity of limiting free enterprise in order successfully to prosecute a war is strikingly brought out in the early war career of the railroads directly involved in the struggle. Railroad presidents were forced in some instances to travel the narrow path between complete laissez-faire and government regulation.

For some months after the war broke out, President James Guthrie of the Louisville and Nashville Railroad carried on a profitable trade in provisions with Alabama and Georgia, a trade made all the more lucrative for him because his competitor, the Mobile and Ohio Railroad, was deprived of its outlet on the Ohio River at Cairo, Ill., by the concentration of Northern troops at that point. Guthrie was an outstanding president of a railroad every bit as strategically located as the Baltimore and Ohio. Striking south from Louisville through Kentucky and Tennessee, the line was the only important Western railroad link between North and South. The secession of the Southern states, far from cutting off its business, as it had that of the wholly Northern Illinois Central, actually increased the business of the Louisville and Nashville because the South was importing large quantities of provisions and supplies to meet the expected outbreak of war.[1] In fact, the business became so great that Guthrie was forced to declare a temporary embargo between April 29 and May 8, 1861, because the railroad was getting more business than it could handle.[2] So many provisions went south that panicky Louisville citizenry, alarmed at a rumor of starvation, obliged Guthrie to furnish armed guards for his trains.[3] Guthrie refused to give up this trade, however, until he knew what action the state of Kentucky would take.[4] Lincoln's policy was to allow the commercial intercourse to continue, because he did not wish to do anything to antagonize this vital border state.[5] To limit the trade as much as possible, the Treasury Department on May 2 issued an order forbidding the carriage of munitions and provisions into the Confederacy, and this order was enforced by a decision of a Federal Circuit Court on July 11.[6] The trade still went on, however, through the subterfuge of hauling goods by wagon a few miles below Louisville, then transferring them to the railroad.[7] The Louisville *Courier* commented that any prohibition of this contraband trade would be so economically disastrous that grass would grow in the streets of Louisville. Besides, Kentucky and Tennessee had built the L & N for commerce, and if Lincoln interfered, he would be violating the Constitution.[8] But there was opposition, too. Kentucky farmers were afraid to sell wood to the L & N for use as fuel.[9] It was the action of the Confederates themselves which finally drove Guthrie, the L & N, and Kentucky into the Union camp. In May the Confederate Congress placed an embargo on the exportation of cotton to the North, later extending it to sugar, rice, molasses, tobacco, syrup, and naval stores. The strict enforcement of this blockade, coupled with the permit system of the North, tended to reduce sympathy for the South in Kentucky.[10] On July 2, 1861, Governor Isham G. Harris of Tennessee placed an agent on the L & N in Tennessee to prevent contraband goods from being shipped North.[11] Finally, on July 4 all L & N rolling stock in Tennesssee was confiscated (5 locomotives, 3 passenger and baggage cars, and 70 freight cars) by order of Governor Harris.[12] Guthrie tried, unsuccessfully, to get it back, and finally the L & N was forced to cease operations south of the state line. The railroad was soon to be an important central point in military operations in Kentucky.[13]

Samuel Felton and the Philadelphia, Wilmington, and Baltimore Railroad could hardly do otherwise than submit to government demands, because this railroad was a vital connecting link between the nation's capital and its largest city. Yet Felton was in full voice against the construction of a government railroad between New York and Washington because of alleged inefficiency and delay in the operation of his road, and he was first to protest Cameron's charge of fraud in settling accounts for troop transportation, and the government's subsequent action of using the Northern Central to carry troops to Washington. Nobody had to tread more warily in this respect than John W. Garrett of the Baltimore and Ohio Railroad. Accused by Cameron of traitorous conduct, Garrett had to worry about keeping the main line west open for business, and at the same time keep his Washington Branch operating at peak efficiency, subject to the threat of government seizure. On at least two occasions, Garrett diverted precious stocks of repair materials to reopening the main stem, when those materials had originally been acquired to construct a double track on the Washington Branch. Certainly this was not an easy decision to make. War business helped the B & O tremendously in financing its necessary repairs. But Garrett did not hesitate to point out the disadvantages of this business. His annual report for 1861 said that regular passsenger travel had been adversely affected by United States authorities,

who for long periods required, even for the merest local traffic, tests and securities which much lessened the use of the road. For considerable periods, also, the regular passenger trains of the Company were altogether suspended, either from apprehensions of interruption by the Confederates, or to secure the exclusive use of the Road and its equipment for government purposes.

As for freight, government authorities not only forbid "certain productions" from passing over the line, but "Much revenue was . . . lost by absorption of the cars . . . in military uses, or by occupying them for long periods as warehouses for army materials."[14]

The Illinois Central, another railroad destined to do a large government business, hastened to inform Secretary of War Cameron on April 26, 1861, through its president, W. H. Osborn, that "the Directors are desirous to serve the Govern-

ment to the best of their ability."[15] With 110 locomotives,
2,600 freight cars, and 3,500 employees, the railroad was
ready to set aside its regular business and to give preference
to that of the government. Yet the annual reports complained
to the stockholders that the normal business of the road was
constantly interrupted by the demands of the government.
Regular operation was delayed by the necessity of sending
troops, ammunition, grain, and meat south to Cairo, and the
company was compelled to pay damages for failure to furnish
cars.[16] The superintendent said that operations in 1861 were
seriously deranged by service required by the state of Illinois
and by the national government: "the necessity to make up
large trains for troops, munitions, etc., has obliged us to sacrifice, at times, our local traffic."[17]

Although troop movements were of necessity secret, the
railroad complained that the short notice it received made
the necessary concentration of motive power and cars take
double the usual time. The actual cost per passenger mile to
move troops in 1861 was 1.8 cents, and the railroad was
receiving only 1.3 cents for this service from the government.[18]
Naturally, the necessity of furnishing rolling stock for an unprofitable business reduced profits from civilian activity.

This skeptical attitude on the part of the railroad companies
did not last long. The great increase of general business which
the war effort brought them soon changed the early fears of
railroad officials. Roads favored with a great deal of government business ceased to complain about it, and began to point
with pride to the efficiency with which they handled it. The New
Jersey Railroad reported that government transportation requirements were promptly met, and that as many as 3,000
men, with baggage, had been transported in one day, with little
interference with regular trains. The railroad claimed resources

to carry 10,000 men in one day.[19] The joint report of the Little Miami and Columbus and Xenia Railroad in Ohio said that demands for transportation of troops and munitions had been met promptly; the line received a commendation from the chief of rail transportation of the United States for efficiency and promptness.[20] The Baltimore and Ohio Railroad boasted that from October, 1861, to March, 1862, it was delivering sometimes more than 400 cars daily to supply the needs of Washington.[21] The entire business was met to the satisfaction of the government.

Finally, it is important to note that some of those railroads which had only small amounts of government business continued throughout the war to resent even that little. For instance, the Michigan Southern and Northern Indiana Railroad, in pointing out the insufficiency of their rolling stock to care for increasing East-West business, said:

To add to our embarrassment the General Government *conscripted* 20 cars last Fall in our busiest season, and has since required the indefinite loan of 33 more. Three Locomotive Engines, building for us under contract, were also taken by the Government, and other Engines which were intended to replace those have been seized, greatly to our detriment; but we hope the sacrifice is for the good of the country.[22]

So thought the railroad men. What did government officials think? Except for the Baltimore and Ohio, the Annapolis and Elk Ridge, and railroads operated by the government during the Gettysburg campaign, all the Northern railroads came through the war without being subjected to the humility of government seizure. The only other exception came in the summer of 1864, when rioting of foreign miners in Pennsylvania against the draft, forced the government to operate temporarily the Philadelphia and Reading Railroad, an important carrier of coal for the navy.[23] This record in itself was some indication of the excellent job the railroads did. The government, apparently, was satisfied. In his annual report for the fiscal year ending June 30, 1862, Quartermaster General Montgomery C. Meigs said: "The companies deserve due credit for the patriotic manner in which they have performed the services required of them by the Government."[24] Besides these praiseworthy efforts, the companies had also shown patience with delays in settling accounts. Other agencies affiliated with the government, such as the United States Christian Commission, commented on the patriotic services of the railroads. In 1863 alone, more than 1,200 delegates were transported to the seat of war and return on passes or reduced fares.[25]

On January 24, 1861, a railroad convention was held in Washington to continue business begun earlier at meetings in New York and Saratoga. Attended by railroad men from Massachusetts, New York, Pennsylvania, Ohio, New Jersey, Indiana, and Kentucky, the convention found itself confronted with a civil war which would inevitably destroy much railroad property. A committee was appointed to express the general sentiment of the convention on the national crisis. The committee was composed of Nathaniel Marsh of the New York and Erie Railroad, Erastus Corning of the New York Central, J. Edgar Thomson of the Pennsylvania, John W. Garrett of the Baltimore and Ohio, and S. S. L'Hommedieu of the Cincinnati, Hamilton, and Dayton Railroad. The resolutions of the committee approved the Crittenden Compromise, a proposal introduced into the Senate by John J. Crittenden of Kentucky, providing for a permanent boundary line between free states and slave states, and for the peaceful existence of slavery within the Union. In supporting the compromise, the committee stated that the delegates represented railroad property national in scope, and needed peace and security for the development

of their property. They claimed also to represent public sentiment in their resolutions.[26] The *American Railway Review*
commented favorably on the committee's action, noting that
"Twenty-five millions of free people cannot afford to sacrifice
the glory of their past history, their present interests, their
domestic peace . . . because a mere party clique hold an
accidental majority in the federal capital."[27] Undoubtedly
these sentiments did not endear the railroad interests to the
purely sectional Republican party.

It was in this atmosphere that government policy toward
the railroads evolved. Although the government had already
used its military power to take over part of the Baltimore
and Ohio together with the Annapolis and Elk Ridge, in his
report of July 1, 1861, Cameron urged that this power be
written into a specific law. The War Department, he said, had
taken possession of lines necessary to form a connection
between the Northern states and the capital.

As the movements of the U. S. forces are continued, the supervision
of railroad and telegraph lines will remain a necessity to be met by
the department. I would therefore recommend the propriety of an
appropriation to be made by Congress, to be applied, when the
public exigencies demand, to the reconstruction and equipment of
railroads, and for the expense of maintaining and operating them.[28]

That Cameron's statements were aimed at the Baltimore and
Ohio is borne out by the report of December 1, 1861. In it
Cameron not only recommended that the Washington Branch
be double tracked to Annapolis Junction, but also that an
additional railway be constructed between Washington and
Baltimore by a private company. Such a company with a Maryland charter had already proposed to do this on condition
that the United States government would endorse its bonds.
Proposed rates were 4 cents a ton-mile for freight, 3 cents per

passenger-mile, except that for the duration of the war the latter charge would be 2 cents.[29] This was the proposal that later turned into one for a government railroad the entire distance from Washington to New York. Cameron, a director of the Northern Central, had always been hostile to Garrett and the B & O. The latter was to find a friend in the War Department when Edwin M. Stanton became Secretary in January, 1862, and for the rest of the war the B & O's relations with the government were more cordial.

Upon Stanton's request, Thomas A. Scott, the Assistant Secretary of War, communicated to his new superior certain recommendations. Scott recommended first the creation of a transportation and telegraph bureau to take charge of rail and water transportation and to operate in the War Department. Second, provision should be made for construction and extension of railroads and telegraphs for military purposes. Third, an officer in each state should take charge of transportation of troops and supplies through that state. Fourth, transportation should be by contract for three to six months with bids asked. Fifth, a transportation officer should be placed on the staff of each military department. Finally, an appropriation should be provided for the work of the proposed bureau in order to relieve the Quartermaster of his transportation responsibilities.[30] Though the separate and autonomous transportation corps foreseen in Scott's proposal did not come until the Second World War, it is interesting to note that not only was the proposed bureau established in the War Department but its railroad duties became so important that responsibility for water transportation and for telegraph operation was placed in separate bureaus.

The day before Scott wrote these recommendations, a bill, drawn up under the guidance of Stanton, had been introduced into the Senate by Benjamin F. Wade of Ohio, authorizing the President to take over any railroad in the United States when the public safety demanded it. The introduction of the bill coincided with the beginning of a general land and sea offensive against the Confederacy. Stanton, charged with making the necessary preparations, immediately asked Wade for prompt action in getting the proposed bill passed, in order to make sure that adequate rail transportation would be available.[31]

The debates in the Senate reveal the purpose of the bill. Wade, a Republican whose Committee on the Conduct of the War was intent on securing a vigorous prosecution of the war, assured his colleagues that the bill would not disturb any railroads whose owners were willing to carry on government business.[32] William P. Fessenden of Maine, chairman of the Senate Finance Committee, and one of the great debaters of the Senate, asked that in case the railroad between Washington and Philadelphia refused to transport troops or munitions, should it not be required to do so by force?[33] James A. Pearce, Democrat of Maryland, objected to giving the President such sweeping power over railroads in states not in rebellion. He said that the railroads from Philadelphia to Baltimore and Washington had done everything possible to accommodate the government. Several thousand tons a day were brought to Washington for the use of the military, and he saw no necessity for the government to take over the Baltimore and Ohio. What provisions would the government make for commercial tonnage, and for paying interest on bonds? Why bring railroad employees under the Articles of War?[34] Wade answered that the bill simply regulated a power that the government already had, and that it was thought better to establish the principle of regulation than to mention certain railroads by name.[35] Opinion in Congress was not unanimous as to whether the President had power to seize the railroads regardless of the proposed legislation. Lincoln himself interpreted his war power to include "the right to seize citizens' property if such seizure should become indispensable to the successful prosecution of the war."[36] Henry Wilson of Massachusetts, chairman of the Committee on Military Affairs, made an enlightening statement of the object of the bill:

We have assembled large armies; it is expected that these armies are to move; . . . they have to move over vast spaces of country; railways must be a great means of transportation for them. Now, the object is to have control of the railway lines for the purpose of moving these masses of men. The object is . . . to move large masses of men without the knowledge or consent of anybody, without negotiating with railway directors as to how many men are to be moved, or where they are to be moved, or what rolling stock is wanted . . . and the object is further to concentrate the rolling stock of a large number of railways, if it shall be necessary, on one railway line, so that vast masses of men may be moved rapidly and speedily.[37]

The section of the bill providing court-martial for anyone interfering with the government's carrying out the provisions of the bill became the subject of a prolonged debate between Wade and John Sherman of Ohio on one side, and Fessenden and Orville H. Browning of Illinois on the other. The latter argued first that the President already had the powers the bill gave him and hence the bill was unnecessary, and second that civilians should not be subject to military law without their consent.[38] Browning, predicting wrecks if employees were forced to work against their will, proposed an amendment to the first section requiring the consent of anyone before coming under the military, but the amendment was rejected.[39] Wade and Sherman on the other hand stressed the existence of the war emergency justifying the limitation on constitutional rights.[40] Wade, foreseeing large-scale troop movements where the rolling stock of other railroads would have to be requisitioned, argued that anyone who might interfere with transportation was guilty of treason.[41]

On January 28, 1862, the bill passed the Senate by a vote of 23 to 12. The next day after a short debate the House passed it, 113 to 28.[42] In general, New England and the West favored the bill, with the Middle states divided.[43] On January 31, the bill became law with Lincoln's signature, and on February 4 it was published to the armed forces as General Order Number 10, Adjutant General's Office.[44] The act was in five sections.[45] The first section read:

The President of the United States when in his judgment the public safety may require it . . . is hereby authorized to take possession of any or all the railroad lines in the United States, their rolling stock, their offices, shops, buildings . . . ; to prescribe rules and regulations for the holding, using, and maintaining of the aforesaid . . . railroad lines, and to extend, repair, and complete the same . . . ; to place under military control all the officers, agents, and employees belonging to the . . . railroad lines . . . so that they shall be considered as a post road and a part of the military establishment of the United States.

Section 2 provided that any party attempting to interfere with the government's use of the property would be subject to court-martial and could suffer any penalty the court-martial might direct, including death. The other sections provided for the appointment of three commissioners to assess any damages suffered by seizure and to determine the compensation; made provisions for the transportation of troops and military supplies to be under the Secretary of War and such agents as he might appoint; and provided that the act was not to be in force "any longer than is necessary for the suppression of this rebellion."

The passage of the law did not solve the problem of regulation, however. There were many obstacles in the path of good relations between the railroads and the government. Nothing better illustrates this fact than the quarrels over the line of track between New York and Washington.

Chapter VIII

THE NEW YORK–WASHINGTON ARTERY
BONE OF CONTENTION

There is no route over the whole country over which is passed an equal number of passengers where the accommodations are so disproportionate to the amount and importance of the traffic, or the rates so high or so much time consumed in transit as on this.

American Railway Review, June 5, 1862

THE GOVERNMENT'S CHIEF COMPLAINT against the privately owned railroads focused on the heavily traveled line between New York and Washington. The proposal for construction and operation by the government of a separate rail line on this route raised a point of conflict with the existing roads which was settled only by the end of the war. This important artery was operated in 1861 by several different railroads, and at the beginning of the war, it was impossible to travel the entire distance without changing cars. Garrett of the Baltimore and Ohio operated that road's Washington Branch between Baltimore and Washington. The Philadelphia, Wilmington, and Baltimore continued north to Philadelphia, with a ferry at the Susquehanna River between Havre de Grace and Perryville. From Philadelphia to New York were two lines which connected with ferries between New Jersey and New York. First the Camden and Amboy ran between Camden and South Amboy at the mouth of the Raritan River across from Staten Island. The second route between Philadelphia and New York comprised three railroads: the Philadelphia and Trenton to Trenton, a branch of the Camden and Amboy to New Brunswick, and the New Jersey Railroad from New Brunswick to Jersey

City. The latter route, controlled by the Camden and Amboy, was the route most used.[1]

Of necessity the war threw its heaviest burden on these lines, and because government officials were by the very nature of their travel more familiar with these railroads than with any others, they objected strenuously to delays and inconveniences which actually were no worse than those to be encountered on any other railroad. Another source of grievance was the fact that New Jersey and Maryland were the only two states which levied taxes on railroad traffic. New Jersey collected a tax on fares between New York and Philadelphia, and Maryland took one fifth of all gross passenger receipts between Baltimore and Washington.[2] The existence of the New Jersey tax led the *American Railroad Journal* of February 9, 1861, to suspect that New Jersey railroads maintained expensive lobbies in the state legislature. The *Journal* criticized the Camden and Amboy Railroad for not making available more data than that contained in their annual reports. The conclusion was reached that the railroad was using large sums to influence the legislature and the press and that it wanted to enjoy its monopoly undisturbed. Even in the road's annual statements the *Journal* pointed out the glaring discrepancy that, over a ten-year period, the railroad's dividends exceeded its net earnings by well over $1,000,000. The Camden and Amboy monopoly dated from 1832, when the State of New Jersey gave it exclusive transportation rights between New York and Philadelphia. Run by two brothers, Robert L. Stevens and Edwin A. Stevens, the Joint Companies comprised the Camden and Amboy Railroad and the Delaware and Raritan Canal. Together they had stock control of the Philadelphia and Trenton Railroad and a working agreement with the New Jersey Railroad.[3] In 1854 an act was passed by the legislature of New Jersey which settled the relationship between the Joint Companies and the state. This

act set the year 1869 as the terminal date of the monopoly
and provided that the company could continue to operate until
1888 before being taken over by the state.[4] Thus the existence
of the monopoly and its operation were well established when
the war broke out.

The pressure of war demands brought two improvements in
New York–Washington transportation in the first year of the
war. On May 6, through trains began operating between New
York and Harrisburg via the Central Railroad of New Jersey
to Easton, Lehigh Valley to Allentown, East Pennsylvania
Railroad to Reading, and Lebanon Valley to Harrisburg.[5]
From Harrisburg the Northern Central ran directly to Baltimore. Thus an important supplementary route was opened
between New York and Baltimore. During 1861, 26,000 to
27,000 troops plus a large amount of freight was carried south
over this route.[6] Contrast, however, the PW & B, which up to
November 30, 1861, carried 154,303 troops.[7]

The Central Railroad of New Jersey[8] complained that the
business had been done "at low rate, at great expense, vex-
ation and trouble, and with endless detention of cars." This
railroad was the object of incessant demands to put on express
trains between New York and Baltimore. It did not do so,
however, because it felt that the business belonged legitimately
to the more direct route, and making improvements meant a
waste of money because the business would soon be lost anyway.[9] Improvements made in the direct route brought a sharp
and permanent decrease in government business by the longer
way in 1862 and seemed to justify the Central Railroad's
position. The railroad overstepped its bounds, however, when
it said that for the improvements on the direct line, the government could thank the "circumbendibus route" via Allentown and
Harrisburg.[10]

The second improvement came in November, 1861, when

arrangements were made to run through trains between Washington and New York via the Camden and Amboy. The necessity of changing cars at the Susquehanna River was eliminated by running the cars themselves onto the ferry. Two through trains daily left New York at 7 A.M. and 6 P.M., and left Washintgon at 6 A.M. and 2:30 P.M.[11] These through trains took between 10½ and 12 hours for the journey. Other trains leaving New York at 11 P.M., and Washington at 11 A.M. and 5 P.M., required a change of cars at Philadelphia.[12] The PW & B made a substanial increase in its rolling stock to accommodate this additional business: 45 new freight cars, 15 passenger cars, and 2 engines were added in 1861, while 4 more engines and 30 freight cars were in the process of construction.[13]

But the improvements were insufficient to silence rising criticism. Said the New York *Times*, Feb. 6, 1863, "We do not believe there is a railroad route in the world over which so much business is transacted, in so shameless a condition of inefficiency and discomfort as that between New York and Washington." The 12-hour trip ought to take 8 hours, the track was rough, and the cars, especially south of Philadelphia, were badly ventilated, badly heated, dirty, and with insufficient space for light baggage. The only remedy for this condition, thought the *Times*, was competition.

The proposals of the Metropolitan Railroad Company, brought before Congress, would provide the competition urged by the *Times*. In his report of December 1, 1861, Secretary of War Cameron had stated that "a responsible company" had proposed to build an additional railroad connection between Baltimore and Washington on condition that the government would endorse its bonds. This "responsible company" was the Metropolitan Railroad Company. Created originally in 1856 to build a railroad between Washington and Hagerstown, Md., in

November, 1861, it asked Congress for authority to build a line direct to points on the Northern Central and the PW & B, thus by-passing the city of Baltimore. The plan requested $2,000,000 in United States bonds to be secured by a 36-year first mortgage. The new railroad, it was said, would relieve congestion in Baltimore and place a friendly railroad at the disposal of the government.[14] The *American Railway Review* of April 24, 1862, expressed opposition to this scheme. It pointed out that the line would run through unpopulated sections, and would necessitate heavy grades. Moreover, under the guise of military necessity, the idea would serve merely to rescue a feeble railroad.[15] The *American Railway Times* (January 30, 1864) also opposed a government line because it would be useless once the war was over, and would deprive the existing lines of legitimate business. The House Committee on Roads and Canals, to whom the original proposal was referred, reported that existing facilities were "disagreeable, annoying, and unsatisfactory." The disadvantage of a long journey with several changes, "existing on the most traveled and most vital thoroughfare in the Union . . . assume the proportion of a national wrong."[16] In the hands of this committee, the proposal became a bill to construct under government auspices an independent railroad all the way between Washington and New York. The House asked Stanton to sound out existing railroad corporations to see what arrangements could be made, to find out about improving the routes through Baltimore and Philadelphia and constructing a double track from Relay House, near Baltimore to Washington.[17]

The move for a government railroad did not come from one direction only, however, nor was it based solely on the practical considerations of delay and inconvenience. On December 5, 1861, the New York Chamber of Commerce had drawn up a memorial to Congress urging government construction of a railroad from New York to Washington as a military, postal, and commercial necessity. Within a compass of 240 miles, said the memorial, this line of postal conveyance and commercial traffic embraced the nation's capital and its three largest cities. Because of the location of the cities and towns on the route, the state and municipal authorities controlling the line of communication

hold the postal, commercial, and travelling facilities of the people as completely under their control as they would in the possession of a mountain pass. . . . This jurisdiction has been used for purposes of local profit, to the continued and serious detriment, inconvenience and expense of more than twenty millions of people. . . . We believe they are deprived, in an unjust and illiberal manner, of one of the most sacred rights of a free people—the right of a free and unrestricted highway for the transaction of every description of communication and public traffic.[18]

Citing the broken links in the route and the fact that they were due to the desire for local profits accruing from travelers forced to stop over in various cities, the memorial stated erroneously that such delays did not exist on other leading routes, and added: "We consider such a state of things as derogatory to our character and position as an enlightened people, and antagonistic to the progressive spirit of the age." Furthermore, the war had shown the route to be a military necessity: "the successful prosecution of a war becomes almost solely a question of transportation."[19] The memorial also pointed out that mail, which now took twelve hours to reach its destination, should take no more than six, and that Congress should remedy the situation, acting under its power to establish post roads or military roads for the use of the nation at large.

The city of Washington also presented its complaints via a deputation of prominent men who presented themselves to

Mayor Wallach and to the Postmaster General to ask their influence with Congress to ameliorate the conditions of suffering and inconvenience encountered as a result of inadequate rail communication with the North.[20] The Mayor agreed with the delegation that the lack of a national highway between the commercial and political capitals of the nation was severely felt. The merchants and citizens of Washington and Georgetown were spending tens of thousands of dollars every week in unnecessarily high freight rates and prices, and something should be done about it.[21] There was no suggestion in either of these proposals that the government take over and operate the existing lines, a power which the government was soon to have, but not to use.

Meanwhile Stanton had been sounding out Garrett on the Metropolitan Railroad Company. Garrett opposed the new line vigorously. He pointed out that the present road, 188 miles between New York and Baltimore, was practically an air line, and compared with 267 miles (via Easton, Allentown, Reading, and Harrisburg) or 241 miles (via Reading, Columbia, and York) on other routes.[22] Any new route connecting the Northern Central with the Baltimore and Ohio would by-pass Baltimore and would necessitate deep cuts, high fills, and heavy grades. Taking at least two years to build without effecting any saving in distance would hardly be a war measure.[23] The transfer at Baltimore required only 20 minutes. As for double track from Relay House to Washington, Garrett pointed out that siding had been extended and had proved adequate to handle troops and supplies with the approval and appreciation of the government.[24] When a new bill providing for acceptance of the Metropolitan plan was introduced in the House by Wright of Pennsylvania, chairman of the Military Affairs Committee, Garrett opposed it on the ground that it was unnecessary and that it would be prejudicial to the state of Maryland. The bill was reported back to committee.[25]

The vociferous and energetic Samuel Felton also expressed his opposition to the proposal for a government railroad. Government works cost more, he said, and once built, afford offices to "greedy and unprincipled politicians, who pervert the work to their own selfish purposes."[26] The existing route was the best one because it went through all the principal cities, and was as close to an air line as possible without crossing Chesapeake Bay. He thought the government's true policy should be to spend up to 20 per cent of the cost of a new railroad financing the construction of a double track and a bridge over the Susquehanna River on the existing route.[27]

The act of January 31, 1862, authorizing the President to take over the railroads when the public interest demanded it, was supplemented by a joint resolution of Congress dated July 14, 1862, stipulating that the act was not to be construed as authorizing construction or completion of any railroad, "the greater part of which remained uncompleted at the time of the said act; and so much of the said act as authorizes the President . . . to extend and complete any railroad is hereby repealed."[28] This limitation on the original act was accompanied by further improvements along the line of travel. The PW & B completed 15 miles of double track during the year ending October 31, 1862, and put in service 7 new locomotives, 136 new freight cars, and 2 mail and passenger cars. Felton promised double track to the Susquehanna River, a bridge at that point, and better depots at Baltimore.[29] The New Jersey Railroad added 5 new locomotives and ordered 8 others, along with 6 new passenger cars.[30] Another improvement was the construction of a connecting track between the Philadelphia station of the PW & B at Broad and Prime Streets and the Kensington station of the Philadelphia and Trenton, thereby making possible a through journey without ferrying across the Delaware River.[31] This enterprise, however, was ended by the courts.[32] It was supplemented by the Junction Railroad, completed in late 1863, a joint enterprise of the Reading, Pennsylvania, and PW & B, connecting the Reading line at the west end of the Columbia bridge over the Schuylkill River, crossing the Pennsylvania Railroad, running parellel to Market Street, and turning south to connect with the PW & B at Gray's Ferry.[33] The initiative probably came from the Reading, which wanted the line so as to withdraw rail traffic from city streets, and to facilitate handling of coal in Philadelphia.[34] By 1863 long-distance passengers were routed through Philadelphia via the Reading, Junction, Pennsylvania, and West Chester Railroads to the PW & B. Felton called this arrangement better than the previous one, but not ideal. He hoped eventually to use the Connecting Railroad from Frankford on the Philadelphia and Trenton to Philadelphia, then the Junction Railroad to the PW & B below Gray's Ferry Bridge.[35]

While these improvements were being put into effect, the railroad companies did not relax their efforts to sustain their point of view before Congress. On January 29, 1863, an interesting pamphlet appeared, entitled *Considerations upon the Question Whether Congress Should Authorize a New Railroad between Washington and New York.* It was signed by Joseph P. Bradley, William W. Hubbell, and George Ashmun, attorneys for the railroad companies. The pamphlet attacked the question from a constitutional point of view. "Has Congress the power? And does there exist any necessity for its exercise?" were the two basic questions asked.[36] There was a considerable difference of opinion, it stated, as to the power of Congress to make internal improvements within the limits of a state, citing, first, the opposition to the attempt to convert the old Cumberland Road from a free road to a toll road and the final cession of the road to the individual states, and, second, President Andrew Jackson's veto of the Maysville Road Bill. Concerning the power to establish or construct post offices and post roads, Congress had so far exercised this power only in territories. The method had been "to nominate and declare certain roads already existing to be post roads. . . . Whether the power to establish includes the power to take land and construct has never been declared."[37] (Thus under the act of January 31, 1862, which declared all railroads to be post roads, the government could presumably take over and operate the existing lines, but not construct a new one). By the act of March 3, 1853, the Postmaster General was authorized to make contracts with the railroads for carrying mail. The erection of post offices, as well as navy yards, light houses, and custom houses, had always been done with the consent of the states concerned, a necessary prerequisite to permanent jurisdiction in the area. In time of war, temporary jurisdiction may be secured with the consent of the state, but more usually by the executive than by the legislature. The pamphlet questioned the wisdom of departing from this custom by building the proposed railroad without the consent of the states concerned. It would lead to an antagonistic attitude on the part of those states which had so far been loyal to the national government.[38] The present irregular transmission of mail was a result of the emergency conditions of war, but, through great exertion on the part of the railroads, all requirements of the government had been met and measures were being taken in cooperation with the Post Office Department to facilitate the mails and "remove the delays consequent upon a single line of track."[39]

Having disposed of the power to build internal improvements and to establish post offices and post roads, the pamphlet went on to examine the war power of the executive as Commander-in-Chief to construct as a temporary expedient military roads and forts. Undoubtedly the power existed and could be used, but any works constructed under it should be returned to the jurisdiction of state laws as soon as the war emergency had passed, or else require action by Congress to make the area a federal territory.

No loyal state will object to a public work necessary for the defence of the country. But it must be a public work—the property of the government . . . not of a corporation, to be fattened on franchises conceded to them by Congress. . . . The military power of the government cannot be delegated to a corporation.[40]

Thus arguing that such a railroad could be built only under the temporary military power of the executive, provided the government built and operated it, the remaining question was considered, Does any necessity for the road exist? With a resounding "No," the pamphlet cited the fact that the War Department itself had expressed complete satisfaction with the transportation of troops and military supplies. Over 6,000 troops had been transported from New York to Philadelphia in one day without interfering with regular mail and passenger trains, and railroads south of Philadelphia had on occasion done even better.[41] All existing railroads between New York and Washington were being double tracked, in addition to which there existed a thriving canal and ocean commerce between the important cities. Thus the plea of necessity was an "utter absurdity."[42] Briefly presenting other considerations, the pamphlet stated that the existing line was the most direct one; that a bridge over the Susquehanna River was being built; that the war would be over before a new road could be completed; and that existing business did not warrant two lines. Existing roads had entered into a mutual contract to construct double track,

complete connections, substitute embankments for trestles wherever possible, straighten the right of way at Trenton and at
Newark, acquire more rolling stock, and shorten the over-all
time to 8¼ hours.[43]

The truth of the matter seems to be that though the roads
did accomplish what was here set forth, it was still not enough
to keep up with the insistent demands of the military; but those
demands were of a temporary nature, and after the war a second
competing railroad would have been disastrous to either or
both of the railroad companies. It is of interest to note that
the double tracking of the Washington Branch was not completed until December, 1864, and that the bridge across the
Susquehanna River was not placed in service until a year and a
half after the end of the war.

Regarding rates, the pamphlet admitted that other roads
charged less, but that they had coal or freight business to make
up the difference, and even so the New York–Washington roads
did not charge as much as they were entitled. First-class fare
was $8.25, reduced to about $7.00 after deducting taxes and
the cost of transit from one station to another in Philadelphia.
(But of course that was one of the things objected to.) Troops
were charged $5.00 (Cameron had said $6.00), or about 2 cents
a mile, and government freight was carried at the rate of 3 cents
per ton mile.[44] The transit taxes collected by New Jersey and
Maryland were in lieu of all other taxes and were taxes on
property, not on citizens of other states.[45] The conclusion was
reached that the power of Congress to construct the proposed
railroad was at best doubtful, and that the need for it was
absolutely nonexistent.

The 1861 memorial from the New York Chamber of Commerce had mentioned delay in the carriage of mail between New
York and Washington. Continued complaints came before Con-

gress on the subject, and in December, 1863, the Senate asked the Postmaster General to determine the explanation for the alleged delay. Then on January 6, 1864, the House appointed a nine-man committee to examine the proposed route. The committee passed a resolution asking the Secretary of War and the Postmaster General for particulars as to transportation and rates.[46] The railroads' explanation was not long in coming. The primary cause of mail delay was the lack of a double track on large portions of the route, a condition which limited the number of trains, and made each one bigger, heavier, and hence slower.[47] Two recent changes were expected to alleviate the conditions complained of. Two trains (one morning and one evening) were set aside for New York–Washington business exclusively. Also one special military train was added to the route, and a general superintendent established for the entire line.[48] The unfortunate destruction by fire of the Gray's Ferry Bridge and winter ice at Havre de Grace were untimely incidents which tended to counteract improvements inaugurated by the railroads.[49] As for double track, the basic difficulty, the situation was improving rapidly. The New Jersey Railroad from Jersey City was double tracked except for the last three miles north of New Brunswick.[50] The Camden and Amboy was double tracked four more miles toward Trenton, and work was progressing on the rest. The Philadelphia and Trenton was partly double tracked, with 90 per cent of the necessary grading finished. The Junction Railroad at Philadelphia had been delayed for four months while the government built a fort on a hill being excavated, during Lee's invasion of Pennsylvania. The PW & B was double tracked for 31 miles, and the Washington Branch was double tracked as far as Annapolis Junction, with materials twice diverted to reconstruction on the main stem.[51] The statement ended on the note that all these improvements could meet any emergency, and that, in any case, the roads had always done the necessary government business promptly without failure or detention. It was signed by F. W. Jackson, general superintendent of the New Jersey Railroad, E. A. Stevens, president of the Camden and Amboy, V. L. Bradford, president of the Philadelphia and Trenton, Felton, and Garrett.[52]

A substantial improvement in the mail situation came on May 10, 1864, when a new railway post office car made its initial trip from Baltimore to Jersey City. The car was designed by A. N. Zevely, Third Assistant Postmaster General, and built at the Mount Clare shops of the B & O. It was 45 feet, 9 inches in length, and equipped with two cases containing 200 pigeon holes each, 80 feet of newspaper and package space, and sofas, water coolers, and ventilating system for the convenience of the post office clerks. Regular service was to be inaugurated as soon as a second car could be finished by the Camden and Amboy.[53] On its first trip, the car carried two clerks each from New York, Philadelphia, Baltimore, and Washington, and on its return trip the next day five clerks from the New York post office.[54]

The report of Quartermaster General Meigs to Stanton, January 26, 1864, showed that the railroads had done their best to transact business promptly, but still the New York–Washington route was insufficient for the business to be handled. The ice blockade of the Delaware, Susquehanna, and Potomac Rivers had severely cut the army's receipts of grain and hay. With a daily requirement of 74 carloads of grain and 375 of hay, only 20 carloads of forage had been received in one entire week.[55] Only warmer weather prevented permanent injury to the army's animals. As far as rates were concerned, the railroads on the New York–Washington route were paid under the rates established by the 1862 convention and issued in the circular from the Quartermaster General May 1, 1862. Only the Balti-

more and Ohio received more than the published rates, and that
under the resolution of the convention, March 3, 1862, that the
Secretary of War should compensate railroads in or near the
seat of war.[56] But the insufficiency of the present lines was
enough:

As a military question there can be no doubt of the great advantage
to the United States of another line of railroad between this city
and New York, one crossing the rivers by bridges above the head
of navigation, and not liable to interruption by ice. There have
been times when the government would have gladly availed itself
of the full capacity of several such independent lines. The insufficiency of the present communication has several times caused this
department much anxiety, and the question of taking actual and
entire military possession of these railroads has been discussed
more than once.[57]

Many of the arguments of the 1863 pamphlet of the railroad
attorneys were repeated by Felton in a letter to Charles Sumner,
February 9, 1864. By that time Felton had so exhausted his
energies that he had been obliged to give up the presidency of
his railroad. Though Felton still opposed government construction of a new line, on the ground that competition with private
enterprise was not a legitimate function of government, he was
ready to make a concession when he wrote Sumner to the effect
that, if the government must have a line, it should take the
existing one and operate it as a military road.[58] Felton's letter
was, in effect, a plea for understanding the difficulties that the
railroads were attempting to overcome. Scarcity of labor made
for high wages and unstable employment and at the same time
caused defective workmanship. Five out of eight locomotives
were involved in accidents caused by structural weaknesses
within two months after their purchase.[59] Raw materials had
been withdrawn for use by the military railways.[60] In spite of
the high cost to the railroad, Felton's road and the Camden and

Amboy had reduced troop rates by one third, instead of raising them fourfold, as had frequently been charged. And the PW & B, in cooperation with the United States Sanitary Commission, was the first railroad to provide hospital cars for the transportation of the sick and wounded.[61]

While argument and counterargument raged about various parts of this important line, by 1864 Congress came to center its attacks on the odious New Jersey monopoly, the Camden and Amboy Railroad. This situation came about through the existence of the Raritan and Delaware Bay Railroad.[62] In spite of the fact that New Jersey had given the Camden and Amboy a state monopoly, other small railroads had been built within the state. Some of these combined to form this new line, and in 1863 the Secretary of War was using it to supplement the facilities of the Camden and Amboy.[63] The road ran 65 miles from Port Monmouth near Sandy Hook to Atsion, east of Philadelphia, where it connected with the Camden and Atlantic Railroad, which it owned.[64] What happened was that the Camden and Amboy demanded the money paid for through business by the Secretary of War to the Raritan and Delaware Bay Railroad, since the Camden and Amboy was (by state law) the only legal connection through New Jersey between New York and Philadelphia. When the former railroad refused the demand, the powerful C & A got an injunction from a New Jersey court closing the rival line, and ordering it to pay the required sum to the C & A.[65] The injured road immediately petitioned Congress to declare the route a military and post road of the United States. The report of the House Committee on Military Affairs recommended that Congress honor the petition, pointing out that Congress had ample power under its authority to create post roads and under its control of interstate commerce to free the line from New Jersey's restrictive legislation. The

line was needed to supplement New York–Washington transportation, and, after the injunction, the C & A rates had advanced unexpectedly.[66]

The bill pending in the House was a partial redeclaration of
the principles enunciated in the law of January 31, 1862. One
important section, however, authorized lines declared to be post
roads and military routes to operate in disregard of any state
law. The Camden and Amboy, through the legislature and the
governor, immediately attacked the bill, Governor Joel Parker
claiming that it would be an infringement on the sovereignty
of New Jersey.[67] The New Jersey legislature passed a concur-
rent resolution protesting the bill because it took away the
jurisdiction of the state over its own citizens, because it made
corporations superior to the state (ironically, this situation
already existed), and because it insulted the dignity of the
state by violating a contract which had been upheld by a state
court.[68]

The whole episode brought more forcibly before the public the
existence and power of the Camden and Amboy monopoly. Letters were written to the newspapers, and pamphlets appeared
on both sides of the question. Richard F. Stockton, an official
of the line, wrote two letters to the New York *Evening Post* in
April and May, 1864. He pointed out that the route had been
of military importance as far back as 1812, quoting Calhoun
on the importance of the Delaware and Raritan Canal.[69] Stockton sanctioned the monopoly by pointing to Chief Justice John
Marshall's statement in Gibbons *vs.* Ogden that a state could
regulate its own internal commerce. He justified the transit duty
by saying it was merely a property tax, not a tax on travelers,
and that present fares would continue even if the tax were
dropped.[70] He refuted the charge of inadequate service by
pointing out five different lines which could carry troops and

war materials south faster than the government could take care of them. Government demands "did not approximate anything near the capacity" of the C & A on any day.[71] If this were true one wonders why Stanton was led to use the Raritan and Delaware Bay in the first place, and why Meigs was so anxious to supplement New York–Washington transportation facilities.

The monopoly had its defenders even in Congress,[72] but this body was, of course, the chief sounding board for the opposition, though it did nothing to arrest the monopoly. The veteran Charles Sumner delivered a blast at the C & A on February 14, 1865. Noting the presumptuousness of New Jersey in attempting to regulate transportation between two cities outside its borders, Sumner likened the state to a "baron of the middle ages perched in his rocky fastness."[73] After speaking in favor of a bill which sought to recognize other railroads in New Jersey for the purpose of carrying goods between New York and Philadelphia, Sumner declaimed:

New Jersey is the Valley of Humiliation through which all travelers north and south from the city of New York to the city of Washington must pass; and the monopoly, like Apollyon, claims them all as "subjects", saying "for all the country is mine, and I am the prince and god of it."[74]

And finally, "The present pretension of New Jersey belongs to the same school with that abhorred and blood bespattered pretension of South Carolina."[75]

It is not our purpose here to go further into the controversy concerning the Camden and Amboy. The truth of the matter seems to be that, regardless of important improvements inaugurated by the companies along the through route, the demands of the government were so great that at times delay and partial breakdown were inevitable. When those times came, one of the reasons cited for their occurrence was that the C & A monopolized transportation between New York and Philadelphia, and of course, that the B & O did the same between Baltimore and Washington.

While charges and countercharges were flying back and forth, the railroads themselves continued to make what improvements could be made in their lines. In 1863, the B & O replaced its 40-pound U-rail on wooden stringers between Laurel and Washington with 60-pound T-rail and white oak crossties, a change accomplished without interference with the regular business.[76] During 1864, about one third of the Washington Branch was double tracked.[77] Considering the tremendous hazards and threats of enemy action the B & O main stem was undergoing this year, it was an important accomplishment to get anything done on the Washington Branch.[78] On December 14, 1864, the second track was completed, and the 1865 report showed that all bridges on that line except the granite viaduct near Washington Junction were of iron.[79] During the fiscal year ending October 31, 1864, the Philadelphia, Wilmington, and Baltimore Railroad reported 26¼ miles of second track laid, plus the acquisition of 8 new locomotives, 13 new passenger cars, and 230 new freight cars.[80] The war ended, however, before the Susquehanna River bridge could be completed.[81]

The Federal government never constructed its proposed railroad between Washington and New York. The B & O was able to defend successfully its Baltimore-Washington monopoly, not only against a government railroad, but also against private construction. A bill introduced into Congress in February, 1865, authorizing the Pennsylvania Railroad to build from Washington to a point on the Northern Central was successfully opposed, not only by Garrett, but by the State of Maryland, on the ground that it would be an attack on the state's right to build its own public improvements.[82] But the improvements made in the New York–Washington route, such as through schedules, double track, bridging, and better rails were undoubtedly accomplished more quickly under the lash of war emergency and the threats of government regulation than they would otherwise have been.

Chapter *IX*

GOVERNMENT ACHIEVEMENTS IN
REGULATION

For a time it was impossible to procure a sufficient number of raw
recruits even to run trains.

> William B. Wilson, *History of the
> Pennsylvania Railroad Company*

On May 25, 1862, pursuant to the act of January 31, 1862,
Quartermaster General Montgomery Meigs ordered that "railroad companies . . . shall hold themselves in readiness for the
transportation of troops and munitions of war . . . to the exclusion of all other business."[1] Thus far had government policy
developed since the fateful Baltimore riot of April 19, 1861,
first dramatized the importance of railroads. A significant indication of the good job done by the railroads is that this act
was invoked in the North only during the Gettysburg campaign
for the short railroads in the immediate vicinity of that town,
and in the case of the strike of Pennsylvania miners employed by
the Philadelphia and Reading Railroad. It was under this act
that Daniel C. McCallum and Herman Haupt accomplished
their important work in the ensuing three war years.

The basic problem relating to both government and railroads
was what to charge for troop transportation and for carriage
of military supplies; in other words, the problem of rates. Railroad service was at first handicapped by a lack of uniform compensation. Early in the war the government had attempted to
establish approximate rates it would pay for the transportation
of troops and freight. The charge for troops was to be 2 cents a
mile per passenger.[2] Equipment, munitions, and troop supplies

were to be carried at first-class local rates, the charge varying with the distance, from 10 cents per 100 pounds for 30 miles to 90 cents per 100 pounds for 400 miles. The rate for horses was based on standard weights and carloads. All other supplies were to move at local rates according to classification: provisions and heavy freight at 2-3 cents per ton mile; dry goods and clothing at 3-5 cents per ton mile. This schedule followed closely that drawn up by the Harrisburg Railroad Convention of July, 1861, called by Governor Curtin.[3] The railroads, however, were not forced to keep to this schedule, and overcharging occurred in some instances.

Cameron constantly fought the B & O for overcharging, though the railroad denied doing so. Although there was truth on both sides, Cameron as Secretary of War and a director of the rival Northern Central used his influence against the Baltimore and Ohio. According to Cameron the charge for each soldier from New York to Baltimore was $6.00. Cameron thought that too high, so he had them brought by way of Harrisburg and the Northern Central for $4.00, and the latter rate was then adopted by the direct line.[4] The New Jersey Railroad claimed that, with the exception of the first regiment carried, rates between New York and Baltimore were in accordance with the tariff furnished by the government.[5] The Baltimore and Ohio of course had a monopoly between Baltimore and Washington (the Pennsylvania Railroad did not connect the two cities until 1867), and charged for troops at the rate of 3¾ cents per mile for passengers and 5-8 cents per ton mile for freight.[6]

Felton of the Philadelphia, Wilmington, and Baltimore stated flatly that Cameron's charge that New York–Washington lines did not reduce their fares until the Harrisburg line was opened, was "an error."[7] On the contrary, he claimed, the PW & B, the Camden and Amboy, and the New Jersey Railroad were the first railroads to reduce the fares for government transportation, the reduction being put into effect May 14.[8] In this controversy there was truth on both sides. Accusations of overcharging were based on *total* fare for the distance, including the ferry charges at Philadelphia and Havre de Grace. The railroads' defense was based on its rail fare alone, not including the ferry charges.

The evidence is more certain that Western roads were offenders in this respect. An investigating committee was appointed to examine the accounts against the government in the West, and in December, 1861, they reported their findings to Cameron.[9] Testimony from claimants showed that freight rates published by the War Department were higher than ordinarily charged and that 2 cents a mile for troops was a profitable rate for the railroads. The commissioners stated that there was much competition among railroad terminals at St. Louis for transportation of troops, and much money could have been saved if bids had been invited. They asked two questions of Cameron: Is the War Department circular[10] a contract, or a set of maximum rates?; Is the transportation service performed without a contract and thus subject to reduction? They cited one case involving the cost of transportation of horses per car, for which the charge was about 80 per cent over that charged private shippers. Cameron's answer was that the rates were maximum, not contract and that they were subject to reduction.[11] The Illinois Central Railroad, a land-grant road, was to charge the government one third less than it charged individuals. The inefficiency in government transportation in the West revealed by this report was substantiated by a more extensive report in 1863 and resulted in the removal of John B. Anderson, who had been in charge of government transportation at St. Louis.

The defects and misunderstandings revealed by the investigation prompted Stanton to issue a call to railroad officials to confer in Washington in February, 1862.[12] The conference settled on a charge of 2 cents a mile per man for troops, with 80 pounds of baggage.[13] Freight rates for government business were to be based on the same four classifications already in use by the railroads, with a rate reduction of 10 per cent to the government, provided the charge did not exceed 5 cents per mile (first-class freight) for 50 miles, and 3 cents per mile over 50 miles, using the shortest possible distance. In the regulations issued May 1, 1862, an additional category was entered: from 50 to 83 miles, $2.50 per ton first class. The B & O and certain railroads in Missouri, being considered in a special class, were not to deduct the 10 per cent.[14] Even with the 10 per cent reduction, the service was costly, but, as Quartermaster General Meigs himself stated, "No other mode of transportation could have collected and moved our forces in the same time, or at so little expense."[15] There was no suggestion of overcharging here, and Meigs was the man to whom Scott and McCallum, and through them the railroad presidents, were responsible.

The operation of the military draft act on railroad workers was a particular bone of contention between the railroads and the government.[16] Secretary of War Stanton had decreed that the only exemption to be allowed the railroads was locomotive engineers who were employed by the railroad when the draft act was passed.[17] Thomas A. Scott immediately asked Stanton if railroad employees could not have a blanket exemption in the same manner as telegraph operators, a class then regarded as indispensable in their jobs. Stanton was sympathetic to Scott's plea, and expressed his willingness to issue such an order for railroads engaged in government transportation, but at the same time he was fearful of provoking hostility in the public mind. He ended by asking Scott to draw up such an order for consideration.[18] George W. Cass of the Pittsburgh, Ft. Wayne, and Chicago Railway had also written Stanton on the same subject. Stanton replied that the railway workers' request was justified, and explained that telegraph operators were exempt because so few men had their special skill. He added: "The same principle might justly extend to engineers of locomotives, conductors, and brakesmen, but how much further it should go is a point of difficulty on which I would be glad to be informed."[19]

The days between August 6 and 12, 1862, found an annoyed Secretary of War holding off the futile pleas of railroad officials for draft exemption of their workers. On August 7, Stanton was requested to extend exemption to engineers, machinists, and "other experts,"[20] who could not be replaced without months of previous instructions. The request was signed by the president of the Chicago and Milwaukee Railroad, the receiver of the St. Louis, Alton, and Chicago, and the superintendents of the Chicago and North Western, the Chicago, Burlington, and Quincy, and the Galena and Chicago Union Railroads. On August 8, Samuel Sloan of the Hudson River Railroad asked Stanton if firemen and conductors could be exempt.[21] The same day, Stanton received from Scott the proposed order he had drawn up and which had already been approved by three railroad presidents in Ohio. The order exempted all railroad workers who had been employed at least three months prior to the last presidential call for troops. All employees thus exempt between the ages of 18 and 45 were to be enrolled in companies, to practice military drill once a week, and to be subject to field duty in emergencies.[22] The proposal had come too late to be seriously considered, however, for on August 9, when the Adjutant General's Office published General Order 99, Draft Regulations, the only exemption was for "all engineers of locomotives on railroads."[23] In spite of that order, protests continued to pour in to Stanton's office. George Cass seconded Scott's proposal and added that railroad presidents should be made responsible to the War Department. He pointed out that the excitement among his workers was intense, and would soon result in complete stoppage of trains.[24] President J. N. McCullough of the prosperous Cleveland and Pittsburgh Railroad also supported Scott's proposal:

Exemption is the only thing now that will prevent an utter demoralization of the entire railroad organization of the West. It is now with utmost difficulty that trains are kept running; another week it will be impossible to do so with anything like regularity and promptness, which is very necessary in moving troops successfully.[25]

On August 12, 1862, Stanton passed final judgment on the whole draft question in his letter to Scott:

Locomotive engineers are exempted. If any other employees should be drafted, who being experts cannot be spared, the Government will discharge them, as has heretofore been done, on the ground that their mechanical service is more valuable than service in the field. But the list of exemptions from draft cannot be extended.[26]

The arrangement must have quelled the exaggerated fears of Cass and McCullough, for no more appeals came into the Secretary's office until January, 1865, when Scott wrote to James B. Fry, Provost Marshal General, proposing a new arrangement. Scott suggested that skilled railroad men who had been drafted should be replaced by substitutes furnished by the railroad. These substitutes would be assembled at Philadelphia, Pittsburgh, and Harrisburg for inspection and mustering in, and for the exchange of men to be designated by the railroad. The advantage was to the army, because the substitutes were being furnished for three years, replacing men who had been drafted for one year.[27] Though the proposal was approved by Stanton, the war ended before it could be put into effect. It showed, however, that the railroads were plagued with labor troubles throughout the war.

The railroad convention fixing uniform rates and the settlement of the draft question had eliminated, or at least lessened, two points of friction between the railroads and the national government. One other facet of government policy must be mentioned. Beginning July 1, 1862, railroads were taxed 3 per cent of their gross earnings on passenger service and on dividend and interest payments.[28] This tax was never a source of grievance because the railroads were allowed to add the tax to their rates.[29] Freight traffic was not taxed in this act because of the difficulty of assessment and because the tax might be a discrimination in favor of non-taxed water-borne commerce. These considerations were ignored, however, in 1864 when the tax rate was reduced to 2½ per cent and extended to include freight traffic, while the rate on dividend and interest payments was raised to 5 per cent.[30] For the remainder of the war, this tax furnished an important additional source of revenue for the government.

Chapter X

THE UNITED STATES MILITARY RAILROADS: THE EASTERN THEATER, TO GETTYSBURG

The unfortunate victims of this latest atrocity [the wrecking of a military railroad train by enemy action] were faithful and valuable public servants—men who, knowing the danger incident to their duty, fearlessly encountered it, and lost their lives executing the trust reposed in them. Though not equipped with the implements of war, and sent upon the battlefield, where fame is won, they have none the less sacrificed their lives upon the sacred altar of our country, and deserve a place in our memories among the honored dead who have fallen in its defence.

> Special Order of E. L. Wentz, chief engineer and general
> superintendent of military railroads in Virginia, Oct. 11, 1864

PERHAPS THE MOST IMPORTANT ROLE of the wartime railroads was in the active supply of the Union armies in the field. Now widely accepted in both tactical and strategical planning, the principle of effectively supplying an army in the field via railroad was established during the Civil War. To accomplish this task, the United States Military Railroads, created in 1862, gradually evolved from a simple beginning into a complex and highly skilled organization. Operating in the War Department, it ran the railroads captured in the theaters of war, using them as supply lines for the armies. In addition, a few short lines were constructed by the Department. Beginning with the seven-mile line between Alexandria and Washington, the U.S.M.R. by the end of the war had operated 2,105 miles of railroad, with a combined rolling stock of 419 engines and 6,330 cars, a record of 642 miles of track laid or relaid, 26 miles of bridges built or rebuilt, and a net expenditure of just under $30,000,000.[1]

The act of January 31, 1862, gave the government the necessary power to control the operation of the captured Southern railroads through a central agency.[2] Under this act, Daniel C. McCallum, former superintendent of the Erie Railroad, was appointed on February 11, 1862, to be

. . . military director and superintendent of railroads in the United States, with authority to enter upon, take possession of, hold and use all railroads, engines, cars, locomotives, and equipment . . . that may be required for the transport of troops, arms, ammunition, and military supplies of the United States, and to do and perform all acts . . . that may be necessary and proper . . . for the safe and speedy transport aforesaid.[3]

Stanton added the verbal order, "I shall expect you to have on hand at all times the necessary men and material to enable you to comply with this order, and there must be no failure under any circumstances."[4]

Daniel C. McCallum was an immigrant from Scotland, who as a young boy came to this country with his parents in the eighteen twenties and settled in Rochester, N. Y. After an elementary schooling, young Daniel went to work for the New York and Erie Railroad, where he quickly showed engineering and administrative talents. In due course, he was promoted to become superintendent of the Erie's Susquehanna Division, and in 1854 was made general superintendent of the railroad. Large and powerfully built, he was an autocratic official, running his railroad with strict precision and stern discipline. When he left the Erie for war work, he left his job for good. After the war he lived mostly in retirement, acting occasionally as consulting engineer for the Atlantic and Great Western Railway and as adviser for the Union Pacific. Beneath the stern exterior, there was a genial and cheerful personality. This versatile man was something of a poet and an architect, having had a volume of verses published before the war and having designed St. Joseph's Church in Rochester.[5]

In his Civil War career, McCallum was actually under Meigs, the Quartermaster General, though he regarded himself as independent.[6] At first McCallum did not have the whole power that his title seemingly gave him. Until 1864 it was operative only in the eastern theater of war. In November, 1861, while the field armies still controlled the railroads, General Sherman in the Department of the Ohio had appointed John B. Anderson of the Louisville and Nashville Railroad as railroad director in that department.[7] An investigation late in 1863 uncovered fraud and inefficiency in Anderson's organization, resulting in his removal and the extension of McCallum's authority to the western theater in February, 1864.[8] McCallum never had to use his sweeping powers as far as the vast number of railroads in the Northern states was concerned. Here he fulfilled the function of liaison officer between the government and the several railroad presidents on the one hand, and railroad equipment manufacturers on the other. It was in western operations from Nashville and Chattanooga under Sherman in 1864 that McCallum achieved his most brilliant successes, not only in results accomplished, but in building up the esprit de corps of the organization.[9] The successful supply of Sherman's army in its campaign from Chattanooga to Atlanta was the most outstanding achievement of the military railroads. The principles and methods of operation used in that campaign, however, were worked out in a different theater of war and under the direction of a man who had only very little contact with McCallum. Virginia was the theater, Herman Haupt the man, and the Army of the Potomac the subject, for experiment not only under different commanders but also in supply.

When McCallum was appointed on February 11, 1862, the only railroad actually operated by the government was the seven-mile line across Long Bridge between Washington and Alexandria, recently constructed under a War Department order of January 10, 1862. The line ran from the B & O depot along Indiana Avenue to First Street, across Pennsylvania Avenue to the Capitol, and along Maryland Avenue to Long Bridge.[10] This was the original possession of the United States Military Railroads. During its 3½ years of operation, it ran over 50,000 cars on this line, which formed the single strand connecting Washington with the railroads radiating from Alexandria.[11] For the Peninsular Campaign in 1862, McClellan asked for 5 locomotives and 80 cars to be sent from Baltimore by water to the scene of operations. The rolling stock was purchased from New England railroads,[12] and in May, 1862, shipped to White House, Va., for operation on the Richmond and York River Railroad. With a fifth locomotive sent in June, the army was supplied via the railroad from White House to within four miles of Richmond. At the end of June when the army withdrew to Harrison's Landing, the route was abandoned and the rolling stock destroyed.[13] The Orange and Alexandria Railroad, running generally south and west from Alexandria was an important line of supply throughout the war. In March, 1862, it was opened 26 miles to Manassas Junction and in April, 39 miles to Warrenton. On Pope's retreat in the late summer of 1862, much of the line was abandoned, with the severe loss of 7 locomotives and 295 cars. The Manassas Gap Railroad, running west from Manassas Junction on the Orange and Alexandria to Front Royal and Strasburg, was used to the former place in May and part of June, 1862, then abandoned for several months.[14]

It was during the Peninsular Campaign that Stanton asked Herman Haupt to come to Washington. Haupt found that Stanton wanted him to rebuild the destroyed track and burned bridges of the Aquia Creek and Fredericksburg Railroad. The task was necessary to insure the supply of McDowell's army before it could cooperate with McClellan in the operation against Richmond.[15] Though Stanton wanted Haupt for this job only, possibly for three or four weeks, Haupt remained with the military railroads for a year and four months. In that time and largely on his own responsibility, he organized an efficient construction corps which formed the nucleus for the much larger and more difficult operation in the West, and formulated certain principles of railway operation which were to become fundamental in army supply problems in future wars. It is fitting, therefore, to give here a brief sketch of the man and his life.

Born in Pennsylvania in 1817, Haupt graduated from West Point at the age of 18, in the same class with George G. Meade.[16] Resigning his commission almost immediately, he did some railroad construction work on the Western Maryland Railroad and became interested in bridge construction and its engineering theories. He was appointed Professor of Mathematics and Engineering at the Pennsylvania College in Gettysburg, and while there wrote a book, *The General Theory of Bridge Construction*, (finally published in 1851), which was a definite engineering advance in its field. J. Edgar Thomson, then chief engineer of the Pennsylvania Railroad, visited Haupt in 1848, and was impressed with Haupt's knowledge of bridges. Beginning as Thomson's assistant, Haupt soon rose to general superintendent of the Pennsylvania Railroad, in which position he organized efficiently the operations of the road. One friendship he made was with Thomas A. Scott, then an agent at Hollidaysburg, Pa. In 1853, Haupt became chief engineer of the railroad.

Three years later he resigned to begin construction of the Hoosac Tunnel on the Troy and Greenfield Railroad in Massa-

chusetts, a project which he had previously approved as to
practicality. The change was unfortunate, for it brought him in
opposition to powerful interests in Massachusetts, and the resulting conflict eventually cost him his savings, much of his
property in Pennsylvania, his reputation, and his job with the
Military Railroads. When the tunnel was nearly completed, the
contractors and the railroad company were severely attacked in
the press. Haupt, with his usual thoroughness, eventually traced
the attacks to Chester W. Chapin, president of the competing
Boston and Albany Railroad. The completion of the Hoosac
Tunnel would give the Troy and Greenfield Railroad (now the
Boston and Maine) an advantage over other lines in the trade of
Boston with the West, and it was the Boston and Albany that
would suffer most from this competition. Since the state of
Massachusetts had loaned the enterprise credit of $2,000,000,
Governor John A. Andrew became interested. Chapin had some
influence, through another railroad president and a paper man-
ufacturer, in state politics. Struggling along against press attacks and diminishing finances, the tunnel became the subject of
a state investigation in 1860. The investigation fully supported
Haupt, and the legislature passed a bill placing the enterprise
on a secure foundation. In 1861, however, the outgoing Governor Nathaniel P. Banks neglected to sign the order for payment of the tunnel estimate and the incoming Governor Andrew
refused to sign it. Andrew expressed lack of confidence in Haupt,
and when the executive council tried to uphold Haupt, Andrew
retaliated by removing the state engineer. Another investigation
again supported Haupt and appropriated money to compensate
for damages caused by the actions of the new state engineer.
Andrew opposed the investigation, but let it be known that he
was willing to have the tunnel put in charge of a state commission. The state took over in 1862, and spent 14 years and

$20,000,000 to complete the tunnel. For ten years after the opening of the tunnel an unfriendly attorney-general denied Haupt the right of redemption that he had won through the influence of Jonathan E. Field. In 1884 Haupt finally got $300,-000 damages out of almost $1,500,000 claimed, most of which was distributed among the stockholders, who were reimbursed at the rate of eight cents on the dollar.

After his service in the war, Haupt held office with the Richmond and Danville Railroad. In that post he proposed the plan for the Southern Railway and Steamship Organization and for the Northern Pacific Railroad, and helped complete the road to the West coast. He also aided in the survey and construction of a pipeline from the Allegheny Valley to tidewater against the opposition of the railroads and the Standard Oil Company. Fittingly enough, his death came with a sudden heart attack on board a Washington bound Pennsylvania Railroad train, December 14, 1905.[17]

Herman Haupt was an industrious, hard-working individual, an excellent engineer and a first rate organizer. He knew how to get the best work out of his men, and could adapt himself readily to changing conditions of operation. But he was a hard man to get along with. His pigheadedness had cost him the appointment as assistant secretary of war which went to Scott.[18] His relations with his superiors were not of the best. Only McDowell he knew cordially, and that was an old West Point friendship. He cared nothing for Pope, probably because the latter in turn knew nothing of railroads. He laid down the law to Burnside, and that commander rightfully resented having to take orders from a man inferior in rank. The energetic Haupt was impatient with the do-nothing McClellan. He was resentful of any military interference in his work, and he continually pestered Halleck, when the latter was Chief of Staff, for an order forbidding military interference with the operation of the railroads. When he finally got the order he flaunted it on numerous occasions to warn away would-be trespassers on his authority. Yet he was never afraid to make *his* views known on matters which did not even remotely concern him. He suggested strategic and tactical military moves not only to commanders in the field, but even to Halleck and Stanton in Washington.[19] Undoubtedly Stanton had some cause for losing his temper in his final interview with Haupt. Haupt took pleasure in surmounting difficulties, and was delighted to find a badly tangled situation which he could clear up with his magic touch. But, for all his failures, this humorless man was responsible for developing not only the general principles of railroad supply operation, but also detailed methods of construction and destruction of railroad equipment. To this capable engineer and brilliant organizer is due most of the credit for the successful supply of the Army of the Potomac and its immediate antecedents, and for the principles of operation which achieved their most important fruition in Sherman's campaign in 1864 and 1865.

When Haupt was called by Stanton, negotiations in Massachusetts were at a critical stage, and Haupt wanted to finish the job for Stanton quickly so he could return to Massachusetts.

If [the position of affairs] shall appear to be such as imperatively to require my personal attention, it will be given, although the sacrifices in other important interests will be great. . . . I would expect to continue only so long as public exigencies demanded it. . . . I have no military or political aspirations, and am particularly averse to wearing the uniform; would prefer to perform the duties required without military rank if possible. . . . Pay I do not require or care about. If I take the position you have so kindly offered, it will be with the understanding that I can retire whenever, in my opinion, my services can be dispensed with, and that I will perform no duties on the Sabbath unless necessity imperatively requires it.[20]

Necessity soon revealed its requirements, as Haupt and his in-experienced soldier helpers soon found themselves working through rain, day and night, laying tracks and cutting crossties on the Aquia Creek and Fredericksburg Railroad. "The track was laid in a lake of mud," he reported.[21] One bridge was built in fifteen working hours. Another, 400 feet long across Potomac Creek, and 80 feet high, built in nine days with insufficient supply of tools, inexperienced help, and in bad weather, was a frail looking structure with three stories of trestle work and one of crib work. When completed it carried 10 to 20 trains daily. Soon afterward Lincoln visited McDowell, and upon his return to Washington, told the Committee on the Conduct of the War, "that man Haupt has built a bridge across Potomac Creek . . . over which loaded trains are running every hour, and, upon my word, gentlemen, there is nothing in it but beanpoles and corn-stalks."[22] Besides the bridges, 3 miles of track had been recon-structed, and by May 19 trains were running the 15 miles from Aquia Creek to Fredericksburg, just three weeks after recon-struction was begun. This railroad was part of the main line of the Richmond, Fredericksburg, and Potomac, which termi-nated at Aquia Creek on the Potomac River south of Wash-ington.

Haupt was appointed May 18, 1862, as chief of construction and transportation in the Department of the Rappahannock.[23] He protested that his authority conflicted with that of Daniel Stone, whom Stanton had authorized to construct a bridge across the Rappahannock and thus open the RF & P south-ward, and also with McCallum. Though McCallum nominally was Haupt's superior, an informal arrangement was readily made that prevented any quarreling. "McCallum took the office and I took the field"[24] was the way Haupt put it. One detects a slight note of contempt for the office man. Stanton confirmed Haupt's title and his rank of colonel on McDowell's staff. The authorization included opening all military railroads, using them for transportation, appointing necessary assistants, requisitioning details of men from field commanders for construction or guard purposes, issuing passes to personnel, and purchasing machinery, rolling stock, and supplies for which the Quartermaster would make payment.[25] Haupt commended the soldiers for their willingness and ability to learn. Some of them were detailed permanently to become the basis of a construction corps for future operations.[26] Already Haupt was beginning the formation of a permanent construction corps whose sole duties would be the construction of railroads, bridges, and necessary buildings for supplying the army. Though he was soon to prefer civilians to soldiers, Haupt was willing to begin from a nucleus of what personnel was available.

Relations between Haupt and McDowell were cordial, Haupt having recalled their days at West Point when he was a cadet and McDowell a plebe. This friendship brought willing cooperation from McDowell, an attitude which stood Haupt in good stead in the reconstruction of the Manassas Gap Railroad.[27] The Peninsular Campaign having failed, McDowell was ordered cross country to the vicinity of Front Royal on the Manassas Gap Railroad in order to intercept the Confederate General Thomas J. "Stonewall" Jackson.[28] Haupt arranged for transportation with James A. Devereux, his superintendent at Alexandria, and proceeded at once with the reconstruction of the Gap road. The main depot was at Piedmont, four miles beyond McDowell's headquarters at Rectortown. Five bridges were rebuilt in one day and the road opened in three days.[29] Operations encountered more difficulties than construction. Rolling stock for the railroad had to be requisitioned from other roads. Haupt complained,

The difficulties of the situation were greatly increased by the usual military interference with the running of trains, and by the neglect or refusal of subordinates in the Commissary and Quartermaster Departments to promptly unload and return cars.[30]

Here in his second major reconstruction job, Haupt was formulating two principles of operation which he continually emphasized as vital to the task of supplying an army: first, no interference by military officers with the running of trains,[31] and, second, prompt unloading and return of empty cars so that rolling stock would not be used as warehouses. These principles were embodied in an order of June 2: "No officer, no surgeon . . . no paymaster, quartermaster, or commissary, shall have the right to detain a train, or order it to run in advance of schedule time."[32]

Once at Piedmont, Haupt found a blockade of loaded cars, and immediately protested to McDowell, who cooperated to the extent of ordering his chief Quartermaster and chief Commissary to the depot, at night in a pouring rain, in order to superintend personally the unloading of the cars.[33] Another time, a paymaster using an empty boxcar on a track as an office was forcibly ejected along with his money chests, tables, chairs, and papers, so that the track could be used for more vital tasks.[34] A third time, Haupt investigated the non-arrival of four trains at Piedmont, and found that the wife of a prominent officer had stopped the train on which she was traveling, to seek accommodations at a farm for the night, the other three trains necessarily being held up by the delay. In Haupt's own words,

I ordered the conductor to start at once, but just then an elegantly dressed lady came tripping across the field to take her place in one of the cars. I did not display extra gallantry on the occasion, nor even offer the lady assistance. She had detained four trains for three hours in a period of urgency, and I was not in an amiable mood.[35]

Meanwhile the supply trains were not coming through fast enough for Haupt's satisfaction. The explanation came from

Devereux at Alexandria on June 3. He had only five engines, and of those five, one was on its way to Manassas, one was out of order, one could be used only as a switch engine, and the other two were kept busy supplying troops along the line to Manassas. It was thus hard enough to get supplies from Washington, let alone forward more to Piedmont. Inability to use the telegraph because military officials constantly intervened with their own business, and the fact that he had only one telegraph operator, completed the difficulties at the Alexandria end: "I beg to say that day and night I have been at my post, and in action and planning could do no better. But I have *not* control of my trains, or my telegraph."[36] Haupt issued temporary orders to run supply trains through without telegraph, and provided for returning empties to give the right of way to loaded trains. Flagmen were to be sent ahead to avoid collisions on the single track. Haupt informed Stanton that the remedy for this confusion was to use the telegraph only for emergencies and in case of accidents, and to run the trains on a strict schedule. He would draw up a timetable which would go into effect as soon as the bridge across Bull Run was completed.[37] From then on, the Virginia Military Railroads operated on a schedule, and relied on the telegraph only in emergencies.[38] The proof of the schedule system was to come at Gettysburg, when the Western Maryland Railroad under Haupt's direction ran 15 to 18 trains a day to supply Meade, although the ordinary capacity of the road was three or four trains a day.[93]

In June, 1862, Jackson eluded McDowell at Front Royal, and McDowell moved his army out of the Shenandoah Valley east to the line of the Orange and Alexandria Railroad, with headquarters at Manassas. There he was made the scapegoat for his failures and was replaced by Pope on June 26.

Through most of June, railroad operations ran smoothly,

and Haupt used the lull to reorganize the Construction Corps. He kept employing more civilians and contrabands, using the civilians as foremen and supervisors, but still found it necessary to supplement them with troops. Under regulations issued June 11, 1862, the corps, about 300 men, was divided into 10-man squads, two squads to each officer. All tools belonging to the corps were labeled "Construction Corps, Rappahannock." The regulations stated that the men might have to work all day and at night also. Those unwilling to work 16 hours continuously were requested to return to their regiments. There was to be extra pay for time actually spent on construction work. Civilian superintendents were equal to the military rank of captain, foremen to lieutenant, and laborers corresponded to enlisted men.[40]

In two months Haupt had come a long way from his determination not to work on the Sabbath. On June 20, he wrote Stanton that he considered his organization and construction done and said he wanted to return to Massachusetts to give attention to his financial affairs. He asked for repayment of his personal expenditures, amounting to about $800.[41] He complained also about the conflict of authority. Characteristically, Haupt wanted to do the big things, leaving irksome detail to subordinates: "I wish to have nothing to do with contracts, jobs, or money disbursements, but where necessary to make purchases, I wish to have the power, in general I would get everything through McCallum."[42] No answer was received from Stanton. Haupt soon found that Pope, upon assuming command of the Army of the Rappahannock, thought that railroads were unimportant in a military campaign, and at any rate should not be independent, but should be under the Quartermaster Department.[43] Haupt and McDowell both tried unsuccessfully to change Pope's opinion. Haupt then informed Assistant Secretary of War Peter H. Watson that he was returning to Massachusetts, and asked to be informed of any developments. The military railroads in Virginia held together as an organization for a short time, but soon difficulties ensued which Pope could not cure, and paralysis set in. Watson telegraphed Haupt, "Come back immediately; cannot get along without you; not a wheel moving on any of the roads."[44]

This was just the sort of situation in which Haupt delighted. Returning to Pope's headquarters at Cedar Mountain on August 18, 1862, with the I-told-you-so-now-watch-me-clear-up-the-mess air about him, Haupt was told to dictate whatever orders he considered necessary. The resulting general order placed Haupt in charge of all railroads within the limits of the Army of Virginia, especially the Orange and Alexandria. All orders concerning troop transportation, train movements, and railroad construction were to be channeled through Haupt at Pope's headquarters. Stanton continued Haupt's previous authorization and extended his jurisdiction to include the Army of Virginia.[45] At this time the Orange and Alexandria was open 61 miles to Culpepper, the farthest south this railroad was ever used as a military railroad. No sooner had Haupt set up his headquarters at Alexandria, reorganized the transportation, which was suffering from military interference and from neglect in unloading, and undertaken the retreat from Culpepper ordered by Pope, than the Confederates began the activity which opened the second battle of Bull Run. J. E. B. Stuart's raid on Pope's headquarters destroyed the bridge across Cedar Creek, cut off a great deal of rolling stock, and almost claimed Haupt himself as one of its prisoners.[46] Of the 90,000 troops of the Army of the Potomac camped in the vicinity of Alexandria, Haupt succeeded in forwarding 20,500 to Pope, complaining bitterly during those hectic days that the 20 miles between

Alexandria and Bull Run could easily have been covered by marching, and criticizing severely the generals for waiting three or four days demanding rail transportation which could not be furnished because of the sudden jam on the railroad. He concluded that McClellan really cared nothing about going to Pope's aid.[47]

The last ten days of August were the most hectic that Haupt had yet experienced. In energy output and in telegrams sent and received, they resembled the next summer's Gettysburg campaign, but the military railroads were not yet organized efficiently enough to produce the spectacular results of Gettysburg. Confusion of movement, conflict of authority, clash of personalities—these were the salient characteristics of the August days of 1862. Haupt on August 20 ordered 60 empty cars as far south as Warrenton Junction to remove stores. With the power thus concentrated at the south end of the Orange and Alexandria, Halleck (who had become Chief of Staff July 23) informed Haupt that 10,000 to 15,000 troops would arrive at Alexandria within 48 hours, and Halleck ordered Devereux at Alexandria to forward them regardless of train schedule.[48] Haupt immediately flared up in a telegram to Devereux:

Neither General Halleck nor anyone else has any right to give orders in regard to trains in opposition to my instructions. I want the schedule restored tomorrow. You can run extras in between, but the regulars must run, or I will decline all responsibility.[49]

Haupt then informed Pope that troops were being forwarded almost as fast as they applied for transportation. Pope wanted locomotives at Rappahannock Crossing to haul out cars that were there. Halleck telegraphed not to send trains beyond Catlett's Station because of danger.[50] It was up to Haupt to decide whether to stop the trains at Catlett's or to send them on to Rappahannock Crossing. More trouble was caused by delay in unloading not only supplies but also the sick and wounded. Haupt telegraphed Watson, August 22: "Doctors will persist in sending sick, often without papers, to get them off their hands, and we cannot send forward the troops if we must run our trains to Washington with sick, to stand for hours unloaded."[51]

At this juncture Haupt had his most serious quarrel with a general officer. Word came that General Sturgis had ordered four trains stopped outside Alexandria. Haupt immediately reported the situation to Halleck, then went to see Sturgis in person. "I am glad you have come," said the general, "for I have just sent a guard to your office to put you in arrest for disobedience of my orders in failing to transport my command."[52] Haupt replied that arrest would be a relief, because it would mean at least a few hours of needed sleep. He also pointed out to the irate general that the four trains were loaded with wounded, would soon run out of wood and water, and that there would be a consequent delay in unloading and getting reinforcements back to Pope. At the mention of Pope's name, Sturgis exploded, "I don't care for John Pope a pinch of owl dung!" Meanwhile Halleck in Washington backed up Haupt with a dispatch: "No military officer has any authority to interfere with your control over railroads. Show this to General Sturgis, and if he attempts to interfere, I will arrest him." Sturgis, not "in his normal condition," as he later labeled his slight case of drunkenness, was finally made to understand that the dispatch had come from Halleck, not Pope. "Halleck says if you interfere with the railroads he will put you in arrest," an aide said to the general; Sturgis replied, "He does, does he? Well, then take your damned railroad!" The delay, according to Haupt, kept at least 10,000 men out of the battle. Halleck's dispatch to Haupt was confirmed on August 24: "The railroad is entirely under your control. No military officer has any right to interfere."[53]

By August 23, 6,600 men had been forwarded to Catlett's Station, and most of the locomotive power was at the south end. Train orders were to unload at Catlett's, return to Manassas, the only place where trains could pass, there to pass southbound loaded trains, and then to proceed to Alexandria. Haupt sent frantic telegrams to Pope asking the return of empties so more troops could be forwarded. To Watson he telegraphed, "We keep running day and night, eat little, and sleep almost none. 20,000 more troops just arrived."[54] At 4:30 A.M. August 24, Haupt telegraphed Halleck that 1,000 men of the 38th Ohio had just left Alexandria in Baltimore and Ohio cars. Hooker's and Kearney's commands were being transported, and Sturgis was asking to be put in ahead of them.[55] Still there was no word from the returning empties. Morning and afternoon telegrams flew back and forth between Haupt and Watson, the former indicating that transportation was ready, the latter trying to locate the generals in Washington.[56] Not until 7:30 P.M. August 24 did Haupt learn that the returning empties were delayed, now more than 24 hours, because General Sturgis had failed to unload his troops promptly.[57]

By loading troops in Washington and thus keeping the main track in Alexandria clear, by keeping supply trains of forage and subsistence busy moving out of the yard at Alexandria, and by seeing that when cars were sent for 6,000 troops, that number was put aboard (a detail which required the full time of a field grade officer), operations ran a little more smoothly. A system of priority was established: subsistence stores were given first priority, forage second, ammunition third, hospital stores fourth, veteran infantry regiments fifth, and raw infantry sixth.

Artillery and cavalry troops were not to use the railroads. If this system were followed out, and there was no delay in loading and unloading, Haupt claimed that 10,000 men a day could be carried.[58]

On August 26 a Confederate raid on Manassas destroyed the railroad bridge over Bull Run and captured four trains of empty cars.[59] The raid was carried out by an infantry regiment, two cavalry squadrons, and a section of artillery; the defending force approximated three regiments and some cavalry.[60] Unable to get train guards from McClellan, Haupt on his own initiative sent a wreckage and construction train to Burke's Station, 13 miles from Alexandria, from which point the train proceeded slowly with skirmishers out front to Fairfax, three miles further, and under enemy fire brought off a load of wounded. Another train was sent out with workers to repair three bridges on the line, supply trains following closely.[61] On August 27 and 28, telegrams were exchanged directly between Lincoln and Haupt concerning the condition of the railroad after the Manassas raid, and general news of the battle.[62] By August 30, the track to Bull Run was clear, but before the bridge could be repaired, the movements of the enemy forced the project to be abandoned. Haupt blamed McClellan also for not using more initiative in going to Pope's aid.[63]

The last few days of the battle brought another serious problem to the patient but exasperated Haupt. On August 30 Stanton asked for civilian volunteers to help carry wounded from the battlefield, and arrangements for their free transportation to Bull Run were made through Garrett with McCallum.[64] Haupt wanted doctors and surgeons but no one else, and reluctantly sent a train to Washington for the volunteers. The 16-car train, packed with 800 men, arrived in Alexandria at 10 P.M. with about half the occupants already drunk. Haupt sent them on to Fairfax, where most of them wandered about the battlefield, getting in each other's way, and eventually walked back because the trains were loaded with wounded.[65] Field officers telegraphed "send no more citizens," and Haupt asked McCallum to get an order from Stanton placing guards on the Long Bridge across the Potomac to keep civilians out.[66]

General McClellan asked Haupt on September 1 to withdraw all supplies from Fairfax because of the nearness of the enemy. Haupt accordingly telegraphed M. J. McCrickett, his agent at Fairfax, to send out all cars as soon as loaded with wounded, and to abandon forage and any other supplies if necessary. After the last troops had retreated on foot (because they could protect themselves more easily than in a train), McCrickett got out everything except a few stores, and set the latter on fire. "Have fired it. Good-by," said his telegraph of September 2. He was one of the last men to leave the battlefield at Bull Run.[67]

The evacuation of Fairfax meant the end of Pope, and the Army of Virginia was merged into the Army of the Potomac under McClellan. Blame for the failure of Pope in the second battle of Bull Run can hardly be placed on the railroads. Certainly, compared with later successes in railroad supply, Pope's campaign was as close to failure as the military railroads ever came. But it was not a failure that could be placed on railroad personnel. The extreme difficulties of the situation were simply too great to be solved in the short time available. The obstacles overcome in the last two weeks of August, 1862, were never to be met again in equal severity. At Fredericksburg and at Gettysburg, Haupt was to have an experienced corps behind him, something which he lacked in Pope's campaign, partly because that commander had caused the original construction corps to be disbanded. Never again was Haupt to find it necessary to deal with a general who did not realize the importance of his railroad communication. Never again was he to quarrel openly with a general while men and supplies were needed on the battlefield. Perhaps the 10,000 men who failed to arrive in that 24 hours' delay might have turned the tide of battle. Haupt himself blamed McClellan for not supporting Pope more actively, and stressed that McClellan's army should not have waited for three or four days for rail transportation when the march on foot could have been accomplished in much less time. Haupt's energetic attempts to meet impossible obstacles and his services in keeping Washington informed of the progress of the battle as well as possible after communications with Pope had been cut off were recognized by Stanton. "For meritorious services in the most recent operations against the enemy near Manassas," Haupt was thanked in the presence of the Cabinet and Lincoln, and was commissioned a brigadier general of volunteers on September 5, 1862.[68]

The lessons learned in railroad operation in Pope's campaign were soon to be applied. During September, before the battle of Antietam, the Army of the Potomac was supplied by the Loudoun and Hampshire railroad, running in a northwesterly direction generally parallel to and not far from the Potomac River.[69] Haupt himself took no part in the Maryland campaign, but through his agents the railroads performed satisfactory service. The Maryland campaign involved for the first time the use of loyal railroads in the North in the direct supply of an army in the field. Haupt laid down the general principles to be followed in his letter to W. W. Wright, one of his able assistants, whom he sent to assume control, if necessary, of the Cumberland Valley Railroad between Harrisburg and Chambersburg, Pa.

In general it is desirable that roads used wholly or partially for military purposes should be operated by and through the regular officers in charge of such roads; but when the management is characterized by incompetency, or inefficiency, it becomes necessary to assume military possession and place in charge agents and officers who will promptly forward troops and government supplies.

One agent, J. D. Potts, had already taken charge of the Franklin Railroad between Chambersburg and Hagerstown, Md. Three important points, said Haupt, were to be kept in mind (and these were the fruits of Bull Run): (1), do not forward supplies until required, and then only so much as can promptly be unloaded; (2), see that cars are promptly unloaded and promptly returned; (3), establish a schedule and permit no delays or departures from it; if necessary, extra trains may be run.[70] These principles of operation were to be stressed again and again, and were to pay dividends in the efficient supply of the army.

On September 18, Haupt, after conferring with Garrett and W. P. Smith of the B & O, established the rule that supplies to the army in Maryland from Baltimore and points south should be transported via B & O; from north of Baltimore, via the York and Cumberland Railroad, thus relieving the Northern Central of the necessity of transporting government troops northward.[71] The B & O already had an efficient management and a large capacity. The York and Cumberland, however, had to borrow both rolling stock and management personnel from the Pennsylvania Railroad. In addition, Haupt ordered all private sidings vacated, and ordered off the road cars not needed for military purposes.[72] On a personal tour, he cleared a blockade of trains at Hagerstown and another of 200 loaded cars which had been stored on B & O sidings for a week at Monocacy. When the B & O reported a shortage of cars because empties were not returned, Haupt sent two dispatchers from the Orange and Alexandria Railroad over the lines in Maryland and Pennsylvania to round up B & O and U. S. Military Railroad cars.[73]

Part of the Construction Corps was sent from Alexandria to repair the bridge at Harper's Ferry. Most of the difficulties encountered, Haupt reported, were because of failure to observe the three principles of operation he had established.[74] When Lee retreated across the Potomac, McClellan ordered Haupt to reconstruct the Winchester Branch of the B & O. Consultation with W. P. Smith revealed that the road was badly out of order, and an army advancing from Winchester could be better supplied by the Manassas Gap Railroad. On Haupt's recommendation, the Winchester Branch was therefore left alone.[75] When Lee returned the following July, these railroads were to form but a part of Meade's supply line, though the 1862 rehearsal was good practice.

In October about the only railroad suitable for supply purposes was the Orange and Alexandria to Manassas Junction and its extension on the Manassas Gap Railroad as far as Front Royal. Haupt estimated the capacity of this railroad at 700 to 900 tons daily.[76] Crowded depots and lack of cars meant occasional delay in rail supplies to McClellan. But according to Halleck, Haupt was doing excellent work with the equipment he had, and McClellan, being much better supplied than the armies in the West, had no cause for complaint.[77] The Aquia Creek and Fredericksburg Railroad had been destroyed on evacuation by Burnside's Corps in September with a loss of one engine, 57 cars, and several wharves along the Potomac.[78]

While his Construction Corps was repairing the Virginia railroads for future operations, Haupt was developing more effective ways of destroying locomotives and bridges. For the latter, he invented an eight-inch torpedo which could easily be carried in a saddlebag. By boring two holes in the main support of a bridge and inserting two torpedos, a regulation Howe truss bridge could be thoroughly destroyed. If the bridge had an arch, four torpedos were needed, and presumably one torpedo would suffice for a temporary trestle. The best way to destroy a locomotive, Haupt found, was to fire a cannon ball through the boiler. A less effective method was to destroy the flues by letting out all the water and building a fire in the firebox.[79]

In November, 1862, after Burnside had replaced McClellan as commander of the Army of the Potomac, reconstruction and repair of the railroads went on. The work of reestablishing transportation facilities sometimes encountered a great deal of trouble from the Union troops themselves. J. J. Moore, one of Haupt's superintendents, reported broken switch stands and waste of wood and water on the Loudoun and Hampshire line. He complained that soldiers bathed and washed their clothes with soap in water used for the supply of engines. The spectacular result was that "many engines were stopped on the road by foaming boilers caused by soapy water."[80] Water supply was frequently a serious problem. On one occasion, Haupt and General Ingalls, Quartermaster of the Army of the Potomac, were stalled on the Manassas Gap Railroad because their water supply gave out. Luckily the engine carried two buckets, and these were used to dip water from streams along the right of way.[81] Even livestock occasionally presented a hazard. One trainman's diary read, "Backed over a cow, breaking up the engine and depriving us of the use of the machine in a great pressure when the other end of the engine would have laid the cow up and saved the machine." But "the other end" sometimes failed in its task also; as another account put it, "Ran over cow—engine, tender, and eight cars off track."[82]

Operating the Orange and Alexandria as far south as the Rappahannock River, Haupt explained to General Heintzelmann the need for soldiers to guard the bridges south of Manassas Junction. In addition, 350 more cars were needed because McClellan was demanding 1,500 tons a day, almost twice the estimate of the original capacity of the road.[83] Haupt wrote to Watson just before Burnside became commander, that Mc-Clellan was asking for four or five times as much as McDowell had, and in addition the forage for 60,000 animals had to be transported by rail, whereas the previous June it could be gathered from the fields.

Never before . . . has a single track railroad, of such limited capacity, been so severely taxed, and if we can succeed in forwarding necessary supplies, it will only be by the most extraordinary good management and good luck combined.[84]

Burnside promised cooperation with Haupt, but was always bothered by the fact that a man of inferior rank should have more power than he. Haupt was to find in Burnside a man who frequently forgot his promises and whose orders to his subordinates often conflicted with instructions from the military railway department, causing unnecessary delays.[85] On November 9, 1862, Haupt told Burnside in no uncertain terms just what he faced in the matter of supplying the army. It was enough to shake the confidence of a better man than Burnside.

The Orange and Alexandria road by which your army is to be supplied is a single track, without sidings sufficient for long trains, without wood and with insufficient supply of water, a road which has heretofore failed to supply an army of one-quarter the size of that which you command, a road the ordinary working capacity of which is not equal to the half of your requirements, but which, by a combination of good management and good fortune, may be able to furnish your supplies.

At every depot there should be stationed a force large enough to unload all the cars of a train at once. Haupt wanted Burnside to be sure "that cars shall, on their arrival at each and every depot, be immediately unloaded and returned. I say again, that without this the supply of your army is impossible. No man living can accomplish it."

A War Department order of November 10, 1862, laid down as official policy the principles Haupt had been emphasizing since his work under McDowell. Commanding officers were ordered to detail sufficient men to insure the prompt loading and unloading of cars; and under penalty of dismissal, there was to be no military interference with the civilian superintendents of the railroads. McCallum cited this order as the foundation of the success of the military railroads. Without it, the whole system would have failed.[86]

Haupt also told Burnside that a reserve depot was to be established at Manassas, and additional depots constructed at intervals of 30 to 40 miles as the army advanced. The reconstruction of the Fredericksburg Railroad would be necessary because the Orange and Alexandria was not sufficient by itself.[87] This plain talk of the railroad man to his superior officer showed that, like a permanent under-secretary, Haupt was becoming somewhat impatient at the parade of Union commanders in Virginia. He still had two more to go. Again in conference with Halleck and Meigs in Washington, Haupt impressed upon Burnside the necessity for preventing military interference with the railroads and for prompt loading and unloading of cars.[88] Haupt later cited the cooperation of Halleck and Ingalls as responsible for successful supply via the Orange and Alexandria.[89]

By the nature of their personalities it was inevitable that Haupt and Stanton would find an occasion to quarrel. It was only a wonder that it had not happened before. The occasion was Stanton's order of November 12, 1862, ordering railroad agents to give receipts for property delivered to the railroads for transportation.[90] Haupt thought this duty should be performed by Quartermaster personnel and lost no time in pointing out to

Stanton that superintendents could not be responsible, for they had nothing to do with loading and had no means of protecting the cargo. Both Watson and Meigs supported Haupt. The angry Secretary, finding himself alone and fearing that to rescind the order would make him look ridiculous, finally instructed Haupt to consider it a dead letter.[91]

When Burnside moved the Army of the Potomac to its position near Fredericksburg, the reconstruction of the railroad from Aquia Creek was accomplished in the record time of ten days. Five days after the task was begun, a 1,000-foot section of wharf to accommodate larger vessels was completed, and trains were running to Potomac Creek. In five more days, by November 28, trains reached the main depot at Falmouth, on the north side of the Rappahannock across from Fredericksburg. This railroad was to be the main line of supply until after the battle of Chancellorsville in June, 1863. An additional wharf was built at Yuba Dam which could hold 24 cars and accommodate vessels drawing 10½ feet of water at low tide. Sidings were constructed to connect with the main track and to increase the capacity of the yards.[92] From supply depots on the Orange and Alexandria, carloads of supplies were sent to Alexandria. The cars themselves were then loaded on barges, which in turn were floated to Aquia Creek where the rail trip was resumed, the entire trip, without break of bulk, being accomplished in about the same time required to march the army overland.[93] The Schuylkill barges, as they were called, consisted of two separate barges bolted together parallel to each other. Railroad tracks were laid on the barges, enough to accommodate eight cars. Thus the usual 16-car train could be transferred bodily by water from the Orange and Alexandria to the Aquia Creek Railroad in two barges.[94] The feat had never been accomplished before without unloading supplies from rail car to barge and reversing the process at the other terminus. Hundreds of loaded cars used this route, which made for greater efficiency and a saving of personnel in the forwarding of supplies. Six hours were required for the trip between Alexandria and Aquia Creek, with one hour at each end for getting the cars on and off the barges. The saving over land transportation via wagon amounted to about $3,000 per day.[95]

W. W. Wright was appointed superintendent and engineer of the Richmond, Fredericksburg, and Potomac Railroad (of which the Aquia Creek was a part), with instructions from Haupt to establish a schedule, run trains in convoys, and provide for their prompt unloading.[96] Under these conditions, Haupt claimed that a single track railroad could supply an army of 200,000, almost ten times as many as it could if the conditions were not met.[97] Additional regulations required that passes for other than railroad employees were to be given only by the Provost Marshal or Commanding Officer, and no newsboys were to be allowed on trains.[98] That Haupt stuck by his own regulations was demonstrated when the Rev. Alexander Reed, general agent of the Christian Commission, appeared before him to ask passage to Falmouth to attend to the distribution of hospital supplies. Sympathizing with the minister's predicament, but unable to give him a pass, Haupt signed an order making him a brakeman on the railroad, and ordering him to report to Falmouth immediately![99]

On December 12, preparations were made to begin the construction of a railroad bridge across the Rappahannock to Fredericksburg, but when the battle began the next day, the soldier guards immediately deserted their exposed position at the site of construction. When shellfire cut hoisting ropes and shattered bridge timbers, the 30 civilian workers finally took shelter. Haupt found his foreman, E. C. Smeed, behind a tree.[100]

The Construction Corps had worked for some time under enemy fire after its military protectors had deserted.

Haupt's letter to General Joseph Hooker, who replaced Burnside on January 26, 1863, after the disastrous assault on Marye's Heights, pointed out that by observing a strict schedule, the Army of the Potomac never suffered from any deficiency that could be overcome by the railroads (a truer statement than the failure he mentions in his first letter to Burnside). The letter also listed the various superintendents and engineers; as to Haupt's position, "Col. McCallum attends to the routine and red-tape business of the department. . . . For myself, I am generally present when active operations are in progress, organizing and directing where my presence seems essential."[101] On January 1, 1863, an order signed by McCallum and Haupt had separated the Construction Corps from the operating department of the military railroads in Virginia. The railroads ending in Alexandria were headed by James A. Devereux as superintendent, and J. J. Moore as chief engineer. The smaller Aquia Creek road was headed by W. W. Wright, who was both superintendent and engineer. Adna Anderson became chief engineer of the military railroads in Virginia.[102] From January through May, 1863, the supply of Hooker's army ran smoothly. Supplies from the North were received at Washington's B & O station, from where the cars were distributed either to the Sixth Street wharf for general supplies, Buzzards Point for forage, or the arsenal for ammunition. From these points they were forwarded direct to Alexandria and to the railroads there, or by barge to Aquia Creek, thence by railroad to Falmouth. A 16-car supply train was commonly transported from Washington to Falmouth without break of bulk in about 12 hours.[103] From its opening in November, 1862, through March 1, 1863, the Aquia Creek line carried 8,812 loaded cars. Figuring 10 tons per car,

the army was getting 80 cars or 800 tons daily, and in April
the figure climbed to 140 cars daily. More than 50 per cent of
the cars were loaded with forage, another 25 per cent with commissary. Quartermaster stores, mail and passengers, ordnance
and ammunition, and railroad supplies accounted for the rest.[104]

Meanwhile the Construction Corps was busy preparing a
large number of bridge trusses in 60-foot spans which could be
transported in flat cars. Interchangeable parts for military truss
bridges were designed.[105] Concerning itself with destruction as
well as construction, the corps prepared torpedos for blowing
bridges and conducted experiments with methods of destroying
rail. E. C. Smeed, one of Haupt's ablest assistants, invented a
hook to fit under a rail, by which the rail could be pried in such
a way that it would be twisted as well as bent and could not be
straightened except in a rolling mill.[106] Wright thought the best
way was to burn the ends of the ties and the rail would bend
from heat expansion.[107]

The abortive Union advance begun in May, 1863, ended in
a few days with the repulse at Chancellorsville. The position at
Aquia Creek was retained until June 14, when orders were received to abandon it. In the following three days, over 500 carloads of army property, railroad property, and 10,000 to 12,-
000 sick and wounded soldiers from the hospital were moved to
the landing and loaded on vessels. No railroad property was left
behind or destroyed.[108] The efficiency of the railroad men no
longer made it necessary to submit to the destruction of the
base such as had happened in September, 1862, with the loss of
much rolling stock and material. After the abandonment of
Aquia Creek, Hooker marched west toward the line of the
Orange and Alexandria, which again became the main line of
supply. It was only for a short time, however. Confederate
guerrilla raids forced the use of thirty to fifty guards per train.[109]

The month of June brought General Lee's second advance toward Maryland. Hooker, pestered by orders from Washington, began sulking in his tent at Fairfax, and the impatient Haupt promptly informed Halleck.[110] June 27, Hooker, now on the B & O near Harper's Ferry in his pursuit of Lee, asked to be relieved. For the last time, for he was not to serve under Grant, Haupt watched the change of commanders as George G. Meade took over command of the Army of the Potomac. With the advantages of having experienced men behind him, an understanding officer to work with, and a job to be done in territory where he had once lived, Haupt enthusiastically went to work on what was to be his last major supply problem for the army.[111] In late June, with Lee in the Cumberland Valley and Meade on the B & O, Haupt went to Harrisburg to survey the general territory. He found Thomas A. Scott feverishly dispatching troops to protect the Pennsylvania Railroad bridge at Harrisburg from a threatened cavalry raid. Though Scott reported the enemy retreating from the west bank of the Susquehanna, Haupt thought Lee was concentrating for a strike at Meade.[112] Haupt telegraphed Halleck on June 30 that the point of concentration was Chambersburg; a second telegram early on the morning of July 1 to Meade named Gettysburg as the place.[113]

On July 1, Haupt went to Baltimore to organize transportation on the Western Maryland Railroad, a line running northwest from Baltimore to Westminster and Union Bridge, Md. The road was a single-track line, laid with scrap-iron rail on poor supports, with no adequate sidings and no telegraph line. A route west to Hagerstown had been surveyed, but the war deferred completion until 1872. Engines, which used wood for fuel, were repaired in the shops of the Northern Central, and, until well after the war, trains used the tracks of the Northern

Central for entry into Baltimore.[114] When Haupt went to Westminster he found complete confusion because the railroad was running trains off schedule to prevent capture. Once again, as with Pope the preceding August, it was a situation to delight Haupt.

I asked them to give me a few minutes to think, and to escape the crowd I crept into a covered wagon and hid myself. In a short time I emerged, having organized a plan of operations, and, as soon as I could reach the wires, commenced to put it in operation.[115]

Haupt immediately wired Adna Anderson in Virginia to bring 400 men and a train of wood (for fuel), lanterns (for night work), and buckets (for water supply).[116] With no time to build either sidings or a telegraph line, Haupt had to dispense with a schedule and with special trains. Borrowing rolling stock from the Military Railroads, Baltimore and Ohio, Pennsylvania, Northern Central, and Philadelphia and Reading, the road was operated with Anderson as superintendent from July 2 to July 7 by running five or six trains in convoy, protected by guards.[117] The train convoy had to be unloaded and returned before another could be sent. By operating three convoys daily each way, Haupt figured the capacity of the road as 1,500 tons to the front each day, with a return load of 2,000 to 4,000 wounded soldiers.[118] This task required about 150 cars daily; each convoy thus had 50 cars, or five 10-car trains. Twice a day, at 10 A.M. and 5 P.M., a long train of baggage cars, each car supplied with straw and open at either end, left the battle area for Baltimore.[119] Every three hours an express train left for Westminster with dispatches for Frederick.[120] On a line which ordinarily ran three or four trains daily with a schedule of about five hours for the 30 miles to Westminster, this was truly a remarkable achievement. The B & O to Frederick and the Northern Central to Hanover Junction were also being used.

By July 4 Haupt reported to Halleck that the plan was working well.[121]

The Construction Corps meanwhile was working on the repair of the Northern Central between Hanover Junction and York, and Haupt himself directed repair work on the Littletown branch of the Gettysburg Railroad.[122] When Lee retreated from Gettysburg on July 4, Haupt informed Meade that communication with Washington by rail and telegraph would be possible by noon of July 5, at which time he also hoped to have the Northern Central open to York.[123] Haupt, finding that Meade was not prepared to pursue Lee, returned to Washington on July 5, seeing separately Halleck, Stanton, and Lincoln, urging that Meade be ordered to pursue Lee, and that Lee could be intercepted by forwarding troops by rail to Front Royal.[124]

Unable to do more in Washington, Haupt returned to Harrisburg on July 8 to open the Cumberland Valley Railroad to Chambersburg. The Confederates had torn up the track of this road and also that of the Franklin Railroad to Hagerstown, in addition to destroying 19 bridges on the Northern Central between Hanover Junction and Harrisburg.[125] Haupt expected communication with Harrisburg to be open by July 9. The Construction Corps of necessity was using so much material on this road that much of the reconstruction of the Hagerstown road was done by Pennsylvania Railroad workers with 400 tons of iron from Cambria. Haupt sent to Devereux at Alexandria for oxen and teams to haul ties for the Hagerstown road.[126] The 30-mile line of track between Hanover Junction and Gettysburg (comprising two railroads: the Hanover Branch Railroad to Hanover, and the Gettysburg Railroad to Gettysburg) was under military possession from July 9 to August 1, 1863, and in that time transported 15,580 wounded men to the rear.[127]

Meigs telegraphed Haupt on July 14 to withdraw the Construction Corps from the Northern Central and return to Alexandria.[128] Lee had successfully retreated across the Potomac. The reconstruction of the Hagerstown road was abandoned, and Haupt sent Anderson with tools, equipment, and oxen back to Virginia to secure the Orange and Alexandria and the Manassas Gap railroads.

The miraculous transformation of the Western Maryland Railroad in the successful supply of Meade's army showed the ability of Haupt to adapt his principles to different situations. The use of train convoys instead of a schedule proved that. But his insistence on prompt unloading and return of empty cars was the keystone of Haupt's successful operations. Speed and efficiency Haupt was capable of himself and demanded in his subordinates. In the reconstruction of the Cumberland Valley Railroad, rails bent less than one foot out of line were straightened in a few minutes without heating.[129] Lack of speed and efficiency in others only exasperated and disgusted Haupt. Beneath the pressure of the Hoosac Tunnel litigation in Massachusetts, Haupt was soon to retire from active responsibility with the military railroads. But his principles of operation, applied on a much larger scale in the West, came to be recognized as axiomatic in the successful supply of an army in the field.

Haupt's last summer of service with the military railroads was spent in Virginia, where he tried as always to bring the railroad supply to 100 per cent efficiency. Confederate guerrilla activity in the summer of 1863 kept Haupt and his railroaders always on their mettle. Devereux reported to Haupt on July 26,

No. 1 train this A. M. found, when a mile and a half east of Burke's, a rail taken out of the track and horseshoe on rail. Engine was reversed and brakes put hard down. Engine jumped the break, and, with two cars, passed on. . . . Before train was checked, 12 rebels in grey and blue coats and pants, and all with guns, pushed out of bushes, whilst the guard of the 4th Delaware then took a hand and, after a few shots, jumped off the train and had a foot-race through the woods. One fat rebel particularly distinguished himself in getting out of sight. The guard saved the train and its convoy, and Providence saved a smash-up which, for some time, would have prevented the Army of the Potomac from receiving supplies.[130]

Devereux asked for 200 men as railroad guards. Haupt reported the raid to General Ingalls, asking for men to guard the gaps in the Blue Ridge, and recommended the arrest of all civilian inhabitants within a 10-mile radius if the damage continued.[131] That some positive action was regarded as necessary may be seen from the fact that the Orange and Alexandria was doing a heavy business. On July 26, 127 loaded cars moved the 40 miles to Warrenton Junction, and 159 on July 27. Some trains hauled over 1,000 tons of supplies and equipment.[132] Haupt's recommendation resulted in Meade's order of July 30 that residents of territory within 10 miles of the railroad were responsible for injury done to the railroad by guerrillas, and were liable to impressment to repair the damage to the road. If the damage did not stop, the inhabitants would be put across the enemy lines and their property confiscated.[133] In August, some of the companies of the Construction Corps began arming and drilling for self-protection.[134]

It was at this juncture that Haupt again encountered his old enemy in the Hoosac Tunnel litigation, Governor Andrew. As a result of conferences between Andrew and Stanton in the latter part of August, Stanton issued an order dated September 1, 1863, that all commissions would be vacated if they were not formally accepted within five days. Haupt wrote to Stanton on September 5, just one year from the date of his commission. Haupt said he would not accept his commission unconditionally, because that would mean he could be ordered anywhere and so prevented from returning to Massachusetts to defend his private interests. He reiterated his desire to serve his country, but stressed that his fortune, his reputation, and millions of dollars were at stake. He claimed that certain parties in Massachusetts had already brought fictitious claims without giving him notice, and that they had received favorable judgment because of non-appearance of the defendant. Why would it not be possible for him to continue as chief of the Bureau of Military Railroads as a civilian? He pointed out that since Pope's campaign he had had no official title, merely signing himself "in charge of United States Military Railroads."[135]

Upon receipt of the letter, Stanton summoned Haupt to his office, explaining that the commission had been given for meritorious service, had been confirmed by the Senate, and that not to accept it would be construed as a mark of disrespect to the President. In addition, if it were not accepted, Haupt legally could not receive any pay. Haupt replied that he did not care about the pay, and that he was losing many times the amount of his pay in neglecting other interests. He said he was willing to stay as long as his services were needed, but when they were not, the Secretary could relieve him. Thereupon Stanton exploded, "I will relieve you at once, sir!"[136] On September 14, Haupt was relieved and officially turned over his office to McCallum. His sudden removal brought an expression of surprise from Representative John Covode, chairman of the Congressional Committee on the Conduct of the War. Watson, the Assistant Secretary of War, sent a letter of regret. Apparently Haupt harbored no ill feeling toward Stanton. He later characterized the Secretary as of "marked ability . . . honest, patriotic, and fearless . . . but impulsive and headstrong."[137] So Herman Haupt, still young at 46, with a wealth of achievement behind him, left Washington, to go on to new accomplishments in a brilliant postwar career.

Chapter XI

THE UNITED STATES MILITARY RAILROADS: THE EASTERN THEATER,
1864–1865

[The railroads'] undulations were so striking that a train moving along it looked in the distance like a fly crawling over a corrugated washboard.

> Robert U. Johnson and Clarence C. Buel, editors,
> *Battles and Leaders of the Civil War* (Horace Porter)

It is arguable that without the railroad the South would have proved unconquerable.

> Carl R. Fish, *The American Civil War*

THE ORANGE AND ALEXANDRIA RAILROAD to Culpepper supplied Meade throughout the fall of 1863. In October, the Confederates destroyed 22 miles of line from Manassas Junction south to Brandy Station, but the break was repaired the last week in October. The Construction Corps rebuilt the Rappahannock River bridge (625 feet long and 35 feet high) in 19 working hours.[1] May 4, 1864, the line was abandoned by Grant beyond Burke's Station. In the fall of 1864 it was operated to Manassas, and from November 10 until the war's end to Fairfax.[2] Like the Orange and Alexandria, the Manassas Gap Railroad played only a minor part in the campaigns of 1864 and 1865. Operating to Piedmont in October, it was abandoned in November, the rails being taken up and carried to Alexandria.[3] Grant's spring campaign began on May 2, 1864. A week later repairs began on the Aquia Creek Railroad, and by May 17 the line was open 14 miles to Falmouth, a job which included the construction of a 414-foot bridge over the Potomac Creek.[4]

The line operated until May 22 to remove 8,000 wounded from the battle of Spotsylvania Courthouse, and was abandoned shortly afterwards.[5]

Even though the railroads centering in Alexandria played a minor role in the final military campaign in the east, they were nevertheless kept busy in various necessary tasks. The Construction Corps built 100 flat cars of 5-foot gauge, of which 56 were sent to the Military Division of the Mississippi.[6] Sometimes the operating personnel saw service on other roads. When a strike occurred on the Philadelphia and Reading Railroad, delaying coal shipments for the Navy, McCallum on July 10 ordered a force of conductors, brakemen, engineers, and firemen from Alexandria for temporary service.[7] Two weeks later the strike was ended and the men were back in Virginia.

Repairs on the Orange and Alexandria and the Manassas Gap railroads entailed combatting a great deal of guerrilla activity. The repair of the latter road to Piedmont in October, 1864, occurred at the expense of the death of the superintendent, M. J. McCrickett, and four other trainmen who were killed when a doubleheader plunged down an embankment owing to the removal of a rail.[8] Just after the road was completed to Piedmont, orders were received to abandon it after taking up the iron. By mid-November this task had been accomplished and most of the iron sent to the Winchester and Potomac Railroad. From mid-November until July, 1865, the Orange and Alexandria was operated to Fairfax, with one regular train and two wood trains daily each way.[9] During the last month of its military operation, the road ran supplies south to Sherman, and in return carried a large number of troops north to Washington. On June 27, it was turned over to the Virginia Board of Public Works.[10] The Loudoun and Hampshire in 1864 and 1865 ran one mail and supply train daily each way, plus several wood trains destined for the Quartermaster in Washington. In May and June, 1865, the Army of the Potomac camped along its line before disbanding.[11]

Grant's plan of capturing Richmond from the South through Petersburg made necessary the extension of military railroad operations to two new railroads. About June 1 the Richmond and York River Railroad was opened for 14 miles between White House on the Chickahominy River and Dispatch. That portion of the line between the Chickahominy and the Pamunkey Rivers was torn up and the track and material removed to Alexandria.[12] Toward the end of June, the City Point and Petersburg Railroad was occupied for eight miles from the former terminal to Pitkin Station.[13] Much of this first section was reconstructed from the track of the Richmond and York River Railroad. Wharves and buildings were constructed at City Point, rolling stock checked in, and by July 7 regular trains began running.[14] July 22, J. J. Moore was ordered to survey a proposed extension of the City Point and Petersburg Railroad from Pitkin Station to Yellow House on the Weldon River, headquarters of the Fifth Army Corps. The nine miles of construction was finished during the first ten days of September, 1864.[15] Earthworks were constructed for defense against ever-present guerrillas, sidings built for hospitals and bakeries, and warehouses for Quartermaster, Commissary, and Ordnance. Wharves were constructed or extended at City Point, Bermuda Hundred, and Light House Point, and temporary hospitals set up.[16] By October the railroad line was scheduling an average of nine trains daily, excluding specials.

November and December of 1864 were months of expansion, both in number of trains and in mileage of track. Grant, besieging Petersburg, was perfecting his line of supply for the inevitable showdown in the spring. In November, two and a quarter miles of line were constructed from Yellow House to Peebles House. This extension, completed amid heavy rain, included 850 feet of trestle work and some steep grades, the maximum being 228 feet per mile, or about 4 per cent.[17] After the construction of necessary buildings, barracks, and wharves, the line was soon averaging 15 trains daily each way. In December a branch was built from Hancock Station to Fort Blaisdell, and in January extended to the headquarters of General Crawford.[18] On January 25, Grant ordered part of the Construction Corps to Beaufort, N. C., to repair the railroad there in anticipation of Sherman's advance north through the Carolinas.[19] This force put in a week's work in North Carolina between January 30 and February 8, until the arrival of the permanent corps from the West. In the two weeks after the Virginia crew returned to its original station on February 12, the 11-mile City Point and Army line was extended five miles from Warren Station to Humphreys Station. Hampered again by continuous rain, the crew built the necessary sidings, platforms, and water stations, and 2,781 feet of trestles.[20] The location of the railroad was at first opposed by engineer officers because of the heavy grades involved, but the Construction Corps was able to overcome its difficulties, and soon the 22-mile line (including branches) was carrying trains averaging 15 loaded cars, with a maximum of 23 cars. In addition to the supply trains, two passenger trains were operating daily each way.[21] In his account of Grant's final campaign, General Horace Porter has left this impression of the City Point and Army Railroad:

The military railroad connecting headquarters with the camps south of Petersburg was about 13 miles long, or would have been if it had been constructed on a horizontal plane, but as the portion built by the army was a surface road, up hill and down dale, if the rise and fall had been counted in, its length would have defied all ordinary means of measurement. Its undulations were so striking that a train moving along it looked in the distance like a fly crawling over a corrugated washboard.[22]

On April 3, 1865, Grant began the final offensive of the war with the occupation of Petersburg. The track of the South Side Railroad (Petersburg and Lynchburg) was relaid and trains were operating into Petersburg by April 4. The Construction Corps continued their work by changing the 5-foot gauge in the Petersburg yards to 4 feet, $8\frac{1}{2}$ inches, and by repairing the badly worn ties and rails of the South Side Railroad west of Petersburg. By April 11, just a week later, the railroad had been repaired, the gauge had been changed, and trains were running the 62 miles from City Point to Burkesville. Until after the end of the war, the line was used to supply General Meade, to transport some of Sherman's army north from the Carolinas, and to carry south the paroled soldiers of Lee.[23] On July 24, 1865, the South Side Railroad was turned over to the Virginia Board of Public Works.

Largely concerned with postwar operation was the Richmond and Danville Railroad. This road, of scrap rail laid on pine scantling, had been thoroughly destroyed in July, 1864.[24] On April 27, General Ingalls ordered necessary repairs to be made. Three days later, McCallum ordered suspension of all but whatever was nearing completion in order that the bulk of the Construction Corps might be sent to Alexandria for discharge. This was in response to Meigs's order of April 29 to discontinue construction and repair except what was needed for supply of troops.[25] The men not immediately discharged completed the necessary repairs, and readied a rolling stock of 24 new locomotives and 275 new box cars in the Manchester shops.[26] Most of this new motive power, however, remained in storage.

The line used 10 of its own locomotives, in addition to 5 from the East Tennessee and Virginia Railroad, 2 from the Nashville and Chattanooga Railroad, one from the Norfolk and Petersburg, and one recaptured U. S. Military Railroad engine which had been lost in Pope's retreat in 1862.[27]

May and June, 1865, were extremely busy months on the 140-mile line to Danville. Between May 2 and 5, an entire division of 8,000 men was transported from Danville to Burkesville in 21 trains of 253 cars. In the nine days immediately following, 30 trains of 360 cars of captured ordnance and equipment passed over the line on its way to City Point. Between May 10 and 22, 18,000 men of the Sixth Army Corps were transported from Danville to Manchester in 45 trains of 468 cars. June brought not only the northward movement of Carolina troops but the southward movement of paroled prisoners, who after June 15 arrived at Danville at the rate of over 800 a day until a total of 15,600 had been passed over the line. By July 4, the business was over and the road was turned over to the Virginia Board of Public Works.[28]

The Virginia Military Railroads also operated two lines in the Norfolk area. The Norfolk and Petersburg Railroad carried wood from the vicinity of Suffolk to Norfolk over one of the best constructed lines in Virginia. The second line was the Seaboard and Roanoke which had its seaboard outlet at Portsmouth, and it was via this route that over 15,000 railroad ties were shipped to the North Carolina railroads.[29] Through this port too had come the new rolling stock intended to open communication with Weldon, N. C., but which the war's end diverted to Manchester for storage.

It remains to speak only of the Winchester and Potomac Railroad. On August 12, 1864, McCallum ordered this line repaired 6 miles to Halltown, and a week later the line was in use. Traffic on the line was light until its extension in November, 1864, 22 miles to Stevenson, with iron rail from the Manassas Gap Railroad. Equipped with 13 engines, 75 cars, and a staff of 600 men, the railroad was the main line of supply for Sheridan's Army of the Shenandoah in the winter and spring of 1865. In seven months operation at the close of the war the Winchester and Potomac operated 2,238 trains, carrying almost 200,000 passengers in an excellent demonstration of the efficiency which the railroad corps had achieved. It could point with pride to the transportation of the Sixth Corps from Stevenson to City Point via Washington, the first division of which was moved in 44 hours, and the second in 52 hours.[30]

The United States Military Railroads operated 611 miles of railroad in 17 lines radiating from Alexandria, Norfolk, Petersburg, and including also the Aquia Creek Railroad, the Winchester and Potomac, and the lines operated temporarily in Maryland and Pennsylvania. A total of 72 locomotives and 1,733 cars were either purchased or built by the government for use on these lines. Approximately 177½ miles of track was laid, and about 129 taken up. A total of 34,931 lineal feet of bridges was constructed, of which all but about 1,600 feet was trestle or temporary work. Of tonnage hauled or personnel transported, it is impossible to obtain accurate figures.[31] The chief significance of the work done by the Military Railroads in Virginia lay not only in the active supply of armies in the field, but the working out of principles of operation and standards of efficiency which were to be applied on a much larger scale in the Mississippi Valley, and were to reach a pinnacle of success in the supply of Sherman's army from Chattanooga to Atlanta, and again in his march north through the Carolinas. Many of the railroad men to see service in the West, such as W. W. Wright, Adna Anderson, and E. C. Smeed, had received their original training in the field under Herman Haupt. To him must go the credit for evolving principles of operation which were to remain valid in subsequent military conflicts over a wide area. To his lieutenants must go the credit for applying the lessons learned on a larger and more dramatic scale. It is time to turn, then, to railroad operations in the West.

Chapter XII

THE UNITED STATES MILITARY RAIL-ROADS: THE WESTERN THEATER, TO 1864

Of the skill and ability of General D. C. McCallum . . . and of the able body of engineers, superintendents, and assistants . . . it is impossible to speak too highly.

Report of QM General Meigs to Stanton for the year ending June 30, 1865

IT WAS THE WORK OF Lewis B. Parsons at St. Louis which laid the foundation for the expansion of military railroad activities in the West. After helping to furnish transports for the use of Grant in his expedition against Fort Donelson and Fort Henry in February, 1862, Parsons was promoted to Colonel in April and was made an aide on General Halleck's staff.[1] His work from late 1862 until after the end of the war was little short of Herculean. In December, 1862, on seven days notice, Parsons provided river transportation for 40,000 men under Sherman from Memphis to Vicksburg, a movement requiring the use of 70 to 80 ships. After fighting a two-day battle, these troops were reembarked in 16 hours, transported 300 miles via the Mississippi, the White, and the Arkansas Rivers, successfully captured a fortification on the Arkansas River, reembarked within five days, and were carried 300 miles back to Vicksburg to take part in the siege of that city.[2] In June, 1863, Parsons provided transportation for Burnside with 10,000 men from central Kentucky, by rail through Ohio, Indiana, and Illinois to Cairo. There the troops were transferred to river boats and dispatched to Vicksburg to reinforce Grant. The entire movement, over 1,000 miles long, required only four days.[3] The important part played by Parsons in the movement of Schofield's 23rd Corps from Tennessee to Virginia in January, 1865, and in the postwar movement of disbanding troops will be discussed later. Suffice it to say here that Parsons did important work both in rail and in river transportation in 1862 and 1863, and was responsible for correcting at least the most flagrant abuses that had developed in 1861 in Western transportation.[4] His career at St. Louis, and later at Washington, where in August, 1864, he took up his duties as head of all rail and river transportation for the Armies of the United States, contrasted sharply with the career of John B. Anderson, who for a short time in late 1863 and early 1864 was general manager of all railways in possession of the government in the Departments of the Cumberland, the Ohio, and the Tennessee.

Lewis Parsons was not a civilian, and was not a member of the United States Military Railroads.[5] He was an officer in the Army Quartermaster Corps, and hence his work is not directly comparable to the work of the military railroads. Also, of course, a great deal of his time was concerned with river transportation, which was outside the province of the military railroads. On the other hand, the few times Parsons arranged for rail transportation for troops in the North, he had to deal with Northern railroad officials in somewhat the same manner that McCallum did in arranging the transfer of Hooker's corps from Virginia to Tennessee in 1863. The importance of Parsons lay in the fact that he created an orderly basis for the work of the United States Military Railroads in the West in 1864 and 1865. Since the active work of the Western military railroads did not come until the later years of the war, McCallum was never forced to explain or to emphasize the importance of the railroads to army generals in the West as

Haupt was obliged to do in Virginia. One dramatic episode illustrated the importance these generals attached to railroads in the South as means of communication and transportation. In April, 1862, a small party led by a 22-year-old spy, J. J. Andrews, under the command of General Don C. Buell, undertook to capture a train on the Western and Atlantic Railroad for the sole purpose of cutting rail communication between Atlanta and Chattanooga. The spies captured the train at Marietta, Ga., while the train crew and passengers were eating breakfast in the station, and started north at full speed. They were pursued first on foot, then by hand car, and finally by another locomotive. The spies detained the pursuers at various places by pulling up track, releasing freight cars from their train to be left standing in the way, and by throwing ties across the rails. But the pursuers reached Dalton in time to send a warning to Chattanoooga two minutes before the raiders had cut the telegraph wire. The party was captured soon after when their engine broke down.[6]

The armies in the West had already been shown that transportation was a vital factor in their success. Not only was the Western arena large geographically, but also the work of Parsons had proved that railroad and river transportation was necessary to army operation. Hence when the United States Military Railroads set out to organize a network of supply lines in the West, fortified with principles of operation learned through experience in the East, the problems they were concerned with and the situation they faced were entirely different from those with which Haupt had coped in Virginia. By 1864 the principles had been learned, and the armies appreciated their importance. The Military Division of the Mississippi now provided a large area in which the military railroads could demonstrate their real effectiveness.

In spite of these advantages, however, the early career of the military railroads in the West was anything but auspicious. Rumors that all was not going smoothly caused Stanton to ask Haupt in March, 1863, to investigate charges of speculation and inefficiency in government transportation in the West. Hooker wanted Haupt to stay in Virginia for the coming campaign, so Haupt appointed F. H. Forbes, a Massachusetts newspaper reporter and personal friend to go in his stead.[7] Apparently the agent uncovered what was suspected: "Some large game was hit in these reports, and I had letters of remonstrance from parties who wished me to suppress the reports. I replied that the reports must go to the Secretary of War."[8] With the occupation of Chattanooga on September 9, 1863, the army had encountered immediate supply difficulties. The Louisville and Nashville Railroad was sending only 16 carloads daily when 65 were required.[9] Some of the line's rolling stock had been used for the Nashville and Chattanooga Railroad, but it was Charles A. Dana's opinion that that excuse was not a sufficient explanation for the fact that the Louisville and Nashville charged 25 per cent higher than other roads and that it persisted in preferring private business over that of the government: "It will be impossible to maintain the army without a complete change in the management of the road."[10]

The defeat of Rosecrans at Chickamauga later in the month brought Quartermaster General Montgomery Meigs on a trip through the West to inspect the supply lines of the army. Meigs found that railroad communication with Nashville had been cut through destruction of the railroad bridge at Bridgeport, Ala., on the Nashville and Chattanooga Railroad. The rail line in general was badly run down because it had been overworked supplying the Confederates at Murfreesboro. Grant, taking over the Army of the Cumberland, ordered General Allen, the

Quartermaster at St. Louis, to move to Louisville preparatory to controlling the supply of the army via the Tennessee River.[11]

In addition, the army at Chattanooga was reinforced by the transfer of Hooker's 11th and 12th Corps from Virginia to Alabama, the most dramatic rail operation of the entire war, and a task carried out all the more effectively through the active cooperation of many railroads and railroad officials. Rosecrans's defeat at Chickamauga caused Dana to telegraph Stanton September 23, 1863, to send 20,000 to 25,000 troops to Bridgeport for the defense of Tennessee and for future operations in Georgia.[12] The telegram was received at 9:45 P.M. and an immediate council of war was held the same night.[13] Present at the conference were Lincoln, Stanton, Seward, Chase, Halleck, Hooker, Watson, Hardie of the War Department, and McCallum.[14] Stanton asked Halleck how long it would take to move 20,000 men from Virginia to Tennessee. Halleck replied three months, which would make the proposed move impractical. T. T. Eckert, chief of the telegraph of the U. S. Army, later brought into consultation, at first gave as his opinion 40 to 60 days.[15] After carefully studying the timetables, however, he thought that, using pontoon bridges at Louisville, and establishing food depots at 50-mile intervals where cooks could have food ready, the move could be made in 15 days.[16] Lincoln suggested reinforcements be sent from Burnside's army in east Tennessee, and Halleck, concurring, said the necessary number of men could get from Burnside to Rosecrans in 10 days.[17] Stanton opposed this suggestion and countered with sending 30,000 men from the Army of the Potomac. Chase and Seward supported Stanton, and they, together with Hooker who had been skeptical at first, convinced Halleck and Lincoln after a long debate.[18] It was decided to send the 11th and 12th Corps of Meade's Army of the Potomac, 20,000 troops, under the command of General Joseph Hooker.[19] Stanton sent telegrams to Garrett, Felton, and Scott, and next day, September 24, those three and W. P. Smith, master of transportation of the B & O, arrived in Washington to confer with McCallum and set up the all-rail route over which the transfer would be made.[20] Brigadier General Boyle at Louisville was asked for data on the capacity of the Louisville and Nashville Railroad.[21] In reply, Boyle secured the cooperation of the Louisville and Nashville, the Nashville and Chattanooga, and the Kentucky Central Railroads.[22] At Culpepper Courthouse on the Rappahannock River, the troops would use the Orange and Alexandria to Washington, and the Baltimore and Ohio to Benwood on the Ohio River below Wheeling. After ferrying to Bellaire, Ohio, the troops would travel on the Central Ohio Railroad to Columbus, and the Indiana Central to Indianapolis. There they would transfer to the Jeffersonville, Madison, and Indianapolis Railroad, which would take them to Jeffersonville on the Ohio opposite Louisville. After another ferry trip, the Louisville and Nashville would take over to Nashville, and then the Nashville and Chattanooga to Stevenson and Bridgeport, Ala.—a total of about 1,200 miles. A shorter route lay by way of Cincinnati and Covington, but was not used because a change in gauge would necessitate a transfer at Lexington.[23] McCallum took charge of the movement to Washington, where Garrett and Smith took over supervision all the way to Jeffersonville. South of the Ohio, Scott and John B. Anderson at Louisville saw the transfer through to completion, with the help of Frank Thomson at Nashville and Meigs at Chattanooga.[24] For the duration of the transfer these railroads were under the military control of the government.[25]

The planners of this movement were not groping entirely in the dark. In February, 1862, Scott, then Assistant Secretary of

War, had drawn up a comprehensive report on transportation of troops westward. The report stated that the combined rolling stock of the participating railroads could move 15,000 men a day from Washington to Pittsburgh; the Pittsburgh, Ft. Wayne, and Chicago and the Cleveland and Pittsburgh could move about 6,000 men a day to Cincinnati; and 30 to 40 steamboats could move 4,000 a day to Covington or Louisville. The time from Washington to Cincinnati by rail was figured at 78 hours, with the trip by river from Pittsburgh to Covington requiring a total of 30 hours longer.[26] Scott considered it impossible to use Lincoln's proposed railroad into east Tennessee for troop transportation, and hence opposed its adoption. On the other hand, the Louisville and Nashville could be used if the government built rolling stock for use on its 5-foot gauge line.[27]

On September 25, 1863, the first elements in this vast movement came through Washington, the 11th Corps from Manassas Junction, the 12th from Brandy Station,[28] and for 72 hours a steady stream of traffic crossed the Long Bridge with its human freight. The B & O had sent 390 troop and stock cars in two days south on the Orange and Alexandria to load the troops and their equipment, thereby exceeding McCallum's request for 140 cars a day for three days.[29] By 10 A.M. of September 25, 3 trains with 2,000 men (more than 60 cars) had passed Martinsburg 30 minutes apart, and 9 more trains, with 7,000 men, had passed Relay House.[30] McCallum reported everything running smoothly, and said that the B & O had done a good job, though it had not met all his demands.[31] Meanwhile Garrett was busy preparing the way westward. Low water on the Ohio prompted him to order a pontoon bridge constructed between Benwood and Bellaire, a job finished in two days. He also telegraphed H. J. Jewett of the Central

Ohio Railroad to concentrate 125 passenger cars and 50 baggage cars at Bellaire on each of three successive days to take care of the movement.[32] All business which might interfere was to be suspended. Help in furnishing rolling stock was asked of Presidents L'Hommedieu of the Cincinnati, Hamilton, and Dayton, Clement of the Little Miami, McCullough of the Cleveland and Pittsburgh, Hubby of the Cleveland and Columbus, and Neaman of the Indiana Central.[33] By 9:15 A.M. of the 27th, 12,600 men, 33 cars of artillery and 21 cars of baggage had left Washington, and the first train was just arriving at Benwood 42 hours away, closely followed by others at 15-minute intervals.[34] B & O railroad agents had instructions from Stanton and Hooker (through Smith) not to stop or delay any train, a policy which was followed to the letter. When General Carl Schurz of the 3rd Division of the 11th Corps fell behind his troops and attempted to stop the division so he could catch up, Smith told the conductor not to delay the train, and Stanton threatened to arrest Schurz if he interfered with the railroad officials.[35] By 1.30 P.M. on the 28th all troops had left the starting point, and by September 30 the last of 30 troop trains had arrived at Benwood.[36] The B & O had discharged its obligations with only minor delays.

Ohio was crossed without difficulty, but getting through Indianapolis proved a more trying task. Lewis M. Cole, who had supervised the construction of the pontoon bridge at Bellaire, was the B & O agent at Indianapolis. The first train reached Indianapolis at 3:40 P.M. September 28.[37] In accordance with his instructions, he sent troops a mile across town for hot rations; the troops then marched a mile back to the depot of the Jeffersonville line, adjacent to the Indiana Central.[38] This necessary delay was complicated by a quarrel between Cole and William P. Innes, Rosecrans's superintendent of railroads, over supply priority.[39] The movement was thus delayed an average of six hours in Indianapolis, a delay which caused both Scott and Smith to hazard the guess that water transportation from Cincinnati or Parkersburg would have been better.[40] Early on the morning of September 29, the head of the column arrived at Jeffersonville, where ferries were waiting to take them to Louisville and the Louisville and Nashville Railroad. Scott got the first train through Louisville at 5:30 A.M., the second at 7, and the third at 10.[41]

James Guthrie, president of the Louisville and Nashville, had been engaging in a continuous quarrel with Innes over the effort being exerted by the L & N to help the Union cause. Innes, dissatisfied with the railroad's efforts, wanted to monopolize the railroad for government business only, and if necessary to seize the road. He supported Dana in accusing Guthrie of transporting the military only when private trade was not more lucrative, an argument which had some factual basis early in the war. Guthrie, on the other hand, charged Innes with violation of the contract between the railroad and the government.[42] Scott tried unsuccessfully to bring about some settlement of these difficulties. His sympathies, however, were with the railroad, and he felt that, except for the supervision and approval of the Secretary of War, military officials should not interfere with railroad operations,[43] a feeling in which Herman Haupt would have heartily concurred.

The friction between Innes and Guthrie caused Stanton to order Scott to change the gauge of the Louisville and Lexington Railroad, as a precaution against trouble on the L & N.[44] Also 43 new cars belonging to the government at Jeffersonville were transferred to the L & N.[45] Other cars came from Cairo and from Missouri.[46] The first four trains arrived at Bridgeport September 30, five days from Washington; there the troops detrained because the railroad bridge was still out.[47] By October 3, the first regiments of the 11th Corps began arriving at their base camp 26 miles from Chattanooga.[48] October 6, the last regiment passed through Indianapolis, and by October 8, the troop movement was complete.[49] In 14 days, 23,000 men had been moved 1,233 miles,[50] an accomplishment not to be surpassed during the war, and one to be compared only with the movement of the 23rd Corps from Tennessee to Virginia in January, 1865, and with the demobilization movements in the spring of that year. The baggage of the two corps, including horses, wagons, ambulances, and commissary, moved west over the same route during the first two weeks of October.[51] House cars were altered to carry horses, and 50 wagons were requisitioned from the Northern Central Railway.[52] Thus the complete transfer of men and equipment took only about three weeks, a time so far under the general estimate that it must have greatly surprised Halleck and Lincoln. Besides pointing to the strategic value of the railroads, the movement also proved that sufficient outside pressure would generate enough cooperation between different men and different railroads, and produce enough efficiency in coordinating transportation over a long distance to effect dramatic and far-reaching results.

The motive power and rolling stock of the Louisville and Nashville and the Nashville and Chattanooga proved insufficient to supply the larger armies. Dana recommended military operations to gain control of the Tennessee River and use river transportation.[53] The serious bottleneck was the lack of a railroad bridge across the Tennessee River at Bridgeport, which meant that wagons took eight days to get from Stevenson to Chattanooga.[54] To secure a more efficient line of supply, Stanton on October 19, 1863, with the advice of Meigs and Grant, appointed John B. Anderson general manager of all

railways in possession of the government in the Departments
of the Cumberland, Ohio, and Tennessee. Anderson was to
appoint his own assistants, provide the transportation asked
by the army, and make requisitions for necessary supplies.[55]
Anderson, originally with the transportation department of the
Louisville and Nashville, had been appointed in November,
1861, by Sherman as railroad director in the Department of the
Ohio.[56] Anderson's work was not on the same plane as his
recommendations, however, and the battle of Chattanooga in
November, 1863, had highlighted certain deficiencies in army
supply by railroad. Stanton did what he could to correct these
conditions. He immediately acted to secure additional motive
power. He telegraphed M. W. Baldwin & Co. at Philadelphia
to complete and forward to Chattanooga with the utmost
dispatch the three locomotives which the company had been
building for the New York and Harlem Railroad. The seizure
was necessary for a military purpose. "The supply of the
army and the success of military operations is greatly dependent
upon there being no delay."[57] On the same date (November
20, 1863) Stanton sent the following telegram to Cornelius
Vanderbilt, president of the New York and Harlem:

Your letter of the nineteenth has just been received. The engines
referred to were seized by order of this Department from an absolute
and paramount necessity for the supply of the armies on the Cumberland. They are absolutely essential for the safety of those armies,
and the order cannot be revoked. Whatever damages your company
may sustain the Government is responsible for but the military
operations and the supply of arms at Chattanooga in the judgment
of this Department and no doubt also in your judgment are superior
to any other consideration. Nothing by a controlling necessity would
induce the Department to interfere with the business of any individuals or companies. This however is a case when the safety and
support of an army depends upon the exercise of the authority of
the Government and prompt acquiescence by loyal citizens. I hope

therefore that you will not only throw no obstacle in the way of a speedy forwarding of these engines to Louisville but that you will use your well known energy in aid of the government to hurry them forward.[58]

Finally on November 30 the War Department issued an order forbidding interference by military officials in train operation and transportation of troops and supplies.[59] Then on December 19, 1863, a War Department order sent McCallum with part of the Construction Corps to Tennessee to examine the railroad supply lines to the armies at Chattanooga and help in the reconstruction of the Nashville and Chattanooga Railroad.[60] W. W. Wright was in charge of one division of the Construction Corps (285 men) which accompanied McCallum. In January, 1864, this division repaired the Nashville-Chattanooga line from Bridgeport to Chattanooga, opening the latter city to trains three weeks ahead of schedule. Wright reports the rejoicing of the army over this job, as the chief commissary was able to issue full rations for the first time since the occupation of Chattanooga.[61]

The government had previously got wind that all was not quite as it should be in railroad supply, especially via the Louisville and Nashville. Andrew Johnson, the military governor of Tennessee, had been ordered to construct a new rail line from Nashville to Reynoldsburg on the Tennessee River, thus eliminating an exclusive dependence on the L & N for supplies from the North.[62] The revelations of Anderson's inefficiency made Grant suspicious of some sort of collusion between Anderson and Guthrie, since Anderson had formerly worked for the L & N.[63] Thus the ground was laid for Anderson's removal. That Grant would not allow a quarrel between the railroad and the military, however, was possibly a contributing factor to the replacing of Rosecrans by Thomas as head of the Army of the Cumberland.[64]

McCallum had called on Anderson at Nashville, saying he was to aid Anderson in the repair of the railroad between Brideport and Chattanooga. That accomplished, McCallum offered Anderson the entire construction force to work on the Nashville-Chattanooga line. Anderson for some reason refused to adopt this course and turned instead to repair of the Chattanooga-Knoxville line. Meanwhile the Nashville and Chattanooga Railroad languished in very bad condition. Trains were running only eight miles per hour, and still frequent accidents occurred. McCallum thought the best thing to do would be to relay the whole line of track as soon as new rail could be procured.[65] For this purpose, McCallum recommended completion of the rolling mill at Chattanooga, which had been started by the Confederates. In addition, shops and repair machinery would be needed if Chattanooga were to become an important base of supplies. Nothing had been done to accomplish this task, and even the shops at Nashville were deficient and run down. Parsons at St. Louis had also stressed the importance of securing a constant supply of railroad machinery: "We require arsenals of railroad machinery as much as arsenals of arms."[66]

Nor had anything been done to put the Nashville-Decatur line in order. Dana reported that General Grenville M. Dodge wanted to repair this railroad himself but could do nothing because the whole line was under Anderson's control.[67] After no improvements were noted in a period of three weeks, Grant relieved Anderson, who claimed trouble with bridge contractors, and ordered Dodge to fix the road. Dodge went to work energetically, at first with only axes, picks, and spades. Blacksmith shops of the enemy were appropriated so that railroad tools could be made. Rolling stock and rails came from other Tennessee railroads or from Vicksburg. In 40 days, Dodge repaired over 100 miles of track, incluuding 182 bridges.[68]

There is no direct evidence here that Anderson was deliberately trying to sabotage the railroads, though the circumstantial evidence is strong. That he was inept and inefficient is certainly true. Probably he saw that the war had so disrupted the normal business of the L & N that there was not much point in exerting himself to help those whose effect would be to disrupt it further. In the L & N organization there were undoubtedly sympathizers for both sides. The members included not only the questionable Anderson, but the loyal and energetic Albert Fink, chief engineer and superintendent of the road and machinery department during the war.[69]

The complete inadequacy of rolling stock was also pointed out by McCallum. On the 519 miles of military railroads soon to be in operation in the Military Division of the Mississippi, there were only 70 locomotives and 600 freight cars. Almost the same amount of equipment was used on the 70 miles between Washington and Culpepper, Va., on the Orange and Alexandria: "It is apparent that with the present equipment no advance of army can be made, if I am correct in assuming that it must depend upon railroads for supplies."[70] McCallum recommended that a total rolling stock of 200 locomotives and 3,000 cars was necessary initially, and provision should be made to augment it as the army advanced. Stanton later expressed doubt that so much rolling stock would be necessary, but McCallum pointed out that the military character of the problem necessitated more equipment than that based simply upon tonnage. It was also necessary, of course, to use some of the rolling stock for construction purposes.[71] A construction corps of 1,000 men, plus all their necessary tools and equipment, would be needed to keep the line of supply in repair. The railroad could best be worked by divisions, with divisional officers responsible to the operating department. In contrast to these recommendations, McCallum found that the railroad organization in the Chattanooga area was defective and characterized by a lack of energy. The men in charge showed little or no ability to understand the magnitude of their undertaking.[72]

The incompetence revealed by McCallum's report and the increasing importance of the Western theater of war after the victory at Chattanooga, resulted in Grant's order of February 4, 1864, from Nashville headquarters of the Military Division of the Mississippi, giving McCallum the position of general manager of military railways in the West, with the power, authority, and duties of John B. Anderson, who was relieved.[73] Upon taking up his duties, McCallum found the 151-mile Nashville and Chattanooga Railroad, the main line of supply, in frightful condition.

The track was laid originally on a unballasted mud-road bed in a very imperfect manner, with a light U-rail on wooden stringers, which were badly decayed and caused almost daily accidents by spreading apart and letting the engines and cars drop between them.[74]

In use beside the Nashville-Chattanooga line were 39 miles Nashville to Dark's Mill, 60 miles Stevenson (Ala.) to Huntsville, and 42 miles Chattanooga to Charleston, making 292 miles in all. To operate these lines, McCallum had 50 locomotives, of which 47 were U. S. Military Railroad engines, and 3 were borrowed from the L & N. Eleven of the 50, however, were tied up in the repair shop. There were, in all, 437 U.S.M.R. freight cars, plus about 100 borrowed from the L & N, and of that total about 400 were in running condition.[75]

Colonel McCallum began his job of organization by creating two departments, a transportation department to manage train movements and do general maintenance work on track and equipment, and a construction corps to do major repair work and to build new roadbeds wherever necessary. Thus the separation of construction and operation into two departments, originally established in Virginia January 1, 1863, was carried out in the West as a tried and proven system of organization.[76] On February 10, 1864, McCallum appointed Adna Anderson superintendent of transportation and maintenance, and W. W. Wright chief engineer of construction.[77] Anderson had earlier been engineer of the Virginia railroads ending in Alexandria, and since January 1, 1863, chief engineer of the military railroads in Virginia. He was to retain his position in the West until November 1, 1864, when he was again promoted, this time to the position of chief superintendent and engineer of all the U. S. Military Railroads, thus becoming second only to McCallum. Wright came to his new job with experience gathered on the Aquia Creek Railroad and in the Gettysburg campaign under Haupt. He was later to distinguish himself again as head of the military railroad organization in North Carolina.

It will be instructive at this point to examine more closely the detailed organization set up by these men and the functions they fulfilled. Anderson's instructions from McCallum included the power to hire and fire and to establish pay rates with McCallum's approval. He could make supply requisitions on the assistant quartermaster detailed to service with the military railroads, and he could requisition men and material from the chief engineer. If McCallum were absent, Anderson's superior would be General Grant, or the Commanding Generals of the three departments. Wright had similiar powers of hiring and requisitioning supplies. He was also obliged to honor requisitions on him by the chief superintendent, but to carry out necessary repairs Wright was obliged also to secure the approval of the Commanding General.[78]

The Transportation Department, which reached a maximum

of 12,000 men in the Division of the Mississippi, was divided
into three subordinate departments: one to run the trains; one
to maintain the rolling stock; and one to maintain the track.
Under the first subdepartment, each railroad was operated by
a superintendent of transportation who was assisted by one or
more masters of transportation, who moved freely over the line
as checkers to see that all was going smoothly. Dispatchers
were placed at the principal stations to control the engine
crews and supervise any necessary repairs to locomotives. The
second subdepartment was headed by a superintendent of
repairs, and under him were supervisors, roadmasters, foremen,
and laborers. The maintenance of rolling stock by the third
subdepartment was under the control of a master machinist
and a master of car repairs. The heads of the three subdepart-
ments reported independently to Superintendent Anderson.[79]

The Construction Corps, developing on a much wider base
than in Virginia, was divided into six divisions. The nucleus of
the corps was one division of the Virginia Construction Corps,
consisting of a subdivision of trackmen, who were sent to
Chattanooga in December, 1863, to work on the railroad to
Nashville. In January, three new divisions were organized to
work on the same railroad and also the line between Chattanooga and Knoxville.[80] Though reaching a maximum strength
of 6,000 men (for the six divisions), the basic unit of the
Construction Corps was a division of 682 men. Headquarters
consisted of the division engineer and his assistant, a rodman,
a clerk, and two messengers. Each division had a train crew of
11 men, consisting of conductors, firemen, engineers, and brakemen. The rest of the unit was broken down into five subdivisions,
of which the two most important were the bridge builders and
track layers. Each of these consisted of 356 men, of whom 300
were mechanics and laborers, the remainder including a super-

visor, a clerk, a timekeeper, a commissary, a quartermaster, a surgeon, a hospital steward, six foremen, 30 subforemen, a blacksmith and his helper, and 12 cooks. The other subdivisions, those in charge of water stations, masonry, and ox brigade, contained a personnel of 48 in all. Any or all of the subdivisions could be expanded or contracted to meet a particular situation.[81] All personnel received regular pay, except the surgeons, who were paid from a voluntary fund contributed by the men.[82]

With the organization under Anderson and Wright beginning to function in a systematic way, McCallum turned his attention to the task of obtaining the necessary rolling stock. In this work he had the active cooperation of Stanton. On March 23, 1864, Stanton issued this appeal to the country's locomotive manufacturers:

Gentlemen: Col. Daniel C. McCallum . . . has been authorized to procure locomotives without delay for the railways under his charge.

In order to meet the wants of the military departments of the government you will deliver to his order such engines as he may direct, whether building under orders for other parties, or otherwise, the government being accountable to you for the same. The urgent necessity of the government for the immediate supply of our armies operating in Tennessee renders the engines indispensable for the equipment of the lines of communication, and it is hoped that this necessity will be recognized by you as a military necessity, paramount to all other considerations.[83]

The response was immediate from the manufacturers, who completed and delivered the locomotives as fast as they were able. Twelve arrived at Nashville in April, 1864, 24 in May, 24 in June, and 26 in July.[84] By the end of 1864, 140 new locomotives had been delivered.[85] Car deliveries were high in April, and again in August and September, averaging, throughout 1864, 202 cars per month. Besides this new rolling stock, Mc-

Callum also used equipment borrowed from Kentucky railroads of 5-foot gauge. The L & N loaned 14 engines and 120 cars, the Louisville and Lexington 2 engines and 15 cars, and the Kentucky Central 2 engines and 60 cars.[86] By the end of 1864, McCallum could show that his original aim of having 200 locomotives and 3,000 cars in service was very nearly accomplished.[87] To care for this additional rolling stock, it was necessary to expand the machine shops, car shops, and other repair facilities at Nashville and at Chattanooga. At times during the momentous year 1864, the Nashville shops alone were repairing 100 engines and 1,000 cars. The material to build the necessary facilities at these two cities was either purchased from Northern manufacturers or seized in the South.

The general intention was to make these two cities the great centres toward which all operations should converge; where supplies of all kinds could be obtained in case the roads were cut in their rear; where repairs of any kind or to any extent could be made, and in case communication was destroyed between them, operations would be conducted from either with facility in any direction.[88]

The stockpiling of supplies in preparation for Sherman's campaign in 1864 brought four months of feverish activity to the military railroads. The single-track supply line of the 185-mile Louisville and Nashville was augmented by the construction of the 78-mile Nashville and Northwestern, which was to bring supplies to Nashville from Reynoldsburg on the Tennessee River, to which the supplies had been carried by water. The necessity for supplementing the carrying capacity of the L & N had been foreseen in October, 1863, when Stanton ordered Andrew Johnson to take charge of construction of the railroad under the direction of the Quartermaster General, and to turn the line over to the military railway organization when it was completed.[89] The work progressed slowly, however, and finally Grant ordered McCallum to take active charge of the job on February 17.[90] In less time than three months the road was completed, using Johnsonville instead of Reynoldsburg as the river terminus. To reconstruct the road, Wright, on Grant's order, brought 2,000 laborers and mechanics from the North, and their work was supplemented by the 1st Missouri Engineers, the 1st Michigan Engineers, and the 12th and 13th Regiments of Colored Infantry. On June 21 the operation of trains was taken over by the transportation department.[91] Confusion of authority between Johnson, Sherman, and the military railroads was not straightened out until August 6, 1864, when Lincoln gave control of the line to the U. S. Military Railroads.[92] By the end of the war, 115 miles of track and ballast had been relaid, sidings long enough to accommodate five to eight trains had been constructed at eight-mile intervals, and 45 new water tanks had been built.[93] At Johnsonville, two large transfer freight houses were built, to transfer cargo from ships to cars. Small cars were used to transfer the cargo, and at full capacity the cars could unload four or five ships at once and load the cargo into an entire train. Just as the work was completed, a raid by the Confederate General John B. Hood forced the evacuation of Johnsonville. The new freight house was burned, and because of confusion of authority between Wright and the Quartermaster Department, never completely rebuilt.[94] The line carried a great many supplies in the late summer and fall of 1864, a season of low water on the Cumberland River which prevented the direct water shipment of supplies to Nashville.[95]

The 151-mile single-track Nashville and Chattanooga Railroad did Herculean work in the supply of Sherman's army until the end of the Atlanta Campaign. The line was reconstructed with T-rail, replacing the old U-rail; longer sidings and larger water stations were built to accommodate the heavier traffic.[96]

Confederate raids forced a good deal of extra construction. One bridge had to be rebuilt five times, another four times. Extra construction helped explain the fact that the material and labor cost on this railroad alone in 1864-65 was over $4,000,000. Altogether, 130 miles of main line were rebuilt, and 35 water tanks constructed.[97] During the period just before Sherman's campaign 130 10-ton cars arrived at Chattanooga each day. The railroad was restricted to carrying food, ammunition, and army supplies; troops and cattle were sent on foot; until June, private freight was allowed only on the return trip.[98] Until its capacity could be increased sufficiently to supply both Burnside and Sherman, and because of its heavy grades,[99] the railroad had to be supplemented by another route in the early days of Sherman's campaign. This route ran directly south from Nashville 120 miles to Decatur, Ala.; then the route turned east over the Memphis and Charleston 80 miles to Stevenson, where it joined the Nashville and Chattanooga. This route was 87 miles longer than the direct way, and was used in the early days of the campaign exclusively by trains returning from the front.[100] A hospital train on this line made three trips weekly from Bridgeport in the spring of 1864. It was made up of one passenger car, one mail car, three box cars, and three hospital cars. During the Atlanta Campaign, trips were more frequent, and trains longer. One 10-car hospital train in July, 1864, carried 314 passengers.[101]

Besides the roads listed thus far, three other minor lines played a supplementary part in supply work before and during Sherman's campaign for Atlanta. The East Tennessee and Georgia Railroad, running from Chattanooga to Knoxville was opened in May, 1864, after laying 35 miles of track, mostly after Wheeler's raid, and building 10 water tanks. The huge truss bridge across the Tennessee River at Loudon, 1,700 feet long and 85 feet high, was the largest such structure on any military railroad.[102] About 1,000 men were employed on this line February to April, 1864, transporting supply trains.[103] The East Tennessee and Virginia continued this route for a short distance northeast of Knoxville, though the line was not opened to Bristol until the spring of 1865.[104] Finally in the summer of 1864 a rail connection with the lower Cumberland River helped to keep the Nashville supply depot well stocked. The route consisted of the Edgefield and Kentucky Railroad 47 miles from Nashville, then 15 miles of the Memphis, Clarkesville, and Louisville Railroad to the Cumberland River.[105] The history of this route shows that guerrilla raids were not the only hazard. Spring freshets in 1865 twice carried away the railroad bridge across the Red River, necessitating its rebuilding on each occasion.[106] Finally the U. S. Military Railroads controlled for a time 75 miles of the Western end of the Memphis and Charleston Railroad, along with 48 miles of the Mississippi Central south into Mississippi from Grand Junction on the Memphis and Charleston to the Tallahatchie River. This line was abandoned and reopened no less than five times between the summers of 1864 and 1865. It partially supplied Grant in the Vicksburg campaign.[107] Part of the Mobile and Ohio, and the Memphis and Little Rock from Duvall's Bluff to the Little River, were also used in 1865.[108] Sherman, while in Atlanta, also occupied the Atlanta and Macon to Rough and Ready, the rails of which later went to replace those destroyed by Hood on the Western and Atlantic Railroad.[109]

Chapter XIII

THE UNITED STATES MILITARY RAILROADS: SHERMAN IN GEORGIA AND THE CAROLINAS

The railroad revolutionized warfare, but it was McCallum who made the revolution manifest.

> Carl R. Fish, *The American Civil War*

The Atlanta Campaign would simply have been impossible without the use of the railroads from Louisville . . . to Atlanta.

> William T. Sherman, *Memoirs*

GENERAL SHERMAN'S ARMY jumped off from Chattanooga May 1, 1864, and from then until the capture of Atlanta it was dependent on the transportation corps to bring its supplies over lines protected and maintained by the Construction Corps. The Western and Atlantic Railroad was reconstructed as fast as Sherman's army advanced, and together with the Nashville and Chattanooga, and the Louisville and Nashville, made a 472-mile supply line from Louisville to Atlanta. In a single paragraph in his memoirs, Sherman records his debt to that route:

That single stem of railroad supplied an army of 100,000 men and 35,000 horses for the period of 196 days, viz; from May 1 to Nov. 12, 1864. To have delivered that amount of forage and food by ordinary wagons would have required 36,800 wagons, of 6 mules each, allowing each wagon to have hauled two tons 20 miles a day, a simple impossibility in such roads as existed in that region.[1]

Sherman's campaign was the supreme test for the military railroad organization. All the lessons learned in 1862 and 1863 in Virginia and in Kentucky and Tennessee were to be applied with startling effect in Tennessee and Georgia. The men themselves shared the enthusiasm of their leaders, and took tremendous pride in their duties, accomplished at times under extremely hazardous conditions. McCallum pointed out that the hardships and dangers to the railroad workers were much greater than to any other class of civilian employees, and their endurance and bravery was not exceeded by any branch of miltary service, especially in the Atlanta campaign.

It was by no means unusual for men to be out with their trains from 5 to 10 days, without sleep, except what could be snatched upon their engines and cars while the same were standing to be loaded or unloaded, with but scanty food, or perhaps no food at all, for days together, while continually occupied to keep every faculty strained to its utmost.[2]

And again,

All were thoroughly imbued with the fact, that upon the success of railroad operations, in forwarding supplies to the front, depended . . . the success of our armies; that although defeat might be the result, even if supplies were abundantly furnished, it was evident that there could be no advance without; and I hazard nothing in saying, that should failure have taken place either in keeping lines in repair, or in operating them, General Sherman's campaign . . . would have resulted in disaster and defeat.[3]

Here was the core of the situation. Defeat or victory might hinge on military strategy or tactics in actual battle, but adequate supply was necessary to the undertaking of an offensive campaign, and in the Atlanta campaign the sole means of transporting supplies was by railroad.

The reconstruction and maintenance of the Western and Atlantic Railroad from Chattanooga to Atlanta in the wake of Sherman's army was perhaps the most difficult task faced by the military railroad organization. Dramatic work was done by the bridge builders, who constructed 11 major bridges on the line, doing their fastest work on the 780-foot Chattahoochee River bridge, built in four and a half days by the first and third divisions of bridge builders.[4] Chief Engineer Wright kept his men close behind the advancing army in their reconstruction work. By May 9, the army and the railroad had progressed to Tunnel Hill, May 15 to Tilton, May 16 to Resaca.[5] There Sherman found the bridge over the Oostenaula River destroyed. Wright told Sherman it would take four days to repair, to which Sherman replied, "Sir, I give you 48 hours or a position in the front ranks." With 2,000 men working steadily, the bridge was actually finished in 72 hours, and Wright was excused for the delay.[6] He had driven his men as fast as possible: "The work of reconstruction commenced while the old bridge was still burning, and was somewhat delayed becauses the iron rods were so hot that the men could not handle them to remove the wreck."[7]

By May 20, trains were running through to Kingston. Five and a half days in early June were required to build the 600-foot bridge over the Etowah River, and trains then ran through to Big Shanty until after the capture of Kenesaw Mountain. On July 3, Sherman ordered construction resumed, and three days later the railroad was open to Vinings Station, 10 miles from Atlanta. One more river, the Chattahoochee, stood between the army and Atlanta. Construction began on the bridge July 23, then was stopped on army orders until August 2, when it was resumed. The bridge, 780 feet long and 92 feet high, was completed on August 5, in the record time of four and a half working days, and trains approached to within three miles of Atlanta. General Slocum entered Atlanta September 2, and the railroad followed him the next day. The job had been done with no night work, the men working during the day from dawn to dark, with one hour for dinner.[8] Much of this work was done under the direct supervision of E. C. Smeed, formerly one of Haupt's most able assistants in Virginia. Smeed had superintended the construction of the Rappahannock River bridge during Burnside's campaign, and had been in charge of the reconstruction of the Northern Central Railway during and immediately after the battle of Gettysburg. He was later to accompany Wright to North Carolina in 1865. It was Smeed also who invented the device for twisting rails without the necessity of heating them first. In his memoirs, Haupt credited most of the success of Sherman's campaign to the quiet, unpretentious Smeed. With veteran bridge builders and all the necessary tools, Smeed built the Chattahoochee bridge in half the time of the Potomac Creek bridge, which in turn required only half the amount of timber of the former bridge.[9]

The career of E. C. Smeed amply illustrates some of the detailed work done by the Construction Corps. In the fall of 1863, Smeed was ordered to report to McCallum at Bridgeport, then the base of supplies for the army at Chattanooga. Smeed repaired the bridge connecting the railroad line to Chattanooga, and was then ordered by Wright to open communication with Knoxville, for which task he had two companies of the Virginia Construction Corps. Before that job was finished, Smeed turned over the railroad to the superintendent, E. L. Wentz, and turned his attention to the completion of the railroad between Nashville and Johnsonville. By laying track first and grading the road after it was opened, Smeed had 45 miles in operation in 30 days. At the beginning of the Atlanta campaign, Smeed joined the Construction Corps at Big Shanty, Ga. Here his work was made easier because by now the corps was properly equipped with bridge tools, track tools, hooks for prying up rails, proper box cars and flat cars for materials, and stock cars for animals. Timber for a bridge was cut in the vicinity and sent by rail to the framers and raisers at the site, the work being done from both ends. Water tanks 12 feet in diameter and 8 feet deep were constructed for the use of regular trains, and in the case of advance engines, bucket brigades were formed to carry water from any nearby stream.[10]

About 75 miles of new track was laid between Chattanooga and Atlanta, the rest being repaired from what remained after Johnson's retreat. All the lines in Tennessee and Georgia, of course, had to be strongly defended against both organized and guerrilla attacks. This was especially true of the Western and Atlantic. By 1864, the Confederates realized the importance of railroads and they continuously attempted to knock them out of operation. To defend the railroad, detachments of the Construction Corps (bridge builders and track layers) were stationed at various points along the right of way; in addition, frequent depots were established with stocks of iron, rails, ties, spikes, and timber.[11] To supplement these measures, railroad guards were placed at Ringgold, Dalton, Resaca, Kingston, Etowah Bridge, Allatoona, Kenesaw, and Marietta.[12] These precautions usually sufficed to repair guerrilla damage quickly and efficiently. To meet full-scale raids, fully equipped construction trains were kept ready both at Chattanooga and at the front to move up at a moment's notice.[13]

In spite of these precautions, Hood on October 6 attacked the line at Allatoona, and destroyed eight miles of railroad between that place and Big Shanty. The thorough destruction required a week to repair, using up six miles of new rails and 35,000 new ties.[14] At the same time, manoeuvering in Sherman's rear, Hood destroyed 35½ miles of track and 455 feet of bridges north of Resaca. The construction gangs, augmented from the 640 monthly average strength to 2,000, were at their work even before Hood left the railroad. The biggest break was 25½ miles between Tunnel Hill and Resaca, including 230 feet of bridges. Working from each end of the break, and also from Dalton, the line was repaired in seven and a half days. Since Hood had destroyed supply depots as well as track and bridges, new ties had to be cut in the woods, and rail had to come either 200 miles from Nashville, or be taken up from railroads south of Atlanta. The entire break was restored and back in operation in 13 days.[15] All of this excellent work was, of course, a fine morale builder for Sherman's troops. There was one story to the effect that

Johnston had determined to blow up an important railroad tunnel in order to stop the invaders, whereupon one of his men remarked, "There isn't no use in that 'cause Sherman carries 'long duplicates of all the tunnels !"[16]

In the spring and summer of 1864, when the Western and Atlantic was the main link in Sherman's supply line, guerrilla raids necessitated the complete reconstruction of 22½ miles of track and 4,081 feet of bridges.[17] But Hood was not active on the Western and Atlantic alone, nor was that railroad the exclusive scene of guerrilla activity in the western sector. After all, it was the Nashville and Chattanooga Railroad which was the principle feeder to the Western and Atlantic at Chattanooga. Statistics alone can demonstrate how much government business this road was doing. South over the single track went clothing, food, equipage, forage, arms, ammunition, and reinforcements. North in return came the sick and wounded, dischargees, refugees, freedmen, prisoners of war, and a varied assortment of military material.[18] From Nashville in 1864 the following numbers of loaded cars were sent forward: February, 2,108; March, 2,450; April, 3,445; May, 3,769; June, 3,217. Troop shipments were: February, 17,444; March, 16,490; April, 18,737; May, 32,051; June, 18,333.[19]

It would be strange indeed if all this business were carried on without attempted interference on the part of the Confederates. On September 1, Wheeler destroyed 7 miles of line between Nashville and Murfreesboro, and in December Hood took up 7¾ miles, including 530 feet of bridges.[20] The alternate route via the Nashville and Decatur was the scene of two September raids by Joseph Wheeler and Nathan B. Forrest, which together destroyed 29½ miles of track and bridges. Hood's Nashville campaign in November and December, 1864, resulted in the destruction of all the bridges on the line between Nashville and Decatur. It took three months in that winter to effect all the necessary repairs.[21]

Unfortunately it was not only enemy activity which hindered rail operations. Sometimes there were exasperating difficulties which prevented the Military Railroads from operating at full efficiency. Cars and cabooses reserved for railroad personnel were appropriated by troops. One officer even had a roundhouse removed because he could not stand the noise of the trains.[22] Troops sometimes balked at railroad duty, considering it degrading; and to remedy this difficulty, Meigs urged the employment of prisoners of war.[23]

In November, 1864, when Sherman cut loose on his historic march to the sea, 100 miles of the Western and Atlantic between Atlanta and Dalton were abandoned, some of the rail between Dalton and Resaca being carried to Chattanooga, the rest destroyed.[24] The railroads in the Nashville area were to see important service in the spring and summer of 1865, but after the battle of Nashville in December, 1864, the spotlight shifted away from the Mississippi Valley and Georgia to the Carolinas, where Sherman again called on the railroads to furnish supplies for his army of destruction.

The end of Sherman's Atlanta campaign in September by no

means meant the end of work for the military railroads in the Division of the Mississippi. From July 1, 1864, to June 30, 1865, 29,056 cars of stores, each car carrying 8 tons, were forwarded from Nashville to the front, most of the business being done between July and November. At the same time 5,673 cars of troops, each car carrying about 50 soldiers, were forwarded, with the largest business being in November, 1864, when 1,249 cars were sent on their way to the front.[25] These, of course, were loaded cars only. The depot had to handle as well 8,682 empty cars in train movements. While the transportation corps busied itself operating these trains, the Construction Corps renewed track, water stations, bridges destroyed by flood or by enemy action, and built necessary machine shops, roundhouses, engine shops, blacksmith and carpenter shops, storehouses, and offices. Because housing facilities were inadequate, the Construction Corps built their own barracks and mess halls at Nashville, and in December, 1864, when Hood threatened the city, 979 men of the corps worked 12 days on fortifications at strategic points.[26] The Construction Corps also worked at the Chattanooga rolling mill, quarried stone, and built and operated five sawmills.[27] By 1865, the Construction Corps at Nashville had space for 92 engines in repair, construction, or storage. For car repairs, a wrecking car was perfected by George Herrick, superintendent of the car department, which would pick up a train and bring it in for repairs. After January 1, 1865, wrecking trains picked up 16 wrecked locomotives, 530 cars, and 294 carloads of bridge iron, car wheels, and other equipment destroyed in rebel raids.[28] During the year after July 1, 1864, the amazing number of 20,000 cars were repaired or rebuilt and fitted as hospital and troop cars.[29]

It was, of course, necessary, not only in the Division of the

Mississippi, but elsewhere, for the railroad people to work with the Quartermaster, the military branch responsible for supply. Most of the time close cooperation was maintained. The Quartermaster in the area had assistants at Nashville, Chattanooga, and Memphis, each working with the railroads in his particular district. Only toward the end of the war, strangely enough, was there any recorded case of friction. E. L. Wentz, who became superintendent of the Division of the Mississippi November 1, 1864, ignored for the most part his Quartermaster colleagues, and made no property reports to higher authority. The situation was bad enough for General Thomas to appoint a board of survey to investigate. But the end of the war brought also an end to the investigation.[30]

The Military Division of the Mississippi had been the scene of the most extensive and most successful operation of the military railroads. A total of 1,201 miles of railroad were at one time or another operated as military railroads in Kentucky, Tennessee, Georgia, Alabama, Mississippi, Arkansas, and Missouri.[31] The figure was almost exactly double the 611 miles operated in Virginia, and more than four times the 293 miles operated in North Carolina. By all standards, the mission of the railroads was performed successfully, and most of the credit must go to McCallum. An early hesitant and confused military policy concerning railroad operation, executed by an inefficient administrator, was turned by McCallum into recognition of the importance of supply by rail to an army in the field, and beyond that into a practical demonstration of how to secure cooperation between the military and civilian railroad personnel to make the policy effective. Whether the railroads would have been able to accomplish the job without McCallum's leadership is of course unanswerable. It is true that some military leaders, Grant and Sherman among them, did recognize the importance of the railroads in the war picture. But it was McCallum who furnished the necessary initiative and leadership, and who, with able assistants, provided the indispensable factor in the ultimate success of the campaigns in the West. With adequate supplies, Sherman might still have lost, but it is certain that, without them, he could never have accomplished the severing of the Confederacy. The railroads under McCallum had furnished those supplies.

Having accumulated sufficient supplies at Atlanta, Sherman cut himself off from contact with the North, destroyed the railroads in the vicinity of Atlanta, and began his overland march to the sea. At first the military railroad organization thought that Sherman would use the railroads in the vicinity of Savannah, on the ocean. Accordingly, McCallum ordered part of the Virginia Construction Corps to Baltimore, thence by water to Savannah to put the railroads there into usable shape.[32] When, however, information was received that Sherman had no intention of using the Savannah railroads, the destination of the group was changed to Newbern, N. C., from where they were to open the rail line to Goldsboro.[33] The detachment arrived at Newbern on January 30, 1865, and immediately began work.

Meanwhile Wright, who had been busy on the Nashville-Decatur line after Thomas's victory over Hood, received orders December 28 to take one division of the Construction Corps to Savannah to aid Sherman.[34] With the second division, Wright left Nashville January 4, 1865, and arrived at Baltimore on the tenth. After an eight-day wait for transportation, the journey was resumed. On January 29, Wright received orders from Sherman changing his destination from Savannah to Morehead City, N. C., where Wright and his division landed February 5 and 6. Within six hours of arrival, they were working on the railroad.[35] Wright sent the advance Virginia detachment back to City Point and began his task of putting the railroad in operating order from Beaufort, near Morehead City, to Goldsboro by mid-March.[36] This was no easy task. The Atlantic and North Carolina Railroad could be used for 44 miles, but the track was poor and the sidings inadequate. The distance from Morehead City to Goldsboro was 95 miles. Three locomotives and 62 cars comprised the entire rolling stock. Wright requisitioned rolling stock and supplies from McCallum, and when General Cox began his march to Goldsboro on March 3 for his junction with Sherman coming from the South, the railroad kept pace with him. Wright and his men were heartened by the news that the third division of the Construction Corps had been recalled from work on the East Tennessee and Virginia Railroad and were on their way to North Carolina.[37] Supplies were moved from camp to camp and unloaded from the main track as troops marched up the road.[38] Wagon transportation helped of course, but the bulk of supplies was moved by rail. In addition, the Construction Corps built at Morehead City a new wharf covering more than one acre and large enough to accommodate seven or eight vessels at once.[39] Much of this work was done by Negro labor, which was substituted for the more expensive white labor whenever possible.[40]

Naturally, the work did not go unimpeded by the Confederates. They destroyed bridges and water stations and carried away track between Bachelder's Creek and Kingston. Wright and Smeed, his chief engineer, carried on the work day and night to keep up with the advance army under Schofield (who had replaced Cox). At one point, rail was being laid faster than ties were cut, so the railroad workers received the aid of a detail of soldiers who cut 5,400 ties in two days.[41] The Neuse River was reached March 20, and bridged three days later.[42] During that three days track was being laid on the other side of the river so as not to lose any time. At 3 A.M. on March 25, the track workers entered Goldsboro station to find that Sherman had arrived the preceding day.[43] Within three weeks 95 miles of railroad had been rebuilt in a brilliant demonstration of keeping pace with an army in the field.

General Slocum has left an interesting account of exactly how railroads were destroyed by Sherman's army in their march north from Savannah.[44] A thousand men could destroy five miles of track per day. The men would be divided into three sections.

Section #1 . . . is distributed along one side of the track, one man at the end of each tie. At a given signal, each man seizes a tie, lifts it gently till it assumes a vertical position, and then at another signal pushes it forward so that when it falls the ties will be over the rails. Then each man loosens his tie from the rail.

That completed, Section #2 takes the place of Section #1 which moves on to a new part of the railroad.

The duty of the second section is to collect the ties, place them in piles of about 30 ties each—place the rails on top of these piles, the center of each rail being over the center of the pile, and then set fire to the ties. . . . As soon as the rails are sufficiently heated Section #3 takes the place of Section #2; and upon this devolves the most important duty, viz., the effectual destruction of the rail. . . . Unless closely watched, soldiers will content themselves with simply bending the rails around trees. This should never be permitted. A rail which is simply bent can easily be restored to its original shape. No rail should be regarded as properly treated till it has assumed the shape of a doughnut; it must not only be bent but twisted.

The iron was too hot to twist barehanded, so a railroad hook was used which did the job quickly and efficiently. Soldiers, however, did not relish being assigned to the duty of railroad destruction. Slocum said, "This . . . is the only thing looking toward the destruction of property which I ever knew a man in Sherman's army to decline doing."

Sherman expected to resume his march April 10, along the line of the North Carolina Railroad toward Raleigh. It was up to the military railroads to supply him. While the transportation department concentrated on bringing in supplies from Morehead City, the construction department turned their attention to the Wilmington and Weldon Railroad, which ran north from Wilmington to a junction with the other line at Goldsboro. By April 4, this line was open and Sherman, with two lines of supply, and with a fortunate lack of accidents, found his army completely equipped by April 9. Actually, about 150 carloads in excess of Sherman's requirements moved over the Morehead City line in 14 days on a rolling stock of 6 engines and 87 cars, a truly remarkable achievement. The total of almost 3,000 cars forwarded meant that each locomotive and each car had to make an average of two round trips daily between Morehead City and Goldsboro, or 380 miles.[45]

When Sherman resumed his advance, the Construction Corps began reconstruction of the North Carolina Railroad from Goldsboro to Raleigh, taking only nine days to repair and put into operation 48 miles of track, two bridges, and repair miscellaneous damage done by the enemy. On April 19, the construction train and two supply trains entered Raleigh.[46] The task of accumulating supplies at Raleigh was made easy by additions to the rolling stock from the North, and from what was captured by Sherman's troops. On April 21, an agreement was made with the Raleigh and Gaston Railroad to use 4 of its engines and 40 cars in exchange for the rebuilding of the bridge over Cedar Creek. The bridge was rebuilt, but the arrival of more rolling stock from the North and Johnston's surrender made the rest of the agreement unnecessary.[47] Wright's order of May 15, 1865, disbanded the Construction Corps in North Carolina. The men were taken to Fortress Monroe, Va., and those with more than three months service received transportation to their homes.[48]

Since landing at Morehead City, the Construction Corps had

built 33 miles of track, 12 bridges, the large wharf at Morehead City, and made innumerable repairs. The Transportation Corps had sent 3,201 loaded cars to the front between February 15 and May 1, of which 400 cars carried troops; 38 engines were used in this movement (21 were captured from the enemy) and 422 cars (180 captured). The rolling stock, besides U. S. Military Railroads, Wilmington and Weldon, Raleigh and Gaston, North Carolina Railroad, Atlantic and North Carolina, carried the names of the Petersburg Railroad, Seaboard and Roanoke, Petersburg and Weldon, and Virginia Central, and there were even two box cars originally from the Michigan Central.[49] At its busiest time, the corps employed 3,387 men to operate and maintain its 293 miles of track in North Carolina.[50] The Carolina operations of the United States Military Railroads were not so spectacular as those in the Mississippi Valley. But they did show the Transportation Corps and the Construction Corps at their very best in a practically perfect small-scale demonstration of what could be done to supply an army in the field by rail. How far removed was Carolina of 1865 from Virginia of 1861 and 1862!

In Febrary, 1865, Schofield's 23rd Corps was transferred from Tennessee to North Carolina to effect a junction with Sherman. While the U.S.M.R. performed its outstanding work for Schofield in North Carolina, that commander was indebted to the railroads in general and to Lewis Parsons in particular for providing him and his corps transportation over 1,400 miles in 11 days from his headquarters in Tennessee to the Potomac River encampment. Parsons, on Dana's request, originally scheduled the corps to go to Parkersburg by water.[51] Transportation on the Ohio River in mid-winter was uncertain. Parsons therefore arranged with representatives of several Western railroads for a concentration of rolling stock to be available on 12 to 24 hours' notice at either Cairo, Evansville, Louisville, or Cincinnati.[52] Parsons assembled the transports at Paducah, whence McLean's division left on January 18, 1865. By the morning of the 20th, the weather had turned cold and ice had appeared in the river. Parsons ordered the transports to stop at Cincinnati and at the same time telegraphed the Quartermaster there for a concentration of rolling stock. The cars were to have stoves, a supply of hay or straw, one tier of seats, and were to carry about 30 men to a car.[53] On January 21, 3,000 men arrived at Cincinnati and were loaded on cars of the Little Miami Railroad. The next day 4,000 more men were put on cars of the Cincinnati, Hamilton, and Dayton Railroad, and a day later another 4,000 were sent via the Little Miami.[54]

Meanwhile Parsons telegraphed the Quartermaster at Columbus to requisition 200 cars and arranged with President Jewett of the Central Ohio Railroad that trains would travel 10 miles per hour and all other traffic except through passenger trains would be suspended.[55] Trains leaving Cincinnati carried a five-day supply of cooked rations, and arrangements were made at Columbus (transfer point to Central Ohio Railroad) and Bellaire (ferry to Benwood and Baltimore and Ohio Railroad) to have plenty of coffee available.[56] Occasional breakdowns occurred on the Central Ohio when severe cold caused some of the brittle iron rails to snap and some of the overtaxed engines to break down.[57] To aid the line, two engines were borrowed from the Piqua road, and two more from the Cleveland, Columbus, and Cincinnati.[58] The Steubenville and Indiana Railroad was also overtaxed. The 38 trains comprising the movement were too much for the railroad to handle without mishap. A driver on a locomotive broke, derailing the engine and 12 cars, and causing a 12-hour delay; a broken rail caused the derailment of two cars on a bridge and tore up some ties.[59]

The transfer at Benwood was accomplished without incident except that a drunken soldier on one train would not let the train leave Benwood because the officer in charge was across the river in Bellaire. One other train was delayed by a car with a broken axle.[60] Troop cars, of course, were outnumbered by those for horses and equipment. One train consisted of 11 cars for horses, 9 for artillery and baggage, and 7 for troops; another more typical in length, had 11 cars for horses, 3 for troops.[61]

The last troops were loaded on the Baltimore and Ohio at Benwood January 31, and three days later all had arrived at their encampment on the Potomac, having traveled 1,400 miles in 11 days, with only one fatal accident, and that the fault of the soldier involved.[62] W. P. Smith complained that the government cars were not well adapted to the severe grades and curves of the B & O, and he was encountering some difficulty. Many B & O trainmen were frostbitten in the severe cold, and several were killed by accident and exhaustion.[63] Parsons had nothing but praise for the railroad officials and workers in his report, saying that the government was indebted to the railroad men, who realized the importance of their task, and commending especially the B & O because of added difficulties due to the location of its line. Parsons even went to the trouble of contacting the editor of the Wheeling *Register* to deny as untrue the story that nine soldiers had frozen to death on the Central Ohio Railroad.[64] This vast troop movement compares favorably with the transfer of Hooker's Corps west in 1863. More men took part in that movement, but it occurred during a much better season of the year as far as weather was concerned. Then, too, there was more time to prepare for Hooker's move; Parsons had only four or five days. But he of course could easily profit from the experience of the former movement, which was really the first large-scale long-distance troop movement. These were not the only large troop movements of the war. It would be impossible to describe even the important ones, because some were made merely on verbal orders, and there is recorded only the bare statement that such a move took place. In 1865, for instance, the Fourth Army Corps moved 373 miles from Carter's Station in East Tennessee to Nashville, requiring almost 1,500 cars.[65] Enough has been given, however, to show that large-scale rail movements did take place and were of importance in the prosecution of the war.

The end of the war brought with it the problem of how to dispose of the vast amount of railroad equipment and rolling stock which had been accumulated. In the fall and winter of 1864, a substantial reserve of rolling stock had been acquired. The Military Railway Corps had built 35 locomotives and 492 cars of 5-foot gauge, plus 50 cars of 4 feet, $8\frac{1}{2}$ inches. Also ten platform cars of 4 feet, $8\frac{1}{2}$ inches were used on Western railroads to transport 5-foot gauge cars to Jeffersonville, Indiana. All of this rolling stock, except for one platform car destroyed in a wreck, was subsequently sold for cash, mostly to Southern railroads.[66] The total rolling stock of the military railroads amounted to 419 locomotives and 6,330 cars. Of the locomotives, 164 were sold under the executive orders of August 8 and October 14, 1865, 146 for cash, 103 returned to the owners, and 6 destroyed. Of the 6,330 cars, 2,589 were sold under the two executive orders, 2,186 for cash, 510 returned to the owners, and 1,045 lost.[67] Money for the operation of this huge plant came from the Quartermaster. Labor and materials in Virginia cost over $10,000,000, in Mississippi almost $30,-000,000, and in North Carolina about $2,500,000. Income to the U.S.M.R. from the disposal of property and from passenger and freight receipts, totaled over $12,500,000. The net expenditure for the entire war was $29,838,176.72.[68]

Rolling stock was not the only property. Much expenditure had gone into the track itself: 21,783 tons of rails had been purchased, more than a third of this amount in 1864. The price rose steadily from a low of $40 a ton in July, 1862, to $130 in June, 1864. Rails were also secured by taking up lines unnecessary for military use. A total of 142 miles of railroad was taken up in this fashion (62 miles in Virginia, mostly from the Manassas Gap Railroad, 80 miles in Mississippi). Finally, the Chattanooga rolling mill, in operation after April 1, 1865, produced 3,818 tons of rail.[69]

The rising cost of iron prompted McCallum in February, 1864, to recommend to Grant the completion of the rolling mill, which had been started by the Confederates. McCallum figured that the cost of completing the mill, plus the cost of rerolling old iron, would be only a little more than one third the cost of purchasing new iron.[70] Grant agreed, and work was started immediately. Actually McCallum had grossly underestimated the cost of completion of the mill. It was decided to erect a new building at a safer location, and the total cost came, not to McCallum's estimated $30,000, but to over $290,000. The mill was built by the Construction Corps during lulls in field operations, but due to the difficulty of getting materials and machinery, and to overcrowded transportation facilities, the mill was not in operation until April 1, 1865, more than a year after it was started. It operated until October 5, when it was sold at auction for $175,000 to John A. Spooner. The cost of manufacturing the 3,818 tons of iron T-rail came to $135,000, or $35.42 a ton, cheaper than McCallum's original estimate of $50 a ton, and even including the original cost of the mill represented a saving of well over half the cost of buying new iron at prevailing rates.[71] Because the war ended shortly, only a small part of the output was used. Most of the tonnage (3,351 tons) was sold to Southern railroads for $269,000.[72]

Getting the United States Military Railroads out of the railroad business was a job which required decisions of policy on a high level. When the U.S.M.R. wanted to dispose of the Orange and Alexandria Railroad, it found that the line's former president, John S. Barbour, wanted the road, but so did Governor Pierpoint for the Virginia Board of Public Works. Out of this quarrel came specific recommendations from Meigs to Stanton on May 19, 1865:

1. Disposal through the QM General to private parties.
2. No charge against the railroad for the expense of materials or operation.
3. Any materials used in repair or construction of the road to be disposed of with the railroad.
4. Movable property of the U. S., including rolling stock, to be disposed of at auction.
5. Other rolling stock to be returned to original owners.
6. Railroads to be turned over to state Board of Public Works, when it exists.
7. Otherwise, receivers to be appointed by the Treasury Dept., who would if necessary take the oath of allegiance.[73]

Dana suggested the modification that the railroad be allowed to purchase any material and equipment left on the road, but the U. S. government should not give it away.[74] These recommendations for the most part were carried out in actual practice. Unused material in depots was sold to the railroads, but the government did not charge for repairs made. At the same time no claims were allowed against the government for military damages or for profits accrued during operation. The government encouraged reorganization of the roads by the election of loyal managers and directors.[75]

Two executive orders provided authority to dispose of the roads. On August 8, 1865, Stanton ordered General Thomas to return railroads to the original owners under the following regulations:

1. The company was to elect a loyal board of directors.
2. An inventory of rolling stock and other property was to be taken.
3. Inventories of the company and the government were to be kept separate.
4. The company was to give bond that they would pay for government property turned over to them within one year, the government to withhold dues from mail carriage until this obligation was fulfilled.
5. A statement on government expenses for repairs was to be submitted.
6. Tennessee railroads to pay arrears in interest on state bonds issued for aid in construction of roads.
7. Government buildings not useful to the railroads were not to be charged against them.[76]

Under this order, by the end of August all the roads in Virginia except the Winchester and Potomac were turned over to the original owners or to the Virginia Board of Public Works, and in September all lines in the Division of the Mississippi, as well as those in North Carolina, were disposed of in comparable fashion.[77] The Winchester and Potomac, active with postwar business carrying over 40,000 troops, was finally returned to the Baltimore and Ohio on January 20, 1866.[78] Stanton issued a supplementary order dated October 14, 1865, which contained an optional procedure for railroads desiring to purchase rolling stock and materials from the United States. This material could now be paid for in equal monthly installments at 7.3 per cent interest, and, within two years, credit would be allowed monthly on any military transportation rendered by these railroads. The only exception to this installment policy was that serviceable railroad iron in possession of the Quartermaster at Nashville and Chattanooga was to be sold for cash only at War Department prices.[79] Under these two executive orders, 83 engines and 1,009 cars were sold for $1,500,000; 200 engines and 2,000 cars were sold on credit to Southern railroads, helping immensely in their rehabilitation.[80] Of 3,383 cars in the Division of the Mississippi, 2,311 went to Southern railroads.[81] A large amount of railroad material was disposed of, as well. Railroad companies in Virginia, for instance, gave bond for almost $350,000 worth of material.[82]

The summer of 1865 saw the gradual liquidation of the organization which made up the U.S.M.R., as the armies were disbanded and the railroads disposed of. In Tennessee and Georgia 1,000 men were discharged up to June 1, another 1,000 staying until July to rebuild the railroad from the Etowah River to Atlanta which Sherman had destroyed when he left that city.[83] Similarly in North Carolina and in Virginia, the men who had performed such important service were discharged as soon as possible. Many men whose deeds have been chronicled here were to have lucrative postwar careers in the railroad field. J. H. Devereux took a postwar job with the Cleveland and Pittsburgh Railroad. Adna Anderson went to the Northern Pacific. E. C. Smeed, to give only one other example, after the war became chief engineer of the Kansas Pacific Railroad. The war experience of all these men proved useful for their later railroad careers.

The military railroads were an experiment in their early days in 1862 and 1863. No one realized just what might be done or what should be expected from this kind of organization. Sherman's campaign was the greatest experiment of all. McCallum himself said that the supply of 100,000 men and 60,000 animals from a base 360 miles distant over a single-track railroad, mostly through enemy country, was without precedent in the history of warfare.[84] In a mobile war such as the Civil War was, the railroads thus played a leading part in the whole drama. With them, the North might still have lost, but without them, it is certain that victory would not have come.

Chapter XIV

THE WAR AND THE RAILROADS

THE FOREGOING CHAPTERS have set forth some phases of the relationship between the Northern railroads and the Civil War. It will be convenient to summarize these relationships in two ways: first, railroad contributions to the science of war, and second, war contributions to the science of railroading.

1. *Railroad Contributions to the Science of War.* Probably the most important single contribution made by the railroads in the Civil War was mass transportation of troops and supplies. Only a few of the railroads kept separate figures on the number of troops carried, and some of these were comparatively unimportant carriers. Undoubtedly the Pennsylvania Railroad was one of the heaviest troop carriers; according to the figures in its annual reports, the railroad transported a total of 953,-397 troops during the period from April, 1861, to December, 1865. But since more than one third of these were carried in the year 1865 alone, the load was distributed unevenly.[1] The Illinois Central, another important troop carrier, moved 556,421 troops in the years 1862 to 1865.[2] Though definite figures for other railroads are incomplete or nonexistent, we do know that, in general, transportation of troops was only a small fraction of the total passenger business. This is borne out by the practice of not keeping separate figures for military transportation. For the Pennsylvania Railroad, troop travel in 1862 amounted to about 10 per cent of the total passenger business, in 1863 about 12 per cent. Even the extraordinary business done at the close of the war, 378,393 for the year 1865 alone, was only 18 per cent of the total passenger business. The experience of

other roads was similar. In 1862 the Cleveland and Pittsburgh Railroad carried 34,790 troops, about 10 per cent of the 343,-000 passengers of all classes. In the same year the Pittsburgh, Ft. Wayne, and Chicago Railway carried 31,000 troops in a total of over 650,000 passengers, about 5 per cent.[3] But though the percentage was small, it was vital to the successful prosecution of the war.

It is manifestly impossible to determine what percentage of the general freight business of the railroads was military. We do know, however, that the carrying of troops and military supplies took place at a time when both passenger and freight business of the roads was expanding. For instance, the New York Central carried 2,100,000 passengers in 1861, 3,700,000 in 1865; the Michigan Central 328,000 in 1861, 853,000 in 1865; the Central Railroad of New Jersey 400,000 in 1861, 929,000 in 1865.[4] Many railroads showed similar increases in freight business. Again, the New York Central carried 1,100,000 tons in 1861, almost 1,300,000 in 1865. Other railroads experienced similar tonnage increases in 1861 to 1865: Central Railroad of New Jersey, 1,000,000 to 1,400,000; Pennsylvania Railroad, 1,500,000 to 2,800,000; Philadelphia, Wilmington, and Baltimore, 58,000 to 236,000.[5]

As we have previously noted, one result of this expansion was that the motive power and rolling stock of the railroads was used to full capacity during the war years. In addition, the rise in prices and the growing labor scarcity made it difficult to secure additional rolling stock. Some of the railroads were therefore forced to absorb the majority of this increased business, both passenger and freight, without any very substantial increase in rolling stock and motive power. The Philadelphia, Wilmington, and Baltimore Railroad, whose passenger business more than doubled during the war and whose freight business almost quadrupled, could increase motive power only from 32 engines in 1861 to 60 at the end of the war, and rolling stock from 674 to 1,133. The Michigan Central had only 100 passenger cars in 1865 to carry two and a half times as many passengers as it carried in 85 cars at the beginning of the war. The passenger business of the Chicago, Burlington, and Quincy tripled, but the number of its passenger cars rose only from 40 to 72. Motive power was particularly hard to purchase or construct, not only because of the difficulties already mentioned, but also because the government needed engines for the military railroads. The Pennsylvania Railroad, with 229 engines in 1861, actually had only 225 in 1864, due partly to the necessity of outfitting the Philadelphia and Erie.[6] Only a few roads managed to acquire substantial additions to motive power and rolling stock during the war. The Northern Central, the Erie, and the Chicago and North Western were among the lucky ones. Thus the contribution of mass transportation and supply, carried out under controlled conditions in the South by the United States Military Railroads, came at a time when other demands for transportation service were increasing, not only because of the war, but also because of the European demand for grain and the growing domestic desire for new products, chiefly coal, oil, and iron ore; and at a time, too, when labor and materials shortages placed obstacles in the way of any great expansion of available facilities.[7]

That the burden of transportation on government account was shared by many lines can be seen from the list of 75 railroads which presented bills to the government for transportation service rendered up to February 1, 1862.[8] Bills of over $100,000 were presented by the Baltimore and Ohio, the Pennsylvania, the Northern Central, the Illinois Central, the Michigan Southern and Northern Indiana, and the Cleveland and

Pittsburgh. Bills of between $25,000 and $70,000 came from the Philadelphia, Wilmington, and Baltimore, the Cumberland Valley, the Camden and Amboy, the New Jersey Railroad, the Milwaukee and Prairie du Chien, the Portland, Saco, and Portsmouth, and the Connecticut River Railroad. Perhaps the most important fact about this growth in traffic was that most of the increase was in interchange traffic with other railroads, previously only a minor part of a railroad's business. Many railroads were finding their through business becoming more important than their local business.[9] This fact, by laying the basis for postwar expansion of through routes, helped to change the character of the railroads from local companies to national enterprises.

The United States Military Railroads operated solely for the purpose of carrying troops and supplies, and over the war years, particularly in the Military Division of the Mississippi, proved themselves capable of supplying an army operating at some distance from its base of supplies. That was their achievement in Sherman's Atlanta campaign, and over shorter distances in North Carolina and Virginia. The achievements in mass transportation and supply were only part of the military railroads' contribution to the science of war. Certainly one of the reasons for the success of the military railroads was the coordination established between the civilian railroad personnel and the military officers in the field. Engineers, firemen, conductors, train dispatchers, superintendents and other railroad men were all civilians in the employ of the government but not under direct control of the army. The problem of deciding what voice military officers (particularly Quartermasters) would have in railroad operation was one with which Haupt had to cope from the beginning. His decision to keep the roads out of control of the military was a fortunate one for the railroads, though Haupt, a West Point graduate, and a man difficult to get along with personally, would seem to have been the last man to make such a decision. Considering the size of the military railroad operation, there were remarkably few recorded instances of friction between the military and civilian elements, once a working relationship was established. In Virginia, it was probably in spite of rather than because of Haupt's stubborn personality that quarrels were few. Undoubtedly some military men would rather not have worked with Haupt, but the fact that Haupt was supported by General Halleck in an order forbidding any military officer from interfering with railroad operation accounted for ultimate success. By the time railroad operation became important in the Military Division of the Mississippi, not only was the principle of noninterference well established, but also Sherman and Grant themselves recognized the vital role railroads were playing in the war. From 1863 on, coordination and cooperation replaced earlier jealousy and interference. For the military, which in America is always confronted with the problem of relations with the civilian element, it was a valuable lesson which showed how important civilian workers could be in prosecuting a war.

The activities of the military railroads made another contribution to the science of war, that is, the development of more efficient methods of construction and destruction of track and bridges. The development of a Construction Corps, separate from the Transportation Corps, beginning January 1, 1863, was an important step in this direction. Here the engineer training which Haupt had received was invaluable. Track laying became a science worked out in the minutest detail and reaching near perfection from constant practice after Confederate raids. The swift construction of the Western and Atlantic Railroad in Georgia, the Atlantic and North Carolina Railroad in North

Carolina, and the City Point and Army Railroad in Virginia were instances in which the Construction Corps reached its peak of efficiency.

New techniques in bridge construction were also developed, the most important being the use of ready-made bridges and trestles constructed on an assembly-line technique.[10] The Construction Corps might well have been named the destruction corps in its development of ways and means of more effectively destroying the enemy's line of supply. The early method of placing rails on burning ties and bending the hot rails out of shape was used throughout the war, but much more effective methods were developed. Bent rails could frequently be straightened and used again, but the apparatus developed by E. C. Smeed to twist as well as bend them usually rendered the rails useless. The method of setting fire to the ends of the ties without ripping up the rails was sometimes favored because fewer laborers could carry it out.

One final contribution which railroads made to the science of war was the development of special equipment, chiefly hospital cars, hospital trains, and armored cars. Hospital cars were in operation in Massachusetts between Boston and Albany as early as the spring of 1862. These were ordinary passenger cars from which some of the seats had been removed and berths substituted. Each berth had a hair mattress, pillows, and blanket. The car had 12 berths, 6 on a side, and had seats for 18 additional soldiers.[11] But in the theaters of war no such accommodations existed this early. During the Peninsular Campaign in 1862, the wounded were brought from Savage's Station to White House lying on bare floor: "The worst cases are put inside the covered cars,—close, windowless boxes,—sometimes with a little straw or a blanket to lie on, oftener without. They arrive a festering mass of dead and living together."[12]

The alleviation of such conditions as these was due partly to the railroads and partly to the activities of the United States Sanitary Commission. For it was Dr. Elisha Harris who first thought of the idea of hospital cars, while watching the agonies of the wounded being carried in so primitive a fashion.[13] In the war areas, however, the first hospital cars were put into operation October 17, 1862, when the Illinois agent of the Sanitary Commission fitted out two cars for use on the Lebanon branch of the Louisville and Nashville Railroad to help remove the wounded from the battle of Perryville. One of these cars was a combination smoking and baggage car, with the baggage part fitted with 18 bunks.[14] The operation of these two cars proved immediately successful by reducing the time of transportation to Louisville to 24 hours, and hence preventing many cases of gangrene from developing as they had on the slower hospital ships.[15] Morgan's raid shortly afterwards severed the L & N, but after its restoration in February, 1863, river transportation of wounded ceased.[16]

These makeshift hospital cars were really only temporary expedients. The Sanitary Commission drew up plans and specifications of new cars; 10 were in operation in 1863, and new ones were added in the succeeding year.[17] Each car had 24 removable stretchers suspended from uprights on heavy rubber bands. The stretchers were used to carry wounded soldiers from the battlefield to the car and direct from the car to the hospital. The hospital car was also equipped with a medicine closet, and chairs and couch for the surgeon. A kitchen (6 feet by 3 feet) equipped with water tank, wash basin, cupboards, and copper boilers completed the furnishings. Extra stiff springs were placed on the ends of the car and double springs underneath it. Attention was paid to ventilation, heating, and lighting, and the cars were made of variable gauge in order to run on different railroads.[18]

In 1863 these cars made three trips a week from Bridgeport, Ala. to Chattanooga, Nashville, and Louisville, and in 1864 the run was extended to Atlanta. The make-up of the hospital train varied somewhat. Sometimes it carried one passenger car with a special arrangement of seats to be made up into beds if necessary, one mail car, three boxcars, and three hospital cars.[19] One 10-car train carried 314 soldiers (not all stretcher cases), its capacity increased by means of three tiers of cots.[20] Pratt gives the consist of a train as five ward cars, surgeon's car, dispensary car, passenger car, kitchen car, and conductor's car. Hospital trains were protected by distinguishing markings, and were usually not molested by the enemy, though one band of rebel raiders in April, 1863, burned a hospital train after removing the wounded.[21] This incident was unusual, but occasionally hospital trains were involved in ordinary operating accidents. A severe one occurred in Georgia in 1864. The engine hauling a hospital train was detached and had proceeded about a mile up a grade on the way to the water station. Meeting another train on the way down the grade, the engineer reversed his locomotive and jumped. The wild engine crashed full speed into its own train of hospital cars, crushing the fragile cars and killing many battle-wounded soldiers.[22]

Not enough hospital cars were built during the war to use on all fronts. By the end of 1864 cars were running on the route south of Louisville, between Washington and New York, and between New York and Boston via Springfield.[23] The Eastern theater of war, with shorter distances of transportation, was usually supplied with passenger cars in which the backs were removed from the seats and boards covered with bedding were laid lengthwise across them.[24] But this was not until quite late in the war. At Gettysburg, wounded were moved to Baltimore and Harrisburg in baggage cars floored with straw and open at either end for air. Sanitary Commission men brought ice water, crackers, and stimulants to the cars, and each train carried a surgeon and his assistants.[25] Railroad personnel operated the cars while they were en route, but otherwise they were controlled by the army medical authorities and by the Sanitary Commission.[26] Certainly, in a war which saw horrible suffering on the part of thousands of soldiers, this contribution was something of which the railroads and the Sanitary Commission could be proud.

Armored cars were another piece of special equipment developed by the railroads. These could be used for either defensive or offensive purposes, and in either case usually ran ahead of the engine. One ironclad railway battery was constructed of boiler iron riveted on $2\frac{1}{2}$-inch oak plank mounted on a 30-foot platform car. The sides were $2\frac{1}{2}$ feet high and the car was armed with a 6-inch revolving gun.[27] Sometimes the sides were higher and pierced with holes for use by riflemen or by a cannon on a pivot. Such a car was built by Baldwin and used on the Philadelphia, Wilmington, and Baltimore Railroad.[28] A train of these armored cars was encountered on the B & O by Confederate raiders in August, 1864. The six cars and locomotive were protected by railroad rails, two cars had portholes for cannon firing, the others smaller apertures for infantry. The train was stopped when a Confederate artillery shot hit the locomotive boiler and another shot entered a porthole on one of the cars. The raiders destroyed the train by piling railroad ties around it and setting them afire.[29] These beginnings foreshadowed the great railway batteries for coast defense and long range artillery gunning developed in later years.

2. *War Contributions to the Science of Railroading.* The war demands on transportation facilities, urgent as they are in all modern wars, forced the railroads to develop new ways of doing things and new materials for use in equipment and rolling stock.

These developments were just as important to the railroads as
their own contributions were to the military men. One of the
new ways of doing things was the enforced cooperation among
railroads to meet the demands of the war period. Previous to
the war some meetings had periodically been held by groups of
railroads for such purposes as arranging timetables, and these
continued through the war.[30] But, generally speaking, competition was the rule. The existence of different gauges and the lack
of through connections in many cities suggest that what cooperation existed among the railroads was of a limited extent.
But the war, calling for transportation of troops and supplies
over long distances and hence over more than one railroad, enforced cooperation. Fast freight lines were established to overcome slight deficiencies in gauge. The lines comprising the route
from New York to Washington worked together to make improvements in service and even to establish a single superintendent for the whole route. The dramatic transfer of two army
corps from Virginia to Tennessee necessitated cooperation
among the several railroads comprising the route in order to
complete the movement on schedule. Frequently railroaders got
together on their own initiative for one purpose or another. In
March, 1862, representatives of the Illinois Central, Galena and
Chicago Union, Chicago and North Western, Chicago and Milwaukee, LaCrosse and Milwaukee, and Milwaukee and Prairie du
Chien met at the Sherman House in Chicago to establish a uniform system of freight handling and the adoption of various
rules governing passenger trains, rates, and other matters.[31] In
1863, representatives of 19 railroads led by Erastus Corning
of the New York Central and Nathaniel Marsh of the Erie, met
at Buffalo and decided that the four East-West routes should
set up union ticket offices in New York and Boston, and recommended that other cooperating railroads do the same in the

larger cities of the Great Lakes area and the Middle West.[32] It was through the increasing cooperation of the railroads during the war period that the stage was set for the expansion of the postwar years, with the establishment of long through routes, frequently owned or controlled by one company.

A second contribution was an outgrowth of this growing cooperation among lines. The vastly increased mail business brought about the establishment in 1864 of railway post office cars to distribute mail while en route and thus quicken its delivery. The use of these cars on the New York–Washington route was not an isolated circumstance. Heavy army concentrations at such points as Cairo, Ill., brought a sharp increase in this service.[33] Mail had been carried by railroads for a long time, but was first distributed in a car en route by William A. Davis in July, 1862, on the Hannibal and St. Joseph Railroad.[34] The first railway postal route was established August 28, 1864, on the Chicago and North Western's Iowa Division to Clinton, Iowa.[35] The service expanded rapidly after that, being in operation by the end of the war on the New York–Washington run, the Pennsylvania Railroad, the Chicago and Rock Island, the Chicago, Burlington, and Quincy, and the Erie.[36] The business on the New York–Washington line required a full car, but on other lines it could frequently be handled in less than a full car.[37] That the development of this service was encouraged by the war is shown by the fact that a heavy slump in mail business was experienced at the end of the war until after mail communication with the South had been restored.[38] But that occurred quickly and the words "United States Railway Post Office" became a familiar sight on the railroads of America.[39]

A third contribution of the war to railroading was the shift from iron to steel, particularly for rails. It is impossible to determine which railroad made the first use of steel rails. Certainly the experiments carried on by the Pennsylvania Railroad at the Altoona yards in 1863 and 1864 were an important early indication of the necessity for finding some substitute for the universally used iron rail. Heavier wartime traffic and faster trains were wearing out iron rails at a faster pace than they could be economically replaced, what with the rising cost of this item of equipment. Prosperity furnished the capital, and rising costs and heavy traffic the stimulus to experiment. Installation of steel rails was done at high initial cost but their long life was enough to repay the investment. The use of steel rails did not become general during the war, but the war began the trend in that direction and proved the inadequacy of iron under new traffic conditions. Other railroads began to follow the Pennsylvania Railroad's lead. In 1864, the Lehigh Valley Railroad was using some steel rail on its Beaver Meadow Division,[40] and the same year saw advertisements of steel rails being carried in railway periodicals.[41] At first the rails were imported from Europe. It was not until after the war that the first steel rail was fabricated in America.[42] Experiments were made in other uses of steel, as for tires on locomotive wheels, and as early as 1862 the master machinist of the Pennsylvania Railroad was experimenting with steel fireboxes, having found iron unsuitable and copper too expensive.[43]

Closely allied to the change from iron to steel in equipment was the change from wood to coal as fuel. This change was not a direct result of war conditions, since it had begun before the war. The Central Railroad of New Jersey had been using coal as fuel since 1857, and consistently found it 35 per cent cheaper than wood.[44] Other railroads had also used coal as fuel before the war, but the war accelerated the change. In a period of rising costs, particularly from 1863 on, most railroads tried to discover new means of economizing, and many of them found part of the answer in coal. Of course the price of coal as well as of wood rose during the war period, but coal would drive a train relatively farther than wood.

Finally we may note that the service of some men with the military railroads brought invaluable experience to various railroad companies with which these men found employment after the war. J. H. Devereux with the Cleveland and Pittsburgh, Adna Anderson with the Northern Pacific, E. C. Smeed with the Kansas Pacific, and Frank Thomson with the Philadelphia and Erie[45] were only examples of what must have been a large number of military railroad employees who sought and found railroad jobs after the war's end. This relationship was reciprocal, too. McCallum from the Erie, Haupt from the Pennsylvania, and Parsons from the Ohio and Mississippi brought the value of earlier railroad careers to their military tasks.

In these many ways, railroads contributed to the prosecution of the war, and were in turn stimulated by war activity toward further advances in their own technology. It was a relationship from which both sides profited, for certainly the war would have dragged on for years longer without the help of railroad supply, and certainly, too, the advances in railroading would have been delayed years longer without the stimulation of wartime demands.

NOTES

1. *Preliminary Report on the Eighth Census 1860,* p. 104.

2. Henry V. Poor, *Railroad Manual of the United States, 1868,* p. 17.

3. *Ibid.*

4. *Merchants' Magazine and Commercial Review,* XLIII (July-Dec., 1865), 278.

5. *Ibid.,* pp. 429-30.

6. *Ibid.,* p. 292.

7. *Preliminary Report on the Eighth Census 1860,* Table 38, "Railroads of the United States," pp. 214-37.

8. Carl R. Fish, "The Northern Railroads 1861," *American Historical Review,* XXII, 781.

9. *American Railway Review,* June 19, 1862.

10. *Merchants' Magazine and Commercial Review,* XLIV (Jan.-June, 1861), 119. Freight which could use the rail route from Cairo to New York cost $16 a ton, whereas the cost by the river route via New Orleans was $20. *American Railway Review,* Feb. 7, 1861.

11. *Merchants' Magazine and Commercial Review,* XLIV (Jan.-June, 1861), 782-83; *American Railroad Journal,* April 27, 1861. Came a London comment, "If you can see your way . . . to a regulated cotton trade, through the Upper Mississippi and the New York railways . . . John Bull will be the close and faithful ally of the North. . . ." *Merchants' Magazine and Commercial Review,* XLV (July-Dec. 1861), 208.

12. See Chapter V for further consideration of this subject.

13. *Merchants' Magazine and Commercial Review,* XLV (July-Dec., 1861), 134; XLVI (Jan.-June, 1862), 376; *American Railway Review,* March 21 and 28, 1861.

14. *Preliminary Report on the Eighth Census, 1860,* Table 38.

15. See the annual reports of these railroads, which will be cited in more detail in later pages. The Railroad Share List in the

American Railroad Journal listed 242 different railroads in existence in the Northern states, Aug. 24, 1861.

16. *32nd Annual Report . . . of the Boston and Worcester Railroad, 1861*, p. 3; *Ibid., 1864*, p. 3. Eighty-pound rail means that one yard of rail weighed 80 pounds. Rails grew progressively heavier in order to accommodate heavier and faster trains. Today, some railroads with comparatively light traffic still use 80-pound rail, though the important through lines use rail weighing up to 151 pounds per yard.

17. *15th Annual Report . . . of the Pennsylvania Railroad . . . 1862*, p. 36; *United States Railroad and Mining Register,* July 2, 1864.

18. Henry M. Flint, *The Railroads of the United States,* p. 434.

19. *American Railway Times,* Dec. 24, 1864.

20. *American Railway Review,* March 28, 1861.

21. *American Railway Review,* Feb. 27, 1862; *24th Annual Report . . . of the Philadelphia, Wilmington, and Baltimore Railroad,* pp. 10-11. The Central Railroad of New Jersey also used this process; see its *16th Annual Report . . . 1862*, p. 13. The Chicago and Rock Island Railroad adopted it in 1865; see its *Annual Report . . . April, 1866*, p. 16.

22. *American Railway Times,* Dec. 24, 1864.

23. *Ashcroft's Railway Directory for 1862*, pp. 25-50.

24. *Ibid.,* pp. 95, 97, 104.

25. *Ibid.,* pp. 60, 64; so did the Delaware, Lackawanna, and Western, and the Ohio and Mississippi. *Ibid.,* pp. 86, 192.

26. *Ibid.,* pp. 77, 80, 98; *ibid., 1864*, p. 58.

27. *Ibid., 1862*, pp. 76, 91, 96, 106.

28. *Ibid.,* pp. 164, 165, 167, 169, 176, 177.

29. Such Ohio railroads were the Pittsburgh, Columbus, and Cincinnati, Cleveland, Painesville, and Astabula, Little Miami and Columbus and Xenia, Cincinnati, Hamilton, and Dayton. *Ibid.,* pp. 180, 181, 183, 189-91, 193, 202-3, 157.

30. *Ibid.,* pp. 109-49, 160. The important Louisville and Nashville had a 5-foot gauge. Luckily for railroad operations in Virginia, that state stuck pretty much to 4 feet, $8\frac{1}{2}$ inches. To complete the variety, gauges of 4 feet, $9\frac{1}{4}$ inches and 5 feet, 4 inches were also used. *American Railway Times,* Jan. 1, 1861.

31. Emerson D. Fite, *Social and Industrial Conditions in the North during the Civil War*, pp. 56, 58; *Annual Report . . . of the Michigan Southern and Northern Indiana Railroad . . . March 1, 1865*, p. 7.

32. Robert S. Henry, *Trains*, p. 78.

33. *Ibid.* An example was the Crestline, Cleveland, and Lake Shore Fast Freight Line.

34. *American Railway Review, Feb. 7, 1861.* Opposition to the establishment of through connections sometimes reached the point of violence. Erie, Pa., was, for instance, the scene of such a "war." Alexander K. McClure, *Old Time Notes of Pennsylvania.* William Z. Ripley, editor, *Railway Problems,* chapter on "Early American Conditions" (taken from H. G. Pearson, *John Murray Forbes*), p. 77.

35. John T. Scharf, *History of Baltimore City and County from the Earliest Period to the Present Day*, pp. 788-89.

36. Frank H. Taylor, *Philadelphia in the Civil War 1861-1865*, map supplement; Winnifred K. Mackay, "Philadelphia during the Civil War, 1861-1865," *Pennsylvania Magazine of History and Biography* (Jan., 1946), p. 15, note. New York *Times*, Feb. 5, 1863.

37. *Merchants' Magazine and Commercial Review*, XLV (July-Dec., 1861), 572-74. The six included lines radiating to Cleveland, Cincinnati, St. Louis, Chicago, and Detroit.

38. *Report . . . of the New Jersey Railroad and Transportation Co. 1860*, p. 3.

39. *American Railway Review*, Jan. 23, 1862.

40. *1st Annual Report of Milwaukee and Prairie du Chien Railway . . . 1861*, p. 11; Charles E. Fisher, "The Chicago Burlington and Quincy," *Railway and Locomotive Historical Society Bulletin 24*, March, 1931, p. 13; *15th Annual Report . . . of the Pennsylvania Railroad, Feb. 1862*, p. 12.

41. *American Railroad Journal*, Nov. 16, 1861.

42. *Merchants' Magazine and Commercial Review*, LIII (July-Dec., 1865), 358.

43. *25th Annual Report . . . of the Philadelphia Wilmington and Baltimore Railroad . . . 1862*, p. 11.

44. *8th Annual Report . . . of the Northern Central Railway . . . 1862*, p. 20.

45. These distinguishing characteristics of a Civil War engine are evident on the Great Northern's William Crooks, and the Western and Atlantic's General, both exhibited at the Chicago Railroad Fair in 1948. See also, *Railroad Gazette* Jan. 11, 1907, pp. 39-43; T. W. Van Metre, *Trains, Tracks, and Travel*, p. 77; K. A. Herr, *The Louisville and Nashville Railroad, 1850-1942*, pp. 191-92.

46. Diagram of a Camden and Amboy locomotive in *American Railway Review*, March 6, 1862.

47. Henry, *Trains*, pp. 62-63.

48. *Report of the Boston and Maine Railroad . . . 1861*, p. 20; *15th Annual Report of the Central Railroad of New Jersey . . . 1861*, p. 19; Little Miami Railroad Co., and Columbus and Xenia Railroad Co., *Ninth Joint Annual Report . . . 1864*, p. 23; *United States Railroad and Mining Register*, June 21, 1862.

49. *American Railway Review*, Jan. 9, 1862.

50. Two CRRNJ engines ran 34.85 and 57.3 miles on a cord of wood, 28.05 and 52.26 on a ton of anthracite. *15th Annual Report*, pp. 19-20; the Illinois Central got 40-42 miles on wood, 37 on coal; *Illinois Central Railroad . . . Report, 1862*, p. 5. Boston and Worcester engines ran 26-60 miles per cord of wood, 26-57 miles per ton of coal; *32nd Annual Report . . . of the Boston and Worcester Railroad, 1861*, pp. 4-5.

51. *American Railroad Journal*, Aug. 24, 1861, letter from John W. Nystrom of Philadelphia.

52. *Railroad Gazette*, Jan. 11, 1907, p. 43.

53. *Report . . . of the Boston and Maine Railroad . . . 1861*, pp. 21-22; *36th Annual Report . . . of the Baltimore and Ohio Railroad, 1862*, p. 68; *United States Railroad and Mining Register*, June 21, 1862; Herr, *op. cit.*, p. 178.

54. *15th Annual Report . . . of the Pennsylvania Railroad, 1862*, p. 31; *American Railway Review*, June 20, 1861 (Cleveland and Pittsburgh Railroad).

55. *American Railway Review*, May 16, 1861.

56. *Ibid.*, March 13, 1862 (from Milwaukee *News*); Herr, *op. cit.*, p. 178.

57. *American Railway Times*, Feb. 11, 1865.

58. *American Railway Review*, May 29, 1862.

59. Van Metre, *op. cit.*, p. 168; L. K. Sillcox, *Safety in Early American Railway Operation, 1853-1871*, p. 18; A Milwaukee man, A. I. Ambler, invented a car brake which would brake all wheels at the same time and could be controlled by the engineer. *American Railway Review*, March 20, 1862. There is no evidence that this brake was ever put to use on any railroad.

60. *American Railway Review*, March 14, 1861. A train of these iron cars proved their worth in preventing loss of life when the train ran into an open drawbridge. *Ibid.*, March 28, 1861.

61. *American Railway Times*, June 3, 1865.

62. *Report . . . of the Michigan Central Railroad . . . 1862*, p. 27.

63. *Ibid., 1865*, p. 36.

64. *American Railway Review*, March 21, June 13, 1861; *United States Railroad and Mining Register*, Nov. 23, 1861; *American Railway Times*, Jan. 17, 1863.

65. Flint, *op. cit.*, p. 170.

66. Letter from John W. Garrett of the B & O to Secretary of War Stanton, Oct. 6, 1863, *Stanton Papers*, vol. XVII.

67. *American Railway Review*, April 4, 1861.

68. *American Railroad Journal*, May 24, 1862; *Report . . . of the Philadelphia and Reading Railroad . . . 1861*, p. 34. Compare this with the typical loaded coal train of today, which on the Chesapeake and Ohio and other coal roads weighs 5,000 tons or more.

69. *American Railroad Journal*, April 12, 1862 (Report of the State Engineer of New York to the Legislature, Feb. 1862).

70. *Report . . . of the New York and New Haven Railroad . . . 1862*, p. 14.

71. For examples, see *4th Annual Report of the Milwaukee and Prairie du Chien Railway Co., 1864*, p. 41; *14th Annual Report of the Central Railroad of New Jersey . . . 1861*, p. 21; *Annual Report of the Chicago and Rock Island Railroad Co., 1862*, p. 9.

72. *American Railroad Journal*, April 12, 1862; *American Railway Times*, July 4, 1863; *Report . . . of the New York and New Haven Railroad, 1862*, p. 14; *32nd Annual Report . . . of the Boston and Worcester Railroad, 1861*, p. 4; *27th Annual Report of the Western Railroad, 1861*, p. 20; Sir Samuel Morton Peto, *The Resources and Prospects of America Ascertained during a Visit to the*

States in the Autumn of 1865, p. 290. Occasionally express trains attained 55 to 60 miles per hour. *American Railway Times,* Aug. 24, 1861.

73. *Report . . . of the New Jersey Railroad and Transportation Co. . . .* 1861, p. 7.

74. Samuel R. Kamm, *The Civil War Career of Thomas A. Scott,* p. 60; 2,000 cars probably meant about 20,000 tons of freight or 80,000 men. See Robert S. Henry, *This Fascinating Railroad Business,* p. 422.

75. These were divided about evenly among the three railroads. *15th Annual Report . . . of the Pennsylvania Railroad . . . Feb. 3, 1862,* pp. 24, 30; *1st Annual Report . . . of the Erie Railway . . . Dec. 31, 1862,* p. 7; *Annual Report . . . of the New York Central Railroad . . . 1861,* p. 11.

76. *American Railway Review,* May 23, 1861; April 24, 1862; Flint, *op. cit.,* pp. 47-48. Today this route, with the exception of Niagara Falls, is the New York Central's main line via Detroit.

77. Flint, *op. cit.,* pp. 47-48, 188, 212; *American Railway Review,* May 23, 1861. These routes are not used today in these combinations. The Lake Shore and Michigan Southern and Northern Indiana is now the New York Central main line via Cleveland, the Erie having its own line all the way to Chicago. One can no longer travel from Jersey City to Pittsburgh via Central Railroad of New Jersey without changing at Harrisburg. In the sixties, the CRRNJ ran through cars, leaving New York at 8 P.M., arriving Pittsburgh at noon. When the East Pennsylvania and Lebanon Valley Railroad was opened in early 1862, the CRRNJ route was the shortest mileage to Chicago, Cincinnati, and St. Louis. *American Railway Review,* June 13, 1861, Feb. 20, 1862. The Pittsburgh, Ft. Wayne, and Chicago is now the main line of the Pennsylvania Railroad.

78. *Letters 1853-1868 Gen. William J. Palmer,* compiled by Isaac H. Clothier, p. 42 (Sept. 14, 1859). This road is now the main St. Louis line of the Baltimore and Ohio Railroad.

79. Documents 3 and 4 of the Ohio and Mississippi Railroad (New York Public Library, undated); Flint, *op. cit.,* pp. 48-50.

80. Flint, *op. cit.,* pp. 261, 267; *American Railway Review,* May 23, 1861; *United States Railroad and Mining Register,* Nov. 16, 1861. The Chicago and St. Louis Railroad is now the Alton route

of the Gulf, Mobile and Ohio, time now five hours. The Logansport line is now the Pennsylvania, time between Chicago and Cincinnati 6½ to 8 hours. The New York to Washington run is now commonly made in 4 hours.

81. A. B. Hulbert, *The Paths of Island Commerce*, pp. 170-71.

82. E. D. Fite, "The Canal and the Railroad from 1861-1865," *Yale Review*, XV, 199.

83. *Ninth Census of the United States, Statistics of Population,* Table III.

84. Peto, *op. cit.*, pp. 270-71, 277.

85. Harmon K. Murphy, "The Northern Railroads of the Civil War," *Mississippi Valley Historical Review*, V, 324. An exception to this local emphasis was the establishment, early in 1861, of a 3½-day all rail mail and express route from New York to New Orleans, the operation of which was prevented by the outbreak of war. F. B. C. Bradlee, *Blockade Running During the Civil War*, pp. 418-19.

CHAPTER II

1. *Preliminary Report on the Eighth Census,* Table 38. This was an increase of 14,769 over 1850.

2. *American Railroad Journal,* Jan. 7, 1865. Poor, *Railroad Manual of the United States,* (p. 19) gives the increase at 4,550 miles. Most construction was in Pennsylvania (926 miles), with Ohio, New York, New Jersey, California, Illinois, and Michigan following, in that order (pp. 20-21).

3. *1st Annual Report of the Atlantic and Great Western Railway 1863,* p. 22.

4. *Ibid.,* pp. 9-11.

5. *Ibid.,* p. 25; *American Railroad Journal,* Oct. 15, 1864. McHenry alone financed 500 miles of the railroad (*1st Annual Report,* p. 38).

6. *American Railroad Journal,* July 9, 1864, Jan. 31, 1863; *1st Annual Report,* pp. 10-12; see also Henry M. Flint, *The Railroads of the United States,* p. 194.

7. *1st Annual Report,* p. 12. The bad feeling engendered between England and the United States by the Trent Affair in Nov. 1861

brought further, if temporary, obstacles in the financing of the enterprise. *1st Annual Report,* p. 36; *United States Railroad and Mining Register,* May 17, 1862.

8. *1st Annual Report,* p. 36.

9. *American Railroad Journal,* Dec. 20, 1862, Oct. 15, 1864 (from London *Times*); *United States Railroad and Mining Register,* May 17, 1862. The town of Salamanca, N.Y., where the road joined the Erie, was named after its benefactor.

10. *United States Railroad and Mining Register,* May 17, 1862.

11. *American Railroad Journal,* Oct. 15, 1864. Workers also came from Canada. *1st Annual Report,* p. 37. Agents were maintained in Canada and in Ireland to send laborers when needed. Flint, *op. cit.,* p. 195.

12. *American Railway Review,* Jan. 23, 1862.

13. *1st Annual Report,* p. 12; *American Railroad Journal,* Jan. 21, 1863, July 9, 1864; see also Flint, *op. cit.,* p. 195.

14. *1st Annual Report,* p. 18. Another branch, from Meadville to Oil City, finished June 1, 1863, brought coal to the line. *American Railroad Journal,* July 9, 1864.

15. *United States Railroad and Mining Register,* Feb. 7, 1863 (from Meadville *Republican*); *American Railroad Journal,* Jan. 31, 1863.

16. *American Railroad Journal,* May 2, 1863, Aug. 6, 1864.

17. *1st Annual Report,* pp. 15, 17.

18. The line had a contract with the Erie Railway as of May 1, 1863 (*1st Annual Report,* p. 30; *3rd Annual Report of the Erie Railway 1864,* p. 14; the petroleum carried was only one third of the total production (*1st Annual Report,* pp. 16, 19). Not much oil went out by water because the Allegheny River above Franklin was dangerous to navigation (Patrick Barry, *Over The Atlantic and Great Western Railway,* pp. 32-33.)

19. *American Railroad Journal,* July 9, 1864; *1st Annual Report,* p. 22.

20. *1st Annual Report,* pp. 19-21.

21. *2nd Annual Report, 1864,* p. 11. McHenry was deeply involved financially. Much of the floating debt of between $400,000 and $500,000 was in his hands; with cash advanced and bond coupons, the road's debt to him totaled over $1,000,000. The line

paid tribute to McHenry for furnishing this capital, and to Kennard for effectively overcoming the handicap of labor and materials scarcity. *Ibid.*, pp. 5-6, 8, 20.

22. *American Railroad Journal*, Jan. 16, 1864; *1st Annual Report,* p. 12. The line from Salamanca to Galion is now part of the main New York to Chicago route of the Erie Railway.

23. *1st Annual Report*, p. 41.

24. *Ibid.*, pp. 43-44 (letter from Kennard to Reynolds, April 6, 1864).

25. *American Railroad Journal*, June 25, July 9, 1864.

26. *Ibid.*, Sept. 3, 1864.

27. Peto, *op. cit.*, p. 294.

28. July 2, 1864; 60-pound rail was later substituted. The road originally was not well ballasted, and many cuts and embankments were too narrow. Flint, *op. cit.*, pp. 199-200.

29. *1st Annual Report*, p. 13.

30. *Ibid.*, pp. 13-14. By April 1864, four engines a month were being completed. *Ibid.*, pp. 43-44.

31. *Ibid.*, pp. 43-44.

32. *2nd Annual Report*, p. 14.

33. *Ibid.*, pp. 28-29.

34. Barry, *op. cit.*, pp. 62-64, 66-67. The change was necessary because the Ohio and Mississippi was controlled by the Little Miami Railroad.

35. *Ibid.*, pp. 80-81, 110, 112. This same observer thought the railroad lost much trade through lack of a connection at Buffalo, subsequently corrected when the Erie, with its Buffalo branch, came to control the Atlantic and Great Western. *Ibid.*, 100-101.

36. *American Railway Review*, Feb. 20, 1862.

37. April 27, 1861.

38. *7th Annual Report . . . of the Northern Central Railway . . . 1861*, pp. 55-56; *8th Annual Report . . . 1862*, p. 37.

39. *8th Annual Report . . . of the Northern Central Railway . . . 1862*, pp. 4-5. The cars were to be delivered beginning in Jan., 1863. *Ibid.*, p. 2.

40. *16th Annual Report . . . of the Pennsylvania Railroad . . . 1862*, p. 9. Both the Philadelphia and Erie and the Northern Central are now part of the Pennsylvania.

41. Poor, *op. cit.*, p. 233; *American Railroad Journal*, Feb. 21, 1863.

42. *17th Annual Report . . . of the Pennsylvania Railroad . . . 1863*, p. 8; *American Railroad Journal*, July 9, 1864.

43. *American Railroad Journal*, Sept. 3, Oct. 8, 1864.

44. *17th Annual Report . . . of the Pennsylvania Railroad . . . 1863*, pp. 11, 24; *18th Annual Report . . . 1864*, pp. 18-20.

45. *18th Annual Report . . . of the Pennsylvania Railroad . . . 1864*, p. 5.

46. *19th Annual Report . . . of the Pennsylvania Railroad . . . 1865*, pp. 13, 21. A disastrous flood in March after heavy winter snows did much damage along the line. *Ibid.*, pp. 113, 117.

47. Fite, *op. cit.*, p. 60.

48. *American Railroad Journal*, May 14, 28, 1864.

49. *Ibid.*, Feb. 11, March 11, 1865.

50. *American Railroad Journal*, March 19, 1864. See Chapter VI.

51. See Chapter VIII.

52. Flint, *op. cit.*, p. 224.

53. Fish, "The Northern Railroads 1861," *American Historical Review*, XXII, 779-80.

54. F. H. Hodder, "Railroad Background of the Kansas-Nebraska Act," *Mississippi Valley Historical Review*, XII, 3 ff.

55. Grenville M. Dodge, *How We Built the Union Pacific Railway*, p. 10.

56. *Ibid.*, pp. 9-10.

57. *Congressional Globe*, 36th Cong., 2nd Sess., Jan. 5, 1861, p. 252.

58. *Ibid.*, p. 253.

59. *Ibid.*, p. 255.

60. *Congressional Globe*, 37th Cong., 2nd Sess., Part 2, April 19, 1862, p. 1590. This Bill was only slightly different from the Curtis bill, See speech of Representative Campbell (Pa.), *Ibid.*, p. 1579. A foreign war with Great Britain seemed much closer to reality after the *Trent* affair in Nov., 1861.

61. *Ibid.*, 1594, 1579 (the latter Apr. 8, 1862).

62. *Ibid.*, p. 1594. The military necessity argument was of course not the only one advanced in favor of a Pacific railroad. Others pointed to the development of commerce on the Pacific ocean, and

to the agricultural development of the West. See *American Railroad Journal*, Jan. 3, 1863, Jan. 7, 1865. The one argument is emphasized here to show that the government was aware of the military importance of railroads.

63. Nelson Trottman, *History of the Union Pacific*, pp. 8-9.

64. *Congressional Globe*, 37th Cong., 2nd Sess., Part 3, pp. 1971, 2840, 3088; Dodge, *op. cit.*, p. 9.

65. Dodge, *op. cit.*, pp. 11-12; New York *Times* (supplement), March 12, 1864; *American Railway Journal*, Feb. 7, March 7, 1863.

66. Dodge, *op. cit.*, pp. 13, 45, 48. The important work of Dodge did not begin until 1866, when he took the place of chief engineer Peter A. Dey, who had resigned. By the end of the war, the eastern connection of the U.P., the Cedar Rapids and Missouri Railroad, had reached only as far as Boonesboro, Iowa, about 130 miles east of Omaha. *Merchants' Magazine and Commercial Review*, LIII (July-Dec., 1865), 440.

67. *American Railroad Journal*, Dec. 31, 1864; New York *Times*, April 2, 1865.

CHAPTER III

1. Edwin A. Pratt, *The Rise of Rail Power in War and Conquest, 1833-1914*, p. 9; *Army and Navy Journal*, June 11, 1864, April 15, 1865. The use of armored trains for combat and reconnaissance was known somewhat earlier. Charles R. Kutz, *War on Wheels, the Evolution of an Idea*, p. 193.

2. Robert E. Riegel, "Federal Operation of Southern Railroads during the Civil War," *Mississippi Valley Historical Review*, IX, 126.

3. Carl R. Fish, "The Northern Railroads 1861," *American Historical Review*, XXII, 779-80; Carl R. Fish, *The American Civil War*, p. 155. This same argument was used in support of the act of Jan. 31, 1862, authorizing the president to take military possession of the railroads. See Chapter VII.

4. Fish, "The Northern Railroads, 1861," *American Historical Review*, XXII, 782. McClellan already had some railroad experience, having been previously connected with the Ohio and Mississippi Railroad.

5. McClellan to Stanton, 1861 (undated), Stanton Papers, Vol. I.

6. Lincoln to McClellan, Feb. 3, 1863, Stanton Papers, Vol. III.

7. George William Brown, *Baltimore and the 19th of April 1861,* p. 14.

8. *Ibid.,* p. 15.

9. *Ibid.* Winnifred K. Mackay, "Philadelphia during the Civil War 1861-1865," *Pennsylvania Magazine of History and Biography,* (Jan., 1946), p. 14.

10. Brown, *op. cit.,* p. 17.

11. *Ibid.,* p. 133.

12. Frank H. Taylor, *Philadelphia in the Civil War 1861-1865,* pp. 15-16.

13. J. Thomas Scharf, *History of Baltimore City and County from the Earliest Period to the Present Day,* p. 336.

14. *Dictionary of American Biography,* VII, 163-64.

15. In a speech after John Brown's raid at Harper's Ferry. Festus P. Summers, *The Baltimore and Ohio in the Civil War,* p. 45.

16. *Ibid.,* pp. 47-48. See also *35th Annual Report . . . of the Baltimore and Ohio Railroad . . . 1861,* p. 6.

17. Summers, *op. cit.,* pp. 49-50; *American Railroad Journal,* Aug. 16, 1862 (from Baltimore *American*).

18. *The War of the Rebellion, a Compilation of the Official Records of the Union and Confederate Armies* (hereinafter cited as *Official Records*), Ser. III, I, 84. The secession of Virginia was a contributing factor in Garrett's action. Samuel R. Kamm, *The Civil War Career of Thomas Scott,* p. 25. That it was simply inability to render service and not disloyalty on Garrett's part was emphasized by the Baltimore *American,* quoted in *American Railroad Journal,* Aug. 16, 1862. On the other hand, Thomas A. Scott, citing Dennison's telegram and the failure of the B & O to provide decent transportation between Baltimore and Washington, pointed out that a mass meeting of Baltimore citizens on July 28, 1862, had claimed that the controlling authority and a majority of employees of the B & O were disloyal. *United States Railroad and Mining Register,* Aug. 23, 1862, quoting Scott's letter of Aug. 15 to the New York *Times.* Since the activities of Garrett during the war and the loyal service performed by the B & O show overwhelmingly that the railroad was not disloyal, one must ascribe Scott's attitude to the hostility be-

tween the Pennsylvania Railroad and the B & O. This was probably a deeper basis of antipathy than the sharing of Cameron's views pointed out by Kamm, *op. cit., passim.*

19. Brown, *op. cit.,* pp. 40-41.

20. The following account of the Baltimore riot of April 19 is based on Scharf, *op. cit.,* pp. 788-90, and Brown, *op. cit.,* pp. 43-53.

21. *Dictionary of American Biography,* VI, 507-8; Henry G. Pearson, *An American Railroad Builder, John Murray Forbes,* p. 115.

22. The Washington Brigade had left Philadelphia first, at 3 A.M. on the 19th. It was supposed to go through Baltimore at dawn, but the railroad schedule was delayed. Taylor, *op. cit.,* pp. 28-29. If the schedule had been adhered to, perhaps there would have been no riot that day.

23. John G. Nicolay and John Hay, *Abraham Lincoln, a History,* IV, 111.

24. *Official Records,* Ser. I, II, 9-11 (Report of the Baltimore Police Commissioner to the State Legislature, May 3, 1861).

25. Baltimore *Sun,* April 20, 1861, quoted in Nicolay and Hay, *op. cit.,* p. 113.

26. One of the civilians killed was Robert W. Davis, a prominent dry goods merchant. Brown, *op. cit.,* p. 52.

27. Quoted in Scharf, *op. cit.,* p. 791.

28. *Ibid.*

29. *Official Records,* Ser. I, II, 12-13.

30. *Ibid.,* p. 578.

31. Summers, *op. cit.,* p. 56. The Wheeling *Intelligencer* suggested that Garrett turn over his road to the government to prevent Letcher from transporting troops. *American Railway Review,* May 9, 1861.

32. Account taken from Scharf, *op. cit.,* p. 130.

33. Scott to Stanton, Feb., 1862, Stanton Papers, Vol. IV.

34. *United States Railroad and Mining Register,* April 27, 1861, said 60 bridges were destroyed, the largest being 338' long. One of the parties was led by I. R. Trimble, former superintendent of the Philadelphia, Wilmington and Baltimore, who later became a Confederate major general and was captured at Gettysburg. *24th Annual Report of the Philadelphia, Wilmington and Baltimore Rail-*

road . . . 1861, p. 7; Edward McPherson, *The Political History of the United States of America during the Great Rebellion*, p. 393.

35. Extracts from minutes of the Baltimore Police Commissioners, in McPherson, *op. cit.*, pp. 393-94.

36. *7th Annual Report . . . of the Northern Central Railway . . . 1861*, p. 10.

37. *Ibid.*, pp. 35, 37.

38. *24th Annual Report . . . of the Philadelphia, Wilmington and Baltimore Railroad . . . 1861*, p. 7.

39. *Official Records*, Ser. I, II, 582.

40. Scharf, *op. cit.*, p. 130; Nicolay and Hay, *op. cit.*, pp. 131-32; *Official Records*, Ser. I, II, 584.

41. Correspondence between Patterson and Scott, *Official Records*, Ser. I, II, 585-87; Lincoln's letter to Gov. Hicks and Mayor Brown, April 20, 1861, quoted in Clayton C. Hall, ed., *Baltimore, Its History and Its People*, I, 178-79. Fitz John Porter "would march them to the National Capital through Baltimore or over its ashes." See Alexander K. McClure, *Old Time Notes of Pennsylvania*, p. 474.

42. Correspondence between Cameron, Thomson, and Felton, *Official Records*, Ser. I, II, 596-98.

43. Samuel R. Kamm, *The Civil War Career of Thomas A. Scott*, p. 31.

44. *Official Records*, Ser. I, II, 603. Cameron's views were governed by his position as a director of the Northern Central.

45. *Dictionary of American Biography*, XVI, 500-501.

46. William B. Wilson, *History of the Pennsylvania Railroad Company*, I, 416.

47. Stanton to Vice-President Hamlin, Jan. 27, 1862, *Stanton Papers*, Vol. II.

48. *Official Records*, Ser. I, II, 609. Felton took some credit for this new route, having suggested it to Winfield Scott as early as Oct., 1860 (Kamm, *op. cit.*, p. 28). Said the 24th Annual Report of the Philadelphia, Wilmington and Baltimore (p. 7), "The road has thus earned, if it has not received, the grateful remembrances of the government. Though a corporation, it did not forget its duties to the country. . . . It expended its money, its resources, and the energies of all its employees, at a time when the fate of the country seemed trembling in the balance."

49. Kamm, *op. cit.*, p. 36; Burton J. Hendrick, *The Life of Andrew Carnegie*, p. 106.

50. *Official Records*, Ser. I, II, 635-36; Hall, *op. cit.*, pp. 183-85; *American Railroad Journal*, May 18, 1861.

51. Hendrick, *op. cit.*, p. 106.

52. *Dictionary of American Biography*, III, 499-505.

53. Hendrick, *op. cit.*, pp. 106-9.

54. *Official Records*, Ser. III, I, 228.

55. Stanton to Vice-President Hamlin, Jan. 27, 1862, *Stanton Papers*, Vol. II.

56. Slason Thompson, *A Short History of American Railways*, p. 153; H. W. Schotter, *The Growth and Development of the Pennsylvania Railroad Company*, p. 54.

57. Scott's letter of Aug. 21, 1861, to the President and the Board of Directors of the Pennsylvania Railroad is quoted in Schotter, *op. cit.*, pp. 55-56.

58. Wilson, *op. cit.*, II, 244-45.

59. Kamm, *op. cit.*, pp. 9-11.

60. *Official Records*, Ser. III, I, 673-75.

61. See Chapter X.

62. *Official Records*, Ser. I, LII, 704; *In Memoriam—General Lewis Baldwin Parsons*, p. 19; Memo of Transportation Department, Feb. 9, 1862, in *Stanton Papers*, Vol. II.

63. *In Memoriam, General Lewis Baldwin Parsons*, pp. 17-18.

64.' *Official Records*, Ser. I, LII, 704-5.

65. *Ibid.*, Ser. III, III, 398-99.

66. *Official Records*, Ser. III, III, 399.

67. See Chapter VII.

68. C. W. Ramsdell, "The Confederate Government and the Railroads," *American Historical Review*, XXII, 795, 799, 807.

69. Lincoln's awareness of the railroad's importance in war was demonstrated in his request of December, 1861, that a railroad be constructed from Kentucky to the loyal areas of Tennessee and western North Carolina to cement these border areas to the Union. The proposed road was never built, largely because of the opposition of Scott and the adequate capacity of other lines. Lewis H. Haney, *A Congressional History of Railways in the United States, 1850-1877*, p. 157; James D. Richardson, *A Compilation of Messages and Papers of the Presidents, 1789-1907*, VI, 46.

CHAPTER IV

1. *American Railroad Journal,* June 1, 1861, quoting *Railroaa Record.* See also *American Railway Review,* April 18, 1861.

2. The *Review* noted that railway passenger traffic was down, and new construction was stopped by the war. See also *American Railroad Journal,* Jan., 1862.

3. New York *Times,* June 8, 1863, noted that the war was good for the railroads because it enabled them to get rid of their floating debts. See also *Merchants' Magazine and Commercial Review,* LIII (July-Dec., 1865), 177. The Erie Railway reduced its 1861 debt of $2,725,600 to zero in 1863. The detailed comparisons in this and the following two chapters of statistics taken from the railroads' annual reports are limited in value by the fact that no standard methods of accounting existed. Information included in annual reports varied considerably among the companies, making comparison difficult. Even information presented is sometimes incomplete. For instance, it is not always clear to what extent increases in revenue were due to rising rates or to rising tonnage. Items like gross income, net income, and operating ratio were determined differently by different railroads. In addition, fiscal years did not coincide for the companies (see bibliography). Even with these handicaps, however, the general effect of the war on railroad business is clear.

4. Actually, the tide had begun to turn before the war began. Of ten roads centering in Chicago, nine showed increased receipts in 1860 over 1859. *Merchants' Magazine and Commercial Review,* XLIV (Jan.-June, 1861), 537. Grain receipts and shipments at Chicago in 1860 totaled 60,000,000 bushels, more than double 1859. *Ibid.,* pp. 352-53.

5. The shortage was sometimes aggravated by the practice of using cars as warehouses. *American Railway Review,* July 4, 1861, Jan. 23, 1862.

6. *Merchants' Magazine and Commercial Review,* LIII, (July-Dec. 1865), 207. Profits of the Hudson River RR and the Cleveland and Pittsburgh more than doubled in this period. *Ibid.,* pp. 180-81, 207.

7. *Merchants' Magazine and Commercial Review,* LII, (Jan.-

June 1865), 137. An especially bad wreck killed almost 50 soldiers on the Philadelphia and Trenton Railroad. *New York Sun, March 9, 1865,* quoted in Emerson D. Fite, *Social and Industrial Conditions in the North during the Civil War,* pp. 74-75. In general railroads had a good safety record up to 1860. The B & O carried 5,000,000 passengers in eight years with no fatalities. New York railroads in 1860 traveled 35,000,000 miles for each passenger killed. *American Railway Review,* May 23, 1861.

8. *Report . . . of the Boston and Maine Railroad . . . Sept. 11, 1861,* p. 3; *ibid., 1862,* p. 3.

9. *Report . . . of the Boston and Maine Railroad . . . 1862,* p. 3.

10. *Ibid.,* p. 8.

11. *Report . . . 1863,* pp. 3-4.

12. *Ibid.,* pp. 4-5. The B & M shared control of this line with the Eastern Railroad. In 1863 the branch alone carried 14,000 troops, and could not find enough freight cars to meet the demand for their services. *23rd Annual Report . . . Portland, Saco, and Portsmouth Railroad,* pp. 6, 8; *26th Annual Report,* p. 12.

13. *Report . . . of the Boston and Maine Railroad . . . 1864,* p. 3; *Ibid., 1865,* p. 1.

14. *Report . . . of the Boston and Maine Railroad . . . 1863,* p. 19; *1864,* p. 19; *1865,* p. 19.

15. $13,800 to $37,500. *Ibid., 1864,* p. 4.

16. *Ibid., 1865,* p. 1.

17. For all prices, see *ibid.,* pp. 2-3.

18. Each a steady increase from 1,600,000 passengers and 193,-000 tons of freight in 1861. See the various annual reports.

19. *32nd Annual Report . . . of the Boston and Worcester Railroad . . . Nov. 30, 1861,* p. 3.

20. *Ibid.,* p. 3; *1862,* pp. 3-4.

21. *Ibid., 1862,* p. 4.

22. *Ibid., 1863,* pp. 4-5; *1864,* pp. 4, 11. Most of the freight was interchanged with the Western Railroad at Worcester. Six to ten freight trains left Boston daily, and 31 passenger trains. *Ibid., 1864,* p. 11.

23. *Ibid., 1862,* p. 4; *1865,* p. 4.

24. *Ibid., 1864,* p. 5. By 1865 it was 2.052 cents.

25. *Ibid.,* pp. 3, 8; *1865,* p. 5.

26. *Ibid., 1865,* pp. 3, 4.

27. *27th Annual Report . . . of the Western Railroad . . . Jan. 1862,* pp. 13, 3.

28. *Ibid.,* p. 21.

29. *29th Annual Report . . . of the Western Railroad . . . 1864,* p. 5.

30. *Ibid.,* p. 3.

31. *Ibid.,* pp. 5-6.

32. *31st Annual Report . . . of the Western Railroad . . . 1866,* pp. 3, 9.

33. A shore line did exist, however, via the New Haven and New London, the Stonington Railroad to Providence, and the Boston and Providence. All of these lines with the exception of the Boston and Worcester, now make up the New York, New Haven, and Hartford Railroad.

34. *New York and New Haven Annual Report . . . March 31, 1862,* pp. 6, 20.

35. *Ibid.,* p. 7.

36. *Ibid.*

37. *Annual Report . . . May 21, 1863,* pp. 6-7, 12.

38. *Ibid.,* pp. 8, 13.

39. *Annual Report . . . May 19, 1864,* pp. 4, 9.

40. *Ibid.,* p. 14.

41. *Ibid.,* pp. 9-10.

42. *Ibid.,* pp. 10-11.

43. *Annual Report . . . May 18, 1865,* pp. 4-6; 1,800,000 passengers were carried.

44. *Ibid.,* p. 10. A passenger train was added in May, 1864.

45. These lines are now all part of the Pennsylvania Railroad.

46. *7th Annual Report . . . of the Northern Central Railway, 1861,* pp. 28, 11.

47. *8th Annual Report . . . 1862,* p. 20.

48. *Ibid.,* pp. 4-5.

49. *7th Annual Report . . . 1861,* p. 56.

50. *Ibid.,* p. 34.

51. *Ibid.,* pp. 50, 53.

52. *Ibid.,* p. 54.

53. *Ibid.,* p. 12; *8th Annual Report . . . 1862,* p. 17.

NOTES: CHAPTER IV

251

54. *8th Annual Report . . . 1862*, p. 17.

55. *Ibid.*, p. 21.

56. *Ibid.*, pp. 55-56.

57. *7th Annual Report . . . 1861*, pp. 31-32.

58. *8th Annual Report . . . 1862*, p. 37. The Reading, finding that its tracks were not far enough apart to accommodate heavy passenger traffic, had to move its rails in 1862. A. K. McClure, *Old Time Notes of Pennsylvania*, p. 158.

59. *8th Annual Report . . . 1862*, p. 22.

60. *9th Annual Report . . . 1863*, p. 10.

61. *Ibid.*, p. 9.

62. *Ibid.*, pp. 13-14, 30-31. The traffic agreement with the Erie was cancelled in 1865, because of the Erie's inconvenient six-foot gauge. An agreement with the Canandaigua Railroad was substituted. *11th Annual Report . . . 1865*, p. 11.

63. *9th Annual Report . . . 1863*, pp. 11, 14.

64. *Ibid.*, pp. 10-11.

65. *Ibid.*, p. 25.

66. The following account is based on *9th Annual Report . . . 1863*, pp. 31-32.

67. *Ibid.*, pp. 32, 66.

68. *10th Annual Report . . . 1864*, pp. 7-8.

69. *Ibid.*, p. 9.

70. *Ibid.*, pp. 7, 9-10. Compare the experience of the Michigan Central Railroad, Chapter VI. Troops moved in 1864 were more than twice the number in 1863. *Ibid.*, p. 22. Coal was its chief item of transport, being almost one-third the total freight of 1862. *8th Annual Report . . . 1862*, p. 19.

71. *10th Annual Report . . . 1864*, p. 24.

72. *Ibid.*, p. 41.

73. *Ibid.*, pp. 24, 43.

74. *11th Annual Report . . . 1865*, pp. 9, 20.

75. *Ibid.*, pp. 20-21.

76. *24th Annual Report . . . Oct. 31, 1861*, p. 11; Charles E. Fisher, "The Philadelphia, Wilmington, and Baltimore Railroad Company," *Bulletin 21, Railway and Locomotive Historical Society*, Mar., 1930, p. 22.

77. *24th Annual Report . . . Oct. 31, 1861*, p. 11.

78. *Ibid.*, pp. 5, 19.

79. *25th Annual Report . . . Oct. 31, 1862,* pp. 5, 6; Fisher, *op. cit.*, p. 24.

80. Mary A. Livermore, *My Story of the War,* pp. 241-42.

81. *25th Annual Report . . . Oct. 31, 1862,* p. 6.

82. *24th Annual Report . . . Oct. 31, 1861,* p. 11.

83. Fisher, *op. cit.*, p. 17.

84. *25th Annual Report . . . Oct. 31, 1862,* p. 13.

85. Fisher, *op. cit.*, pp. 21-22. Other railroads did not find so great a difference between the cost of the two fuels.

86. *25th Annual Report . . . Oct. 31, 1862,* p. 15; *26th Annual Report . . . Oct. 31, 1863,* p. 11.

87. *25th Annual Report . . . Oct. 31, 1862,* p. 18. A 9 per cent dividend was paid in 1862.

88. *26th Annual Report . . . Oct. 31, 1863,* pp. 6, 8.

89. *25th Annual Report . . . Oct. 31, 1862,* pp. 16-17.

90. *26th Annual Report . . . Oct. 31, 1863,* p. 9.

91. Second track between the Susquehanna River and Baltimore laid in 1864 cost $3,000 a mile. *American Railway Times,* July 23, 1864.

92. *26th Annual Report . . . Oct. 31, 1863,* pp. 10, 11, 14.

93. *Ibid.*, p. 14.

94. *Ibid.*, pp. 16-17.

95. *Ibid.*, p. 11.

96. *27th Annual Report . . . Oct. 31, 1864,* pp. 4-5; Fisher, *op. cit.*, p. 25.

97. $1,960,649.46 to $2,882,979.46.

98. *28th Annual Report . . . Oct. 31, 1865,* p. 7; Fisher, *op. cit.*, p. 34.

99. *Official Records,* Ser. III, V, 303-4, memo of Quartermaster General Meigs. The Northern Central got a good percentage of the westbound traffic.

CHAPTER V

1. *American Railway Review,* Jan. 31, 1861; *Merchants' Magazine and Commercial Review,* LIII (July-Dec. 1865), 176, 177; George W. Stephens, "Some Aspects of Early Intersectional Rivalry

for the Commerce of the Upper Mississippi Valley," *Washington University Studies*, X, No. 2, 296-97.

2. Emerson D. Fite, "The Agricultural Development of the West During the Civil War," *Quarterly Journal of Economics*, XX (Feb. 1906), 261.

3. Fite, *op. cit.*, pp. 264-65; *Merchants' Magazine and Commercial Review*, XLVI (Jan.-June, 1862), 449.

4. Fite, *op. cit.*, p. 260. *Merchants' Magazine and Commercial Review*, XLIV (Jan.-June 1861), 352-53; XLVI (Jan.-June 1862), 363.

5. At Toledo, most grain receipts arrived by rail, and were shipped by water. In 1861, Toledo received 9,000,000 bushels by rail, 1,500,-000 by water; the city shipped only 500,000 bushels east by rail, the rest by water. *Merchants' Magazine and Commercial Review*, XLV (July-Dec. 1861), 573; XLVI (Jan.-June 1862), 367. The *American Railroad Journal* (Sept. 7, 1861) thought the Toledo and Wabash Railroad grain storage facilities were among the best in the West. In New York State in 1861, the Erie Canal carried 4,500,000 tons of freight, mostly lumber and vegetable foods, while the railroads carried 5,500,000 tons in animal products, manufactures, merchandise, and vegetable foods. Most railroad tonnage was transported by the Erie and the New York Central. *Merchants' Magazine and Commercial Review*, XLVII (July-Dec. 1862), 84.

6. *15th Annual Report . . . of the Pennsylvania Railroad . . . Feb. 3, 1862*, pp. 3-4.

7. *Ibid.*, pp. 4-5.

8. *Ibid.*, p. 5.

9. *Ibid.*, pp. 86, 89.

10. *Ibid.*, p. 12. ·

11. *Ibid.*, pp. 5, 7.

12. *Ibid.*, p. 21.

13. *American Railway Review*, May 2, 1861.

14. *15th Annual Report . . . of the Pennsylvania Railroad . . . Feb. 3, 1862*, pp. 78, 22, 30.

15. *Ibid.*, pp. 22, 34.

16. *16th Annual Report . . . of the Pennsylvania Railroad . . . Feb. 2, 1863*, pp. 3, 17; *American Railroad Journal*, April 11, 1863.

17. *16th Annual Report . . . Feb. 3, 1863*, pp. 19, 20.

18. *Ibid.*, p. 4.

19. *Ibid.*, p. 10.

20. *Ibid.*, p. 15. As early as the fall of 1861, the PRR established a temporary embargo on through freight to New York, Boston, and Baltimore because of inadequate rolling stock. *American Railroad Journal,* Oct. 5, 1861. Extra high rates were also used to discourage business. *Ibid.,* Oct. 26, 1861.

21. *16th Annual Report . . . Feb. 2, 1863,* pp. 23-24, 29.

22. *Ibid.,* p. 27.

23. *Ibid.,* pp. 30-31.

24. *Ibid.,* p. 33.

25. *17th Annual Report . . . Feb. 16, 1864,* pp. 5-6.

26. *Ibid.,* pp. 6-7.

27. *Ibid.,* p. 10. The latter had been authorized the year before to shorten by 24 miles the Pittsburgh-Cincinnati line (1862 report, p. 12).

28. *Ibid.,* pp. 8, 12.

29. William B. Wilson, *History of the Pennsylvania Railroad Company,* I, 411.

30. *Ibid.,* p. 412.

31. *17th Annual Report . . . Feb. 16, 1864,* pp. 41 ff.

32. Henry M. Flint, *The Railroads of the United States,* pp. 122-23. Fish plates, small pieces of iron to join rail ends securely together, were not used during the Civil War period. Sir Samuel Morton Peto, *The Resources and Prospects of America Ascertained during a Visit to the States in the Autumn of 1865,* p. 275.

33. *17th Annual Report . . . Feb. 16, 1864,* pp. 12-13.

34. *Ibid.,* p. 13. At this time steel rail was estimated by the *American Railway Times* to cost $112 a ton Bessemer process. Iron rail sold at inflated prices in later years of the war, but in 1863 cost about $58 a ton. *Merchants' Magazine and Commercial Review,* XLVII (July-Dec. 1862), 442-43; *3rd Annual Report . . . of the Erie Railway . . . 1864,* p. 8.

35. *17th Annual Report . . . Feb. 16, 1864,* p. 37.

36. *Ibid.,* p. 19.

37. Wilson, *op. cit.,* pp. 413-15. Thomas A. Scott had charge of these parties, and communicated their information through Gov. Curtin to Washington. See also McClure, *op. cit.,* II, 100.

38. *17th Annual Report . . . Feb. 16, 1864,* pp. 24, 33, 37.

39. *Ibid.,* p. 16.

40. *18th Annual Report . . . Feb. 21, 1865,* pp. 1-3.

41. *Ibid.,* p. 3. About 1,000,000 tons of coal were moved.

42. *Ibid.,* pp. 6-7, 11.

43. *Ibid.,* pp. 11, 39. Using rails with steel wearing surfaces did not prove successful on a large scale.

44. *Ibid.,* pp. 28, 29. Steel tires, established on European railways, were introduced in the United States on the Atlantic and Great Western, and the Buffalo and State Line Railroads. *American Railroad Journal,* Dec. 27, 1862.

45. *19th Annual Report . . . 1866,* p. 9.

46. *Ibid.,* pp. 18-19, 22.

47. *American Railroad Journal,* April 27, 1861 (from Pittsburgh *Post*).

48. *5th Annual Report of the Pittsburgh, Ft. Wayne, and Chicago Railroad Company . . . Dec. 31, 1861,* p. 14.

49. *Ibid.,* pp. 16, 18.

50. *Ibid.,* pp. 19, 32, 42, 52.

51. *1st Annual Report . . . of the Pittsburgh, Ft. Wayne, and Chicago Railway Company . . . Dec. 31, 1862,* pp. 3, 30, 35-6.

52. *Ibid.,* p. 58.

53. *Ibid.,* p. 62.

54. *Ibid.,* p. 79.

55. *American Railway Review,* June 5, 1862.

56. *2nd Annual Report . . . Dec. 31, 1863,* pp. 8, 11.

57. *3rd Annual Report . . . Dec. 31, 1864,* pp. 7-8.

58. *Ibid.,* p. 10. Of course this decrease was not because the army was shrinking, but because it had other sources of supply in 1864. The directors felt that the maximum through traffic had been reached because Eastern roads could not carry off all the business offered at Pittsburgh. *Ibid.,* p. 16.

59. *Ibid.,* pp. 9, 10.

60. *Ibid.,* p. 11.

61. *Ibid.,* p. 12.

62. *Ibid.,* p. 13.

63. *Ibid.,* pp. 14-15.

64. *Ibid.,* pp. 32-33.

65. *Ibid.*, p. 37. This interdependence usually meant that cars of one railroad were freely used on other roads, provided their gauges did not prevent such use. Railroads did not keep track of where their cars were, and hence frequently did not have available all the rolling stock which they owned. See the article entitled, "Railroad Cars Astray," in *United States Railroad and Mining Register*, Dec. 14, 1861.

66. *4th Annual Report . . . Dec. 31, 1865*, pp. 7, 9.

67. *Ibid.*, p. 9. But local tonnage was up 8 per cent. *Ibid.*, p. 17.

68. *Ibid.*, p. 11. The iron lasted only three to five years.

69. *Ibid.*, pp. 17-18.

70. *American Railway Times*, March 19, 1864.

71. *1st Annual Report of the Erie Railway Company . . . Dec. 31, 1862*, p. 6.

72. *Ibid.*, p. 9.

73. Flint, *op. cit.*, p. 183.

74. *1st Annual Report . . . Dec. 31, 1862*, pp. 12-14.

75. *Ibid.*, pp. 15, 16.

76. *Ibid.*, pp. 15, 17.

77. *Ibid.*, p. 31. Origins of these shipments is another illustration of the interdependence of the railroads.

78. *2nd Annual Report . . . Dec. 31, 1863*, pp. 6-7.

79. *Ibid.*, pp. 8-9, 11.

80. *Ibid.*, p. 16.

81. *Ibid.*, pp. 11, 13.

82. *Ibid.*, pp. 12, 13, 16. Seventeen locomotives and 257 cars were added to the rolling stock in 1863. Flint, *op. cit.*, p. 183.

83. *2nd Annual Report . . . Dec. 31, 1863*, p. 17.

84. *3rd Annual Report . . . Dec. 31, 1864*, p. 5.

85. *Ibid.*, p. 8. This was typical. The Milwaukee and Prairie du Chien Railroad paid $115 in 1865. *5th Annual Report of the Milwaukee and Prairie du Chien Railway . . . 1865*, p. 30.

86. *3rd Annual Report . . . Dec. 31, 1864*, p. 15.

87. *Ibid.*, p. 13.

88. *Ibid.*, p. 14.

89. *4th Annual Report . . . Dec. 31, 1865*, pp. 5-7.

90. *Ibid.*, pp. 8, 14.

91. *Ibid.*, p. 13.

92. *Annual Report of the New York Central Railroad . . . for the year ending Sept. 30, 1861 . . . to the State Engineer and Surveyor of the State of New York,* p. 25. The road used the railroad bridge at Troy to carry cars to and from the Hudson River Railroad. *American Railway Review,* April 4, 1861.

93. Quoted in *American Railroad Journal,* May 4, 1861.

94. *Ibid.,* May 25, 1861.

95. *Ibid.,* Nov. 16, 1861 (from Albany *Atlas*).

96. *Ibid.*

97. *Annual Report of the New York Central . . . Sept. 30, 1862,* p. 21.

98. *Ibid.,* p. 23; 1861 report, p. 23.

99. The Rochester–New York flour rate was raised from 20 cents to 90 cents a barrel. This was one method of keeping tonnage from becoming too large for the rolling stock. *American Railroad Journal,* Oct. 26, 1861.

100. *Annual Report . . . Sept. 30, 1863,* p. 37. For the first time the line's total earnings passed $10,000,000. *Ibid.,* pp. 21, 23, 25.

101. *Annual Report . . . Sept. 30, 1864,* pp. 13, 23.

102. *Annual Report . . . Sept. 31, 1865,* pp. 14, 15, 17, 19, 30.

103. *Merchants' Magazine and Commercial Review,* LII, (Jan.-June, 1865), 349. See also *American Railway Times,* Aug. 8, 1863. Farther west even higher prices prevailed (see Chapter VI).

104. *35th Annual Report . . . of the Baltimore and Ohio . . . 1861,* pp. 27, 35.

105. Sometimes even Union troops gave headaches to the railroad. Some Ohio soldiers retreated from Kearneysville on a freight car which careened down a 10-mile grade almost to Harper's Ferry station, endangering both lives and property. Joseph Barry, *The Strange Story of Harper's Ferry,* pp. 154-56.

106. *35th Annual Report . . . 1861,* pp. 6-7. This report was dated Oct. 1, 1863. All the wartime reports were dated two years after the fiscal year to which they applied. Thus even the administrative machinery of this railroad was adversely affected during the war. It was 1870 before this part of the company was functioning normally.

107. *Official Records,* Ser. I, II, 629; Summers, *op. cit.,* p. 101.

108. Summers, *op. cit.,* pp. 71-88; Edward Hungerford, *The*

Story of the Baltimore and Ohio Railroad, 1827-1927, II, 5-6. This campaign demonstrated the military importance of railroads.

109. E. G. Campbell, "The United States Military Railroads, 1862-1865," *Journal of the American Military History Foundation,* II, 75; *35th Annual Report . . . of the B & O, 1861,* p. 36.

110. Campbell, *op. cit.,* pp. 75-6; Robert U. Johnson and Clarence C. Buel, eds., *Battles and Leaders of the Civil War,* I, 122-23 (John D. Imboden).

111. *35th Annual Report . . . of the B & O . . . 1861,* p. 7.

112. *Ibid.,* pp. 6-7; Hungerford, *op. cit.,* p. 8; Summers, *op. cit.,* pp. 65-67; Barry, *op. cit.,* pp. 120-21. The Harper's Ferry bridge was destroyed and rebuilt nine times during the war. *Ibid.,* p. 160.

113. *35th Annual Report . . . of the B & O . . . 1861,* pp. 13, 30.

114. *Ibid.,* pp. 27, 31. Often main-stem rolling stock was transferred to the Washington Branch to accommodate the heavy traffic there. *Ibid.,* p. 36.

115. *Ibid.,* p. 47.

116. *36th Annual Report . . . Sept. 30, 1862,* pp. 6-7, 10.

117. *Ibid.,* p. 31. The Illinois Central Railroad made the same complaint.

118. *Ibid.,* pp. 30, 6.

119. *Ibid.,* p. 37. Of course both the main stem and the Washington Branch were used in these shipments. The census of 1870 gave Washington a population of 109,199 The 40 per cent increase since 1860 was more rapid than in such cities as Baltimore and Philadelphia. *Ninth Census of the United States, Statistics of Population,* pp. 97, 163, 254.

120. *36th Annual Report . . . Sept. 30, 1862,* pp. 41-42, 44.

121. *Ibid.,* p. 49. Oct. 29, 1862, cooking fires got out of control and burned 23 carloads of hay. *37th Annual Report . . . 1863,* p. 6.

122. *36th Annual Report . . . 1862,* pp. 50-53. Loaded coal cars were sometimes placed on bridges to hold them in place.

123. *Ibid.,* 55-56. Over $140,000 was spent for repair of main-stem bridges during this fiscal year, more than half of it at Harper's Ferry. *Ibid.,* pp. 59-60.

124. *37th Annual Report . . . Sept. 30, 1863,* p. 22.

125. *United States Railroad and Mining Register,* Nov. 29, 1862, (from Baltimore *Sun,* Nov. 26, 1862).

126. *37th Annual Report . . . Sept. 30, 1863*, pp. 45-46.

127. *Ibid.*, pp. 47-52.

128. *Ibid.*, pp. 14, 23. *36th Annual Report . . . 1862*, p. 26.

129. *37th Annual Report . . . 1863*, pp. 62-63.

130. *38th Annual Report . . . Sept. 30, 1864*, p. 52.

131. *Ibid.*, p. 51.

132. *Ibid.*, p. 56.

133. *Ibid.*, p. 62. Regular communication was interrupted for 36 hours. New York *Times*, July 19, 1864.

134. *38th Annual Report . . . 1864*, p. 35. The entire main stem was operated for about nine months of the year.

135. *Ibid.*, p. 45. The report cited the untimely death by sickness of Alexander Diffey, supervisor, during his service in helping to forward Hooker's Corps from Washington to Chattanooga.

136. *37th Annual Report . . . 1863*, p. 6. This particular example was after the Gettysburg campaign.

137. *38th Annual Report . . . 1864*, p. 56. In December, watchmen were established along the line to sound a warning when a raid threatened. *39th Annual Report . . . 1865*, p. 41.

138. *39th Annual Report . . . Sept. 30, 1865*, pp. 21, 25. *United States Railroad and Mining Register*, July 29, 1865. See also Edward Hungerford, *Transport for War*, p. 101.

139. *39th Annual Report . . . 1865*, p. 52.

140. *Address of John W. Garrett to the Board of Directors of the Baltimore and Ohio Railroad Company, Dec. 1868*, p. 9.

141. For a convenient statistical summary, see *Merchants' Magazine and Commercial Review*, LIII, (July-Dec. 1865), 176-181, for railroads in New York, 207 for railroads in Ohio.

CHAPTER VI

1. *Report . . . of the Michigan Central Railroad . . . June 1861*, pp. 8, 19, 23, 32-33.

2. *Ibid.*, pp. 19, 28. Charles E. Fisher, "The Michigan Central Railroad," *Bulletin of Railway and Locomotive Historical Society*, No. 19 (Sept. 1929), p. 18.

3. *Report . . . of the Michigan Central Railroad . . . 1861*, pp. 18-19.

4. *Report . . . of the Michigan Central Railroad . . . 1862*, pp. 7, 20.

5. *Ibid.*, pp. 7, 9.

6. *Ibid.*, p. 21; Fisher, *op. cit.*, p. 19.

7. *Report . . . of the Michigan Central Railroad . . . 1863*, pp. 7-8.

8. Fisher, *op. cit.*, p. 31.

9. *Report . . . of the Michigan Central Railroad . . . 1864*, pp. 7-8.

10. *Ibid.*, pp. 11, 22.

11. *Ibid.*, p. 22.

12. *Ibid.*, pp. 24, 31, 34.

13. *Report . . . of the Michigan Central . . . 1865*, pp. 11, 23. Some of this loss was covered by the gain in local traffic.

14. *Ibid.*, p. 25.

15. *Ibid.*, pp. 11-12, 23. The crowded conditions of freight traffic created long delays. Shipments out of Chicago sometimes took 25 to 40 days to reach Buffalo, *American Railway Review*, March 6, 1862 (from Buffalo *Express*).

16. *Ibid.*, pp. 7-8; Fisher, *op. cit.*, p. 31. The increase of $700,000 in expenses was the highest for a single year. *Report . . . 1866*, p. 43.

17. *Report . . . of the Michigan Central . . . 1864*, p. 8.

18. *Ibid.*, *1865*, pp. 10-11; Fisher, *op. cit.*, p. 21.

19. Fisher, *op. cit.*, p. 31.

20. What was then the Chicago branch is now the main line.

21. *Illinois Central Report . . . 1861*, pp. 1, 5-6. *American Railway Review*, July 4, 1861. One train of 26 cars, pulled by two locomotives, left Chicago to the accompaniment of cheers of thousands of onlookers and whistles of other locomotives. Livermore, *op. cit.*, p. 103.

22. *Illinois Central Railroad Report . . . 1861*, pp. 1-2.

23. *Ibid.*, pp. 2-3.

24. *Ibid.* Military companies of Illinois were transported free to Springfield by the Illinois Central, Chicago and Rock Island, Alton, Chicago, Burlington and Quincy, Galena and Chicago Union, Chicago and North Western, and Chicago and Milwaukee. *American Railway Review*, May 2, 1861. See also Chapter IX.

25. *Illinois Central Railroad Report . . . 1861*, p. 3.

26. *Ninth Census of the United States, Statistics of Population*, pp. 3, 110.

27. *Illinois Central Railroad Report* . . . *1862*, p. 1. Company shops were building 550 freight cars as fast as possible. *Ibid.*, p. 5.

28. *Ibid.*, pp. 2, 12.

29. *Ibid.*, p. 12. Passengers carried one mile: 31,800,000; troops carried one mile: 30,700,000

30. *Ibid.*, p. 5.

31. *Illinois Central Railroad Report* . . . *1863*, pp. 1-2, 5.

32. *Ibid.*, p. 5; *1862 Report*, p. 5.

33. *Ibid.*, p. 12.

34. *Illinois Central Report* . . . *1864*, p. 1. Doing government business at cost or less raised the operating ratio to 54 percent from 46 percent the previous year. *Ibid.*, p. 4.

35. *Ibid.*, p. 5.

36. *3rd Annual Report of the Chicago and North Western Railway Company, June, 1862*, pp. 15, 22-23.

37. *Ibid.*, pp. 2, 7.

38. *4th Annual Report* . . . *1863*, p. 3.

39. *Ibid.*, p. 4.

40. *Ibid.*, pp. 6-7; *3rd Annual Report* . . . *1862*, p. 11. Additions to the rolling stock were hampered by government requisitions for 70 freight cars in 1863. W. H. Stannett, comp., *Yesterday and Today, a History of the Chicago and North Western Railway System*, p. 33.

41. *6th Annual Report* . . . *1865*, p. 29. *Merchants' Magazine and Commercial Review*, LIII, (July-Dec., 1865), 444. The Peninsula Railroad was a land grant road before consolidation with the C & N.W.

42. Flint, *op. cit.*, pp. 262-63.

43. *6th Annual Report* . . . *1865*, map insert.

44. *Ibid.*, p. 41.

45. *Ibid.*, pp. 46-47.

46. *Ibid.*, p. 49; *1862*, p. 25.

47. 1865 report, p. 57. These were wages ($1,000,000), track repairs ($813,000), fuel ($656,000), car repairs ($544,000), and engine repairs ($505,000).

48. *1st Annual Report of the Milwaukee and Prairie du Chien Railway Co., 1861*, p. 11.

49. *Ibid.*, 17, 19.

50. *Ibid.*, pp. 22, 23, 28.

51. *Ibid.*, p. 11.

52. *2nd Annual Report . . . 1862,* p. 7.

53. *Ibid.*, pp. 11, 13, 14.

54. *Ibid.*, p. 14.

55. *4th Annual Report . . . 1864,* p. 6.

56. *Ibid.*, pp. 6, 7. The increase in expenses came chiefly from insurance, fuel, train and station supplies, and oil and waste.

57. *Ibid.*, pp. 20-22, 25, 26.

58. *Ibid.*, p. 27.

59. *Ibid.*, p. 28. Other Western roads had similar experiences. In one year wood rose in price from $3.54 to $5.06 a cord. *Annual Report . . . of the Chicago and Rock Island Railroad Co., April 1, 1865,* p. 12. In 1862, this same line paid $37 a ton for new rail; in 1865, $100 a ton (1862 report, p. 7; 1866 report, p. 16).

60. *4th Annual Report of the Milwaukee and Prairie du Chien Railway . . . 1864,* pp. 30-31.

61. *Ibid.*, p. 34.

62. *Ibid.*, pp. 31-32, 46-47.

63. *Ibid.*, pp. 31-32. The 7 passenger engines and 26 passenger cars in 1864 contrasted with 7 engines and 31 cars in 1861. Other roads were doing the same thing. Passenger business on the Chicago, Burlington, and Quincy Railroad tripled between 1862 and 1865, but the number of passenger cars increased only from 40 to 72. Charles E. Fisher, "The Chicago, Burlington, and Quincy Railroad," *Railway and Locomotive Historical Society Bulletin,* No. 24 (March, 1931), pp. 13, 16, 43.

64. *5th Annual Report . . . 1865,* p. 25. On other Chicago railroads, profits of the Chicago and Rock Island rose from $456,000 in 1860-61 to $1,892,000 in 1864-65; of the Chicago, Burlington, and Quincy from $820,000 in 1861-62 to $2,267,000 in 1864-65. *Merchants' Magazine and Commercial Review,* LIII, (July-Dec., 1865), 280-81, 432.

65. *5th Annual Report . . . 1865,* pp. 27-30. This improving railroad was acquired in 1866 by the Milwaukee and St. Paul, headed by the outstanding Alexander Mitchell. August Derleth, *The Milwaukee Road,* p. 87.

CHAPTER VII

1. Kincaid A. Herr, *The Louisville and Nashville Railroad, 1850-1942*, p. 16; *American Railroad Journal*, Nov. 16, 1861 (from L & N annual Report to June 30, 1861).

2. Herr, *op. cit.*, pp. 16-17. Much of the produce was coming from Ohio farmers. Charles H. Ambler, *A History of Transportation in the Ohio Valley*, p. 246.

3. Herr, *op. cit.*, p. 17.

4. John Leeds Kerr, *The Story of a Southern Carrier, the Louisville and Nashville*, p. 20.

5. Lincoln's plan to build a railroad from Kentucky to Cumberland Gap or Knoxville was opposed by Guthrie as impractical. Samuel R. Kamm, *The Civil War Career of Thomas A. Scott*, p. 95.

6. Herr, *op. cit.*, p. 17; R. S. Cotterill, "The Louisville and Nashville Railroad, 1861-1865," *American Historical Review*, XXIX, 702-3.

7. Herr, *op. cit.*, p. 17; Kerr, *op. cit.*, p. 21. In 1862, the Treasury Dept. issued special licenses for trading with the South. *American Railway Review*, April 3, 1862.

8. *American Railway Review*, May 23, June 20, 1861.

9. Kerr, *op. cit.*, p. 21.

10. Herr, *op. cit.*, p. 17.

11. *United States Railroad and Mining Register*, July 6, 1861.

12. In September, the railroad further suffered the destruction of 11 engines, 11 passenger cars, and 159 freight cars. *American Railroad Journal*, Nov. 16, 1861.

13. The illegal and special trade in the Mississippi Valley is treated, but without special reference to the L & N, by E. M. Coulter, "Commercial Intercourse with the Confederacy in the Mississippi Valley, 1861-1865," *Mississippi Valley Historical Review*, V, 379 ff.

14. *35th Annual Report . . . of the Baltimore and Ohio Railroad . . . Sept. 30, 1861*, pp. 30-31.

15. *Official Records*, Ser. III, I, 121-22.

16. Howard G. Brownson, "History of the Illinois Central Railroad to 1870," *University of Illinois Studies in the Social Sciences*, IV (Sept.-Dec., 1915), 66-67.

17. *Merchants' Magazine and Commercial Review,* XLVI (Jan.-June, 1862), 464.

18. *Illinois Central Railroad Report . . . 1861,* p. 3.

19. *Report . . . of the New Jersey Railroad and Transportation Company, 1861,* pp. 6-7.

20. *Little Miami Railroad Company, and Columbus and Xenia Railroad Company, Ninth Annual Joint Report . . . for the Year 1865,* p. 6.

21. *36th Annual Report . . . of the Baltimore and Ohio Railroad . . . Sept. 30, 1862,* p. 37.

22. *Annual Report . . . of the Michigan Southern and Northern Indiana Railroad . . . 1864,* p. 26. Italics are in the report. On the other hand, the Michigan Central Railroad thought the war had dislocated their business, and they did not get enough government patronage to make up their losses. See Chapter VI.

23. Frank H. Taylor, *Philadelphia in the Civil War,* p. 47; Winnifred K. Mackay, "Philadelphia During the Civil War," *Pennsylvania Magazine of History and Biography,* Jan., 1946, p. 15. See also Chapter XI.

24. *Official Records,* Ser. III, II, 794-95.

25. *2nd Annual Report, United States Christian Commission, 1863,* pp. 25, 275.

26. *American Railway Review,* Jan. 31, 1861. See also A. K. McClure, *Old Time Notes of Pennsylvania,* p. 467.

27. *American Railway Review,* Jan. 31, 1861.

28. Report of the Secretary of War, July 1, 1861, in Appendix to *Congressional Globe,* 37th Cong., 1st Sess., p. 11; see also *Official Records,* Ser. III, I, 301-10.

29. *Report . . . Dec. 1, 1861,* p. 18; see also Lewis H. Haney, *A Congressional History of Railways in the United States, 1850-1877,* pp. 159-60.

30. *Official Records,* Ser. III, I, 807-8, Scott to Stanton, Jan. 23, 1862; Kamm, *op. cit.,* p. 84.

31. *Stanton Papers,* Vol. II, Jan. 27, 1862; Eva Swantner, "Military Railroads During the Civil War," *The Military Engineer,* No. 119 (Sept.-Oct., 1929), p. 435.

32. *Congressional Globe,* 37th Cong., 2d Sess., Jan. 28, 1862,

p. 506. Wade later became one of the leaders of the anti-Lincoln Radical Republicans.

33. *Ibid.,* p. 508.

34. *Ibid.*

35. *Ibid.,* p. 509; this argument was echoed by John Sherman of Ohio. *Ibid.,* p. 515.

36. James G. Randall, *Constitutional Problems under Lincoln,* pp. 30-1, 36.

37. *Congressional Globe,* 37th Cong., 2nd Sess., Jan. 28, 1862, p. 510.

38. *Ibid.,* pp. 510, 512, 513. In June, 1862, Browning maintained this position in debate with Charles Sumner who contended that war powers stemmed from Congress, not from the executive. Randall, *op. cit.,* p. 42.

39. *Congressional Globe,* Jan. 28, 1862, 511, 519.

40. This point of view has been sustained in the courts. Randall, *op. cit.,* p. 37.

41. *Congressional Globe,* Jan. 28, 1862, p. 511.

42. *Ibid.,* p. 548. Blair of Missouri guided the bill through the House.

43. Haney, *op. cit.,* p. 158.

44. *Official Records,* Ser. III, I, 879.

45. *United States Statutes at Large,* XII, 334-35.

CHAPTER VIII

1. Roger A. Barton, "The Camden and Amboy Railroad Monopoly," in *Proceedings, New Jersey Historical Society,* (Oct., 1927), new ser., XII, 411.

2. Henry V. Poor, *Railroad Manual of the United States, 1868,* p. 32.

3. John E. Watkins, *The Camden and Amboy Railroad, Origin and Early History,* pp. 44-53. The Trenton–New Brunswick branch was much more important than the main line, which was restricted to freight carriage.

4. *Shall the Extention or Recreating of the Camden and Amboy*

Railroad Monopoly be permitted by the People of New Jersey, and made Perpetual? (an 1864 pamphlet), pp. 2-10.

5. *American Railroad Journal,* Feb. 9, 1861, April 30, 1861; *American Railway Review,* Jan. 9, 1862. This route was longer in mileage but shorter in time because of delays on the direct route at Philadelphia and Baltimore. The establishment of this secondary route, plus the fact that the Philadelphia, Wilmington, and Baltimore Railroad paid for its own repairs while the Northern Central got them at government expense, made Samuel Felton resentful. Kamm, *op. cit.,* p. 59.

6. *15th Annual Report . . . of the Central Railroad of New Jersey . . . Jan. 1, 1862,* p. 11.

7. *24th Annual Report . . . of the Philadelphia, Wilmington, and Baltimore Railroad . . . 1861,* p. 11.

8. *15th Annual Report . . . op. cit.,* p. 11.

9. *Ibid.,* p. 12. About 80 per cent of the traffic used Felton's route. Kamm, *op. cit.,* p. 62.

10. *16th Annual Report . . . 1863,* p. 14. Receipts for government business in 1861 were $53,722.84; in 1863, $21,517.90.

11. *American Railroad Journal,* Oct. 5, 1861; *24th Annual Report . . . of the Philadelphia, Wilmington, and Baltimore Railroad . . . 1861,* p. 7. The route was under the superintendency of Thomas H. Canfield of the Rutland Railroad. Kamm, *op. cit.,* p. 51.

12. *United States Railroad and Mining Register,* Nov. 16, 1861. An additional early evening train from New York was later added, and departure times altered slightly. *Ibid.,* Dec. 27, 1862. Local trains still required a change at both Philadelphia and Havre de Grace.

13. *24th Annual Report . . . of the Philadelphia, Wilmington, and Baltimore Railroad . . . 1861,* p. 8.

14. Festus P. Summers, *The Baltimore and Ohio in the Civil War,* pp. 205-7; Haney, *op. cit.,* 159-60.

15. This general opposition was supported by the *American Railroad Journal,* which advocated that the P W & B should be required to double track its line and build a bridge over the Susquehanna River (June 28, 1862, Feb. 27, 1864). On the other hand, the *United States Railroad and Mining Register* (May 4, 1861)

suggested that the government should own a rail route out of Washington in order to make Annapolis an important shipping center to take the place of Baltimore. The *Register* was published in Philadelphia, and the fact that private companies were using the route via Harrisburg, thus by-passing Philadelphia, undoubtedly prompted the *Register* to favor a government line, which would use the direct route through Philadelphia. See issue of Dec. 14, 1861. *The Army and Navy Journal* (April 15, 1865) called the government failure to build the line "shortsighted."

16. *History of the Railway Mail Service*, p. 59.

17. Executive Document 79, House of Representatives, 37th Cong., 2nd Sess.; Summers, *op. cit.*, pp. 207-8. The bill was sponsored by Washburne of Illinois and Van Wyck of New York. *United States Railroad and Mining Register*, Dec. 14, 1861.

18. *Merchants' Magazine and Commercial Review*, XLVI (Jan.-June, 1862), 39.

19. *Ibid.*, p. 40. The *American Railroad Journal*, Dec. 6, 1862, echoed these sentiments with the comment, "War is now dependant for its successes on railroads and Telegraphs."

20. The delegation consisted of Alderman Semmes, Emile Dupre, George Parker, Pliny Miles, Col. Peter Force, George Lowry, Hudson Taylor, and Messrs. Perry, Jones, Van Vliet, and Riley.

21. *Ibid.*, pp. 73-74. The *American Railway Review* added its voice to the hue and cry, claiming that New York–Washington transportation took 13 hours, when 7-8 would suffice, and that the $8 fare (3½ cents a mile) was exhorbitant (June 5, 1862).

22. Ex. Doc. 79, *op. cit.*, pp. 4-5.

23. *Ibid.*, p. 5.

24. *Ibid.*, p. 3.

25. Summers, *op. cit.*, pp. 213-14.

26. *24th Annual Report . . . of the Philadelphia, Wilmington, and Baltimore Railroad . . . 1861*, p. 9.

27. *Ibid.*, The *American Railway Review* approved these sentiments (May 29, 1862).

28. Appendix to *Congressional Globe*, 37th Cong., 2nd Sess., 423.

29. *25th Annual Report . . . 1862*, pp. 8, 11.

30. *Report . . . of the New Jersey Railroad . . . 1863*, p. 5.

Delivery was delayed until 1864 because the locomotive companies had government orders. *United States Railroad and Mining Register,* Jan. 2, 1864.

31. *25th Annual Report . . . of the Philadelphia, Wilmington, and Baltimore Railroad . . . 1862,* pp. 11-12.

32. *26th Annual Report . . . of the Philadelphia, Wilmington, and Baltimore Railroad . . . 1863,* p. 13.

33. *15th Annual Report . . . of the Pennsylvania Railroad . . . 1862,* p. 48; *25th Annual Report . . . of the Philadelphia, Wilmington, and Baltimore Railroad . . . 1862,* p. 12; *United States Railroad and Mining Register,* Oct. 12, 1861.

34. *Report . . . of the Philadelphia and Reading Railroad . . . 1862,* p. 13.

35. *26th Annual Report . . . of the Philadelphia, Wilmington, and Baltimore Railroad . . . 1863,* p. 13; *17th Annual Report of the Pennsylvania Railroad . . . 1864,* p. 10. One of the assistant engineers on this project was Alexander J. Cassatt, later one of the Pennsylvania's outstanding presidents (*Railroad Gazette,* Jan. 4, 1907). The first train on this route ran Nov. 28, 1863. *United States Railroad and Mining Register,* Nov. 28, 1863. See map in the New York *Times,* Feb. 5, 1863. Beginning about this time, the *Times* supported a government railroad, because existing companies had not carried through the necessary improvements (Feb. 6, 1863).

36. *Considerations . . . ,* p. 1.

37. *Ibid.,* p. 3.

38. *Ibid.,* pp. 4-5.

39. *Ibid.,* pp. 5-6. The emphasis in this whole controversy on the inadequacies of single track point up the importance of recent developments in Centralized Traffic Control, which can make the carrying capacity of a single-track railroad almost equal to that with a double track.

40. *Ibid.,* p. 7.

41. *Ibid.,* p. 8.

42. *Ibid.,* p. 9.

43. *Ibid.,* pp. 9-12.

44. *Ibid.,* p. 13.

45. *Ibid.*, pp. 13-14. In 1948 railroads claimed that they were taxed so heavily in New Jersey that they had to use revenue made in other states to pay their New Jersey taxes.

46. *Official Records,* Ser. III, IV, 47.

47. *Statement Made by the Railroad Companies . . . to the Post-master General,* pp. 3-4. The statement was dated Jan. 14, 1864. Most of its arguments were repeated by W. P. Smith of the B & O in a speech at a Washington dinner given for guests who came on the first through mail train from Jersey City to Washington. *American Railway Times,* Jan. 9, 1864.

48. *Ibid.*, pp. 5-6; *American Railroad Journal,* Jan. 2, 1864.

49. *Statement . . . to the Postmaster General,* p. 5.

50. This was completed by June, 1865. *United States Railroad and Mining Register,* June 10, 1865.

51. *Statement . . . to the Postmaster General,* pp. 7-10.

52. *Ibid.*, pp. 10-12.

53. *United States Railroad and Mining Register,* May 21, 1864 (from Baltimore *Sun,* May 12), Sept. 3, 1864; *American Railroad Journal,* Sept. 10, 1864; Washington *Evening Star,* Aug. 31, 1864 (quoted in *History of the Railway Mail Service,* pp. 154-55.).

54. The exact date of the inauguration of regular service on this route is difficult to determine. On Nov. 26, 1864, it was in operation, but it was the second in the country, the first being the Chicago and North Western to Clinton, Iowa, Aug. 28, 1864. The fall of 1864 is about as close as we can come (*History of the Railway Mail Service,* pp. 83, 153). On March 3, 1865, the railway post office was recognized by act of Congress, and before the war's end RPO cars were operating between New York and Boston via Springfield, on the Hudson River Railroad to Troy, and on the New York Central to Buffalo, on the Erie to Dunkirk, on the Pennsylvania to Pittsburgh, and on the Chicago and North Western, Chicago and Rock Island, and Chicago, Burlington, and Quincy. *Ibid.*, pp. 83, 86, 160, 179; *American Railway Times,* Jan. 28, 1865.

55. *Official Records,* Ser. III, IV, 48.

56. *Ibid.*, p. 49.

57. *Ibid.*

58. *Impolicy of Building another Railroad between Washington*

and New York, p. 23. The *American Railway Times* thought that, if this occurred, neither the government nor the public would be as well served as at present (Feb. 27, 1864).

59. *Impolicy* . . . , pp. 7-8.

60. *Ibid.*, p. 7. ·

61. *Ibid.*, pp. 17-18. See also letter of Felton and W. H. Gatzmer of the Camden and Amboy, June 26, 1861, to Boston *Journal*, reprinted in *American Railway Times*, July 6, 1861. For hospital cars, see Chapter XIV.

62. Also called the Delaware and Raritan Bay, the Raritan Bay and Delaware, and the Delaware and Raritan.

63. Barton, *op. cit.*, p. 415. It carried 17,248 troops and 806,000 tons of freight before it was closed. Emerson D. Fite, *Social and Industrial Conditions in the North during the Civil War*, p. 171.

64. Report 31, March 9, 1864, House of Representatives, 38th Cong., 1st Sess.: Report of Mr. Deming of Committee on Military Affairs on petition of Raritan and Delaware Bay Railroad, p. 1.

65. Barton, *op. cit.*, p. 416; Deming, *op. cit.*, p. 1.

66. Deming, *op. cit.*, pp. 2, 4-5.

67. *Message of Joel Parker . . . to the Legislature . . . Trenton*, pp. 3-4.

68. *Ibid.*, pp. 7-8.

69. Richard F. Stockton, *Defense of the System of Internal Improvements of the State of New Jersey*, p. 29. The second letter is also reprinted in the *United States Railroad and Mining Register*, June 4, 1864.

70. Stockton, *op. cit.*, pp. 10, 39 ff. The tax was 10 cents per through passenger and 15 cents per ton. See *A Defence of New Jersey* . . . , pp. 3-5 (Letters to New York *Evening Post* from "A citizen of New Jersey").

71. Stockton, *op. cit.*, pp. 43-44; the five routes were the ocean, the canal, the C & A direct, the C & A via Trenton, and the New Jersey Central via Harrisburg.

72. See speech of Rep. Sweat of Maine, April 2, 1864, in *A Defence of New Jersey* . . . , pp. 12-13.

73. *Railroad Usurpation of New Jersey* (1865), pp. 4-5 (Speech of Sumner in the Senate, Feb. 14, 1865).

74. *Ibid.*, p. 11.

75. *Ibid.*, p. 12.

76. *37th Annual Report . . . of the Baltimore and Ohio Railroad . . . Sept. 30, 1863,* p. 11.

77. *38th Annual Report . . . Sept. 30, 1864,* p. 49.

78. *Ibid.*, pp. 51 ff.

79. *39th Annual Report . . . Sept. 30, 1865,* p. 7.

80. *27th Annual Report . . . of the Philadelphia, Wilmington and Baltimore Railroad . . . Oct. 31, 1864,* p. 4.

81. *28th Annual Report . . . Oct. 31, 1865,* pp. 6-7.

82. Summers, *op. cit.*, pp. 219-22.

CHAPTER IX

1. United States War Department, Military Railroads, *Order Book of General Orders, Instructions and Reports* (pages unnumbered); hereafter cited as *Order Book.*

2. *Official Records,* Ser. III, I, 325-26, Scott to Maj. Sibley, July 12, 1861. Previously, railroad officials in Pennsylvania had resolved that, on accounts to be settled with the state, charges for passengers would be reduced by one third, but not below 2 cents a mile. *American Railroad Journal,* June 15, 1861.

3. Kamm, *op. cit.*, pp. 69-70.

4. *Official Records,* Ser. III, I, 698-708 (Cameron's Report, Dec. 1, 1861); Appendix to *Congressional Globe,* 37th Cong., 2nd Sess., p. 17.

5. *New Jersey Railroad . . . Annual Report . . . 1861,* p. 7.

6. Appendix to *Congressional Globe,* 37th Cong., 2nd Sess., p. 18; Scott to Stanton, Feb. 2, 1862, *Stanton Papers,* Vol. II (4 cents for passengers; 5 cents for freight).

7. *24th Annual Report . . . of the Philadelphia, Wilmington and Baltimore Railroad . . . 1861,* p. 10.

8. *Ibid.*, p. 10. The New Jersey Railroad said it was charging only 1-1½ cents for troops (1861 report, p. 6). This was in answer to the charge of the New York *Tribune* that the railroad should carry troops for less than the full fare. *American Railway Review,* June 6, 1861.

9. *Official Records,* Ser. III, I, 749.

10. This was the "Castle Circular", issued by E. H. Castle,

superintendent of railroad transportation in the military department of the West. Kamm, *op. cit.,* p. 70.

11. *Official Records,* Ser. III, I, 751-52.

12. *Official Records,* Ser. III, I, 889-90.

13. This military rate for troops was discontinued on Dec. 31, 1865. *Army and Navy Journal,* March 3, 1866.

14. *Official Records,* Ser. III, II, 838-39.

15. *Ibid.,* Ser. III, II, 795.

16. See Chapter V for the effect of the draft on the railroads. This section is concerned with government policy on the subject.

17. *Official Records,* Ser. III, II, 294 (Aug. 5, 1862).

18. *Ibid.,* pp. 309-10.

19. *Ibid.,* p. 310.

20. *Ibid.,* p. 315. "Other experts" probably referred to administrative personnel, who were just as valuable as skilled labor. An item in the *American Railroad Journal* of Nov. 1, 1862, read: "Among those drafted at Scranton, Pa., are John Brisbin, Superintendent; R. A. Henry, general freight agent; W. H. Fuller, ticket agent, and H. R. Phelps, paymaster—all of the Delaware, Lackawanna, and Western Railroad." The efficient operation of railroads was handicapped by such occurrences.

21. *Official Records,* Ser. III, II, 322.

22. *Ibid.,* p. 323.

23. *Ibid.,* p. 334.

24. *Ibid.,* p. 336. Sloan of the Hudson River Railroad also mentioned this danger.

25. *Ibid.,* p. 337.

26. *Ibid.,* p. 358.

27. *Ibid.,* IV, 1049.

28. Haney, *op. cit.,* pp. 171-72.

29. This was usually done by groups of railroads. Those in the Cincinnati area, for instance, agreed on the necessary raise to be charged the public. *American Railroad Journal,* Aug. 16, 1862.

30. Haney, *op. cit.,* pp. 174, 176.

CHAPTER X

1. Report of Bvt. Brig. Gen. D. C. McCallum, Director and General Manager of the Military Railroads of the U. S., May 26, 1866, 39th Cong., 1st Sess., House of Representatives Executive Document 1, pp. 37-38. Hereafter cited as McCallum's Report, it is also printed in *Official Records*, Ser. III, V, 974-1005.

2. Control of the railroads in the military zone at first rested with the Departments of the Army in which the railroads were located. R. E. Riegel, "Federal Operation of Southern Railroads during the Civil War," *Mississippi Valley Historical Review*, IX, 128.

3. McCallum's Report, p. 5.

4. Eva Swantner, "Military Railroads during the Civil War," *The Military Engineer*, XXI, 435.

5. New York *Times*, Dec. 28, 1878; Edward Hungerford, *Men of Erie*, 139-40; *Dictionary of American Biography*, XI, 565-66.

6. Swantner, *op. cit.*, p. 434. An act of Congress, approved July 4, 1864, reorganized the QM Department into nine divisions; the fourth had charge of railroads and telegraphs. U. S. War Department, Military Railroads, *Order Book of general orders, instructions, and reports* (pages unnumbered).

7. Riegel, *op. cit.*, p. 129.

8. *Ibid.*, p. 130; Swantner, *op. cit.*, p. 435.

9. Swantner, *op. cit.*, XXII, 21.

10. *American Railway Times*, March 14, 1863.

11. *McCallum Report*, p. 5. Originally known as the Washington and Alexandria Railroad, it was reorganized in 1862 as the Washington, Alexandria, and Georgetown Railroad. *American Railway Review*, May 15, 1862.

12. Forty cars were purchased from the Boston and Worcester Railroad and 50 from the Providence and Worcester. The government paid $500 for platform cars, and $600 for covered cars. *American Railway Review*, May 8, 1862.

13. *McCallum Report*, p. 6.

14. *Ibid.; Reminiscences of General Herman Haupt*, p. 270.

15. Haupt, *op. cit.*, p. 43.

16. See Haupt, *op. cit.*, Preface.

17. New York *Times,* Dec. 15, 1905. There is a sketch of his career in *Railroad Gazette,* Dec. 22, 1905.

18. Samuel R. Kamm, *The Civil War Career of Thomas A. Scott,* pp. 47-48.

19. Occasionally he even made suggestions to Lincoln. See Haupt to Lincoln, Dec. 22 and 26, 1862, *Stanton Papers,* Vol. X.

20. Haupt, *op. cit.,* p. 44.

21. *Ibid.,* pp. 268-69.

22. *Ibid.,* pp. 46, 48-49.

23. *Ibid.,* p. 47.

24. *Ibid.,* pp. 313, 185.

25. *Ibid.,* pp. 54-55; *Order Book,* May 28, 1862.

26. Haupt, *op. cit.,* p. 47.

27. *Ibid.,* p. 45.

28. *Ibid.,* pp. 53, 55-56.

29. *Ibid.,* p. 269.

30. *Ibid.,* p. 56.

31. Thomas A. Scott had previously expressed this same opinion to Stanton when he said that few army people knew anything about railroads and that transportation of supplies to army depots should not be in army hands. Scott to Stanton, March 1, 1862, *Stanton Papers,* Vol. IV.

32. *Order Book.*

33. Haupt, *op. cit.,* p. 56.

34. *Ibid.*

35. *Ibid.,* p. 175.

36. *Ibid.,* pp. 57, 58.

37. *Ibid.,* p. 59.

38. *Order Book,* June 2, 1862. Only the superintendent and dispatchers could issue train orders.

39. Haupt, *op. cit.,* pp. 214-16, 236; Edward Killough, *History of the Western Maryland Railroad,* p. 63.

40. Haupt, *op. cit.,* pp. 64-65.

41. *Ibid.,* p. 66.

42. Haupt to Stanton, May 28, 1862, *Stanton Papers,* Vol. VII.

43. Haupt, *op. cit.,* p. 69.

44. *Ibid.,* p. 70.

45. *Order Book.*

46. Haupt, *op. cit.*, p. 73; New York *Times,* Aug. 29, 1862.

47. Haupt, *op. cit.*, pp. 74-75, 83-84, 135.

48. *Ibid.,* pp. 76-77.

49. *Ibid.,* p. 77.

50. *Ibid.,* pp. 78-79; Robert U. Johnson and Clarence C. Buel, ed., *Battles and Leaders of the Civil War,* II, 461 (John Pope, "The Second Battle of Bull Run").

51. Haupt, *op. cit.*, p. 80.

52. *Ibid.,* pp. 80, 83 (entire interview).

53. *Order Book.* Sturgis's name was removed from the list of major generals in 1863. Nicolay to Stanton, March 6, 1863, *Stanton Papers,* Vol XI.

54. Haupt, *op. cit.*, pp. 84-85.

55. *Ibid.,* p. 88.

56. *Ibid.,* pp. 89-90, 96.

57. *Ibid.,* p. 90.

58. *Ibid.,* pp. 195-96.

59. *Ibid.,* pp. 94-95, 109; William R. Plum, *The Military Telegraph during the Civil War in the United States,* I, 223-24.

60. *General Fitz John Porter's Narrative of the Services of the Fifth Army Corps in 1862 in Northern Virginia,* p. 58.

61. Haupt, *op. cit.*, pp. 98-99, 103-4, 106, 110.

62. *Ibid.,* pp. 100, 104, 107-8, 110, 114.

63. *Ibid.,* pp. 98, 108-9, 129.

64. Rev. Lemuel Moss, *Annals of the U. S. Christian Commission,* p. 138 (Telegram Garrett to Stuart, Treas. of the Commission, Aug. 30, 1862).

65. Haupt, *op. cit.*, pp. 116-18.

66. *Ibid.,* pp. 126-27.

67. *Ibid.,* pp. 129-30, 133-34.

68. *Ibid.,* p. 135.

69. *McCallum Report,* p. 6.

70. Haupt, *op. cit.*, pp. 138-39. Meigs issued these same orders to QM officers, Oct. 1, 1862. *Order Book.*

71. Haupt, *op. cit.*, pp. 139-40.

72. *Ibid.,* p. 140.

73. *Ibid.*

74. *Ibid.,* p. 143.

75. *Ibid.*, pp. 144-45.

76. *Ibid.*, p. 146.

77. Halleck to Stanton, Oct. 28, 1862, *Stanton Papers,* Vol. IX.

78. *McCallum Report,* p. 6; New York *Times,* Sept. 8, 1862.

79. Haupt, *op. cit.,* p. 149.

80. *Ibid.*, p. 154.

81. *Ibid.*, p. 148.

82. Swantner, *op. cit.,* XXI, 519.

83. Haupt, *op. cit.,* pp. 154-55.

84. *Ibid.*, pp. 155-56.

85. *Ibid.*, p. 158.

86. *McCallum Report,* pp. 33-34.

87. Haupt, *op. cit.,* pp. 158-59.

88. *Ibid.*, p. 160.

89. Haupt to Stanton, Sept. 9, 1863, in *Order Book.*

90. Haupt, *op. cit.,* pp. 160-63.

91. *Ibid.*, p. 165.

92. *McCallum Report,* pp. 6-7; *Official Records,* Ser. III, III, 119-20.

93. Haupt, *op. cit.,* pp. 165-66.

94. *Ibid.*

95. *Ibid.*, p. 179.

96. *Ibid.*, pp. 167-68.

97. *Ibid.*, p. 173.

98. *Ibid.*, p. 168.

99. *Ibid.*, p. 174.

100. *Ibid.*, pp. 176, 272.

101. *Ibid.*, pp. 184-85.

102. *Official Records,* Ser. III, III, 1-2.

103. *Ibid.*, p. 119 (McCallum to Stanton, April 7, 1863).

104. *Ibid.*, p. 120; the *American Railway Times,* April 18, 1863, reported that 1,200 passengers daily traveled the line.

105. Haupt to Stanton, Sept. 9, 1863, in *Order Book.*

106. Haupt, *op. cit.,* pp. 186-87.

107. F. J. Crilly to D. H. Rucker, Aug. 17, 1867, in *Order Book.*

108. Haupt, *op. cit.,* p. 196; Edwin A. Pratt, *The Rise of Rail Power in War and Conquest, 1833-1914,* p. 86.

109. Haupt, *op. cit.,* pp. 204-5.

110. *Ibid.,* pp. 205-6.

111. Haupt was familiar with the territory involved in the Gettysburg campaign. His residence was on Seminary Ridge and one of Longstreet's batteries was set up in his front yard. *Ibid.,* p. 311.

112. *Ibid.,* pp. 208, 211.

113. *Ibid.,* p. 212.

114. Killough, *op. cit.,* pp. 5-13.

115. Haupt, *op. cit.,* p. 213.

116. *Ibid.;* Haupt to Stanton, Sept. 9, 1863, *Order Book.*

117. *McCallum Report* (June 30, 1864), p. 5.

118. Haupt, *op. cit.,* pp. 214-16, 236; Killough, *op. cit.,* p. 63.

119. Katherine P. Wormeley, *The United States Sanitary Commission,* pp. 128, 130, 145.

120. Plum, *op. cit.,* II, 16.

121. Haupt, *op. cit.,* pp. 220-21, 214-15, 244.

122. *Ibid.,* pp. 220-21.

123. *Ibid.,* pp. 222-23.

124. *Ibid.,* pp. 224, 227-28.

125. *Ibid.,* p. 238; *McCallum Report,* p. 8.

126. Haupt, *op. cit.,* pp. 236, 239-40.

127. *McCallum Report,* pp. 7-8.

128. Haupt, *op. cit.,* p. 243.

129. *Ibid.,* p. 255.

130. *Ibid.,* p. 248. For Haupt's work in Virginia this final summer, see also *Official Records,* Ser. III, IV, 962.

131. *Ibid.,* pp. 248, 251.

132. *Ibid.,* p. 252.

133. *Ibid.,* p. 254.

134. *Ibid.,* pp. 256, 259.

135. *Ibid.,* pp. 262-63.

136. *Ibid.,* p. 264.

137. *Ibid.,* p. 301.

CHAPTER XI

1. *McCallum Report,* p. 7. The Manassas Gap Railroad to White Plains had been used for a few days to supply Meade on the march from Gettysburg to Culpepper.

2. *Ibid.,* p. 8.

3. *Ibid.*

4. *Ibid.*

5. *Ibid.; Official Records,* Ser. III, IV, 956. E. L. Wentz was superintendent and chief engineer.

6. *Official Records,* Ser. III, V, 67 (Report of J. J. Moore).

7. *Ibid.*

8. *Ibid.,* p. 68; Plum, *op. cit.,* II, 272-73.

9. *Official Records,* Ser. III, V, 68.

10. *Ibid.,* p. 69.

11. *Ibid.*

12. *McCallum Report,* p. 8; *Official Records,* Ser. III, IV, 956.

13. *McCallum Report,* p. 9.

14. *Official Records,* Ser. III, V, 70.

15. *Ibid.; Battles and Leaders* . . . , IV, 577 (General Grant on siege of Petersburg, extract from report of July 22, 1865).

16. *Ibid.,* pp. 70, 71.

17. *Ibid.,* p. 71.

18. *Ibid.,* pp. 71-72.

19. See Chapter XIII.

20. *Official Records,* Ser. III, V, 72.

21. *Ibid.,* pp. 72-73.

22. Johnson and Buel, eds., *Battles and Leaders of the Civil War,* IV, 708 (Horace Porter, "Five Forks and the Pursuit of Lee").

23. *Ibid.,* pp. 73-74, 582; *McCallum Report,* p. 9. The South Side Railroad is now part of the Norfolk and Western.

24. Dana to Stanton, July 1 and 3, 1864, *Stanton Papers,* Vol. XXII.

25. *Official Records,* Ser. III, V, 101-2.

26. *Ibid.,* pp. 73-74. The rolling stock had been shipped from the North to City Point, then diverted to Manchester for recon-

ditioning, because of three months' deterioration on board. It remained in storage until sold on Oct. 3, 1865. *Ibid.,* p. 596.

27. *Ibid.,* p. 76.

28. *Ibid.,* pp. 75, 79. This line is now part of the Southern Railway.

29. *Ibid.,* p. 76.

30. *Ibid.,* pp. 77-78; McCallum Report, p. 9.

31. *Official Records,* Ser. III, V, 81. J. J. Moore estimated 1,207,474 tons for the Virginia railroads during the war, of which 785,981 were transported over the City Point and Army line.

CHAPTER XII

1. *In Memoriam, General Lewis B. Parsons,* 23; *Official Records,* Ser. I, LII, 709.

2. *Official Records,* Ser. I, LII, 459-60, 709-10. This was General McClernand's expedition.

3. *Ibid.,* p. 711.

4. See Chapter III.

5. With the exception of McCallum and Haupt, the members of the U.S.M.R. transportation corps and construction corps were civilians, a fact which sometimes hampered the efficient operation of railroad superintendents. Haupt to Stanton, Sept. 9, 1863, in *Order Book.*

6. William Pittenger, *Daring and Suffering, A History of the Andrews Railroad Raid into Georgia 1862.* This was one of the most spectacular exploits of the war. The captured engine, the "General," later did heroic service on the railroad, and in 1864 was the last to leave Atlanta before the evacuation by Hood. The engine is now kept on permanent display at Union Station, Chattanooga, by the Nashville, Chattanooga, and St. Louis Railroad. It was temporarily loaned to the Chicago Railroad Fair in 1948.

7. Haupt, *Reminiscences,* pp. 188-89.

8. *Ibid.,* pp. 189-90.

9. Dana to Stanton, Sept. 10, 1863, *Stanton Papers,* Vol. XIV.

10. *Ibid.,* Sept. 16, 1863. In November, Dana complained that the railroad left subsistence stores waiting for days in the depot. Dana to Stanton, Nov. 3, 1863, *Stanton Papers,* Vol. XIX.

11. *Official Records*, Ser. III, IV, 879-80.

12. *Stanton Papers*, Vol. XV.

13. The story of this transfer is ably related in Kamm, *The Civil War Career of Thomas A. Scott*, pp. 165 ff.; Summers, *The Baltimore and Ohio in the Civil War*, pp. 166 ff.; see also Hungerford, *The Story of the Baltimore and Ohio Railroad*, II, 46 ff.

14. Kamm, *op. cit.*, p. 165.

15. David H. Bates, *Lincoln in the Telegraph Office*, p. 174.

16. *Ibid.*, p. 176; Kamm, *op. cit.*, p. 166.

17. Summers, *op. cit.*, p. 167.

18. *Ibid.*, pp. 167-68; Kamm, *op. cit.*, p. 165.

19. Bates, *op. cit.*, p. 175. The total movement was actually 23,000. *Ibid.*, p. 179.

20. *Ibid.*, p. 177; Stanton to Garrett, Sept. 23, 1863, *Stanton Papers*, Vol. XV.

21. Stanton to Boyle, Sept. 23, 1863, *Stanton Papers*, Vol. XV.

22. Boyle to Stanton, Sept. 24, 1863, in *Ibid.*

23. This was the Covington and Lexington Railroad. Bowler to Stanton, Sept. 24, 1863, *Stanton Papers*, Vol. XV.

24. Kamm, *op. cit.*, pp. 167-69; Bates, *op. cit.*, p. 177.

25. Bates, *op. cit.*, p. 177. Order to Gen. Hooker, in James D. Richardson, *A Compilation of Messages and Papers of the Presidents*, VI, 178.

26. Scott to Stanton, Feb. 1, 2, 1862, *Stanton Papers*, Vol. II.

27. *Ibid.*, Feb. 7, 1862.

28. Meade to Halleck, McCallum to Stanton, Sept. 24, 1863, *Stanton Papers*, Vol. XV.

29. W. P. Smith to McCallum, Sept. 26, 1863, *Stanton Papers*, Vol. XV.

30. Smith to Stanton, Sept. 26, 1863, *Stanton Papers*, Vol. XV.

31. McCallum to Stanton, Sept. 26, 1863, *ibid.*

32. Garrett to Jewett, Sept. 24, 1863, *ibid.*

33. *Ibid.* A similiar concentration was ordered at Indianapolis because of the change of gauge.

34. Smith to Stanton, Sept. 27, 1863, *ibid.*

35. Bates, *op. cit.*, pp. 419-20. Stanton also wired Smith to pay no attention to Schurz and to let laggards get along as best they could.

Smith to Stanton, Stanton to Smith, Sept. 27, 1863, *Stanton Papers,* Vol. XV.

36. McCallum to Stanton, Smith to Stanton, Sept. 28, 1863, *ibid.*

37. Smith to Stanton, Sept. 29, 1863, *ibid.*

38. Garrett to Stanton, Oct. 4, 1863; Scott to Stanton, Oct. 5, 1863, *Stanton Papers,* Vol. XVII.

39. Kamm, *op. cit.,* pp. 176-77.

40. Smith to Stanton, Oct. 1, 1863, *Stanton Papers,* Vol. XVI; Scott to Stanton, Oct. 5, 1863, *ibid.,* Vol. XVII.

41. Scott to Stanton, Sept. 29, 1863, *Stanton Papers,* Vol. XV.

42. Kamm, *op. cit.,* pp. 177-79.

43. Scott to Stanton, March 1, 1862, *Stanton Papers,* Vol. IV. *Ibid.,* Oct. 9, 1863, Vol. XVII.

44. Stanton to Scott, Sept. 27, 1863, *Stanton Papers,* Vol. XV. The change was accomplished 8½ days after construction began. Scott to Stanton, Oct. 17, 1863, *ibid.,* XVIII.

45. Scott to Stanton, Sept. 27, 1863, *ibid.,* Vol. XV.

46. Gen. Allen to Watson, Sept. 28, 1863; Scott to Stanton, Sept. 29, 1863, *ibid.,* Vol. XV.

47. Scott to Stanton, Sept. 30, 1863, *ibid.,* Vol. XVI.

48. Hungerford, *op. cit.,* p. 54.

49. Cole to Stanton, Oct. 6, 1863, *Stanton Papers,* Vol. XVII.

50. Bates, *op. cit.,* p. 179; Stanton to Dana, Sept. 24, 1863, *Stanton Papers,* Vol. XV.

51. Smith to Stanton, *Stanton Papers,* Vol. X. The memo is dated Oct. 5, and is placed with the 1862 papers, but the actual date must have been 1863, because it specifically mentions the baggage of the 11th Corps. See also Vol. XVIII, papers dated Oct. 12-18, *passim.*

52. Smith to Stanton, Oct. 6, 1863, *ibid.,* Vol. XVII.

53. Dana to Stanton, Oct. 14, 1863, *ibid.,* Vol. XVIII; Scott to Stanton, Oct. 16, 1863. The Cumberland River could also be used. Meigs to Stanton, Oct. 18, 1863.

54. Dana to Stanton, Oct. 18, 1863, *ibid.,* Vol. XVIII.

55. *Official Records,* Ser. III, IV, 942-43. On the same day, Rosecrans was replaced by Thomas, and the three departments consolidated into the Military Division of the Mississippi. Plum, *op. cit.,* 11, 71.

56. Riegel, *op. cit.*, p. 129; *United States Railroad and Mining Register*, Nov. 2, 1861. Apparently Guthrie was satisfied with Anderson's work on the L & N.

57. *Official Records*, Ser. III, III, 1083-84.

58. *Ibid.*, p. 1083.

59. *Ibid.*, p. 1104.

60. *Ibid.*, Ser. III, IV, 881. *McCallum Report*, p. 12.

61. *Official Records*, Ser. III, V, 934. The thrilling welcome given the first train into Chattanooga is described in Livermore, *op. cit.*, pp. 528-29.

62. *Stanton Papers*, Vol. XVIII, Oct. 22, 1863. Johnson opposed Anderson's appointment because of disloyalty to the North and loyalty to Louisville interests. Johnson to Lincoln, Nov. 2, 1863, *ibid.*, Vol. XIX.

63. Kamm, *op. cit.*, pp. 181-82.

64. Rosecrans's superintendent of railroads had quarreled with both Guthrie and the B & O agent at Indianapolis; and Dana had recommended the removal of Rosecrans. Dana to Stanton, Nov. 1, 1863, *Stanton Papers*, Vol. XIX.

65. *McCallum Report*, pp. 12-13.

66. *Official Records*, Ser. I, LII, 461.

67. Dana to Stanton, Nov. 19, 1863, *Stanton Papers*, Vol. XIX.

68. *Battles and Leaders*, III, 692-93; *Personal Memoirs of U. S. Grant*, II, 46-48. Grenville Dodge had previously won the admiration of Grant and Sherman when he rebuilt the Mobile and Ohio Railroad swiftly and soundly in 1862 after its destruction by Confederates. A railroad engineer before the war, he reentered his profession in 1866 to become chief engineer of the Union Pacific. He once stated his policy for wartime operation of railroads as establishment of a regular schedule, and prohibition of army interference in train operation. Grenville M. Dodge, *How We Built the Union Pacific Railway*, pp. 101-4. These principles had been previously emphasized by Herman Haupt in Virginia.

69. American Society of Civil Engineers, *Memoir of Albert Fink, Past-President, Died April 3, 1907* (pages unnumbered).

70. *McCallum Report*, p. 13.

71. *Official Records*, Ser. III, IV, 219-20.

72. *McCallum Report*, p. 13.

73. *Ibid.; Official Records,* Ser. III, IV, 881, 943-44.

74. *McCallum Report,* pp. 13-14.

75. *Ibid.,* p. 14.

76. *Ibid.,* p. 14; *Official Records,* Ser. III, III, 1-2.

77. *Order Book.* Adna Anderson was no relation to John B. Anderson.

78. *McCallum Report,* pp. 14-15.

79. *McCallum Report,* pp. 15-16.

80. *Official Records,* Ser. III, IV, 957.

81. *McCallum Report,* pp. 16-17.

82. See Charles B. George, *Forty Years on the Rail,* p. 121.

83. *McCallum Report,* p. 18.

84. *McCallum Report* (June 30, 1864), p. 15.

85. Of these, 36 were built by the three companies in Paterson, N.J. (Rogers & Co., Danforth & Cook, New Jersey Locomotive Works). *American Railroad Journal,* July 23, 1864 (from Paterson *Register*). The Paterson works had previously built 30 locomotives for use in Virginia. *United States Railroad and Mining Register,* May 31, 1862.

86. McCallum to A. Anderson, May 8, 1864, in *Order Book; McCallum Report* (June 30, 1864), p. 16.

87. *McCallum Report,* p. 18.

In service Feb. 4, 1864	47 locomotives	437 cars
From manufacturers	140	1818
From other railroads	21	195
Total	208	2450

88. *Ibid.,* p. 19.

89. *Ibid.,* p. 23; *Official Records,* Ser. III, IV, 881.

90. *Order Book.* Col. William P. Innes of the 1st Michigan Engineers was relieved.

91. *Official Records,* Ser. III, IV, 958; V, 948.

92. *Official Records,* Ser. III, V, 944.

93. *McCallum Report,* p. 21.

94. *Official Records,* Ser. III, V, 944-45.

95. *McCallum Report,* p. 23. Parsons at St. Louis did much to pile up water shipments of supplies at Nashville. *Official Records,* Ser. III, IV, 881.

96. *Official Records,* Ser. III, IV, 963.

97. *Ibid.,* Vol. V, 935-37.

98. Riley E. Ennis, "Sherman on Supply vs. Mobility," *Infantry Journal,* XXXVII (Sept. 1930), 297; Sherman's order of April 6, 1864, and Anderson's of April 10 in *Order Book.* Regulations concerning private travel were liberalized early in 1865.

99. Three engines were necessary to conquer the 2 per cent grade over Cumberland Mountain. New York *Times,* Nov. 27, 1863.

100. *McCallum Report,* p. 22; *Official Records,* Ser. III, V, 587.

101. *Bulletin of the United States Sanitary Commission,* March 1, 1864, pp. 259-60; Aug. 1, 1864, p. 600.

102. *McCallum Report,* p. 22. *Official Records,* Ser. III, IV, 957; V, 941-42.

103. *Official Records,* Ser. III, V, 943.

104. *McCallum Report,* p. 22; *Official Records,* Ser. III, V, 956-58.

105. *McCallum Report,* p. 24. The work was done by the first division of the Construction Corps under L. H. Eicholtz. *Official Records,* Ser. III, IV, 958.

106. *Official Records,* Ser. III, V, 955.

107. Plum, *op. cit.,* I, 257.

108. These lines, along with the Vicksburg and Jackson, were located in the Division of West Mississippi. *United States Railroad and Mining Register,* Feb. 11, 1865.

109. *Official Records,* Ser. III, V, 958-59; *McCallum Report,* p. 25.

CHAPTER XIII

1. William T. Sherman, *Memoirs,* II, 398-99.

2. *McCallum Report,* p. 34.

3. *Ibid.,* pp. 34-5.

4. *Official Records,* Ser. III, IV, 958; *McCallum Report,* p. 21.

5. *Official Records,* Ser. III, V, 951.

6. Ennis, *op. cit.,* pp. 298, 300.

7. *Official Records,* Ser. III, IV, 957.

8. *Official Records,* Ser. III, V, 951-52; *McCallum Report,* p. 21.

9. Haupt, *Reminiscences,* p. 290.

10. *Ibid.*, pp. 290, 293-95.

11. *McCallum Report*, p. 35; *Official Records*, Ser. III, V, 950.

12. Ennis, *op. cit.*, p. 299.

13. *McCallum Report*, p. 36.

14. Ennis, *op. cit.*, p. 299.

15. *McCallum Report*, pp. 21, 36; *Official Records*, Ser. III, V, 952, 954.

16. Swantner, *op. cit.*, XXI, 518.

17. *McCallum Report*, p. 21.

18. *Ibid.*

19. *Official Records*, Ser. III, IV, 965.

20. *McCallum Report*, p. 21.

21. *Ibid.*, p. 22.

22. Swantner, *op. cit.*, XXI, 518.

23. *Ibid.*

24. *McCallum Report*, p. 22; *Official Records*, Ser. III, V, 29.

25. *Official Records*, Ser. III, V, 87. Usually a 28-foot by 8-foot box freight car on the U.S.M.R. carried 10 tons, or 40 men. See report of F. J. Crilly, *op. cit.*, Aug. 17, 1867; R. S. Henry, *This Fascinating Railroad Business*, p. 422.

26. *Official Records*, Ser. III, V, 89-90.

27. *Ibid.*, pp. 47, 539.

28. *McCallum Report*, p. 35.

29. The *United States Railroad and Mining Register*, Dec. 3, 1864, gave most credit to Col. John C. Crane of the QM Corps for the success of maintaining an efficient headquarters at Nashville. The locomotive and machine dept. alone employed 3,000 men in a main building 200 feet by 80 feet, which could rebuild locomotives from the boiler and wheels. The machine shop was equipped with lathes, drill presses, bolt cutting and gear cutting machinery. The blacksmith shop had 40 forges, and employed nearly 200 smiths. A paint, glass, and upholstery shop employed 100. The car dept. built a 50-foot armored headquarters car for Gen. Thomas, completely equipped with kitchen, dining compartment, sleeping compartment, toilet facilities, and office. Col. Crane spent over $2,000,-000 monthly to operate these shops. See also New York *Times*, Nov. 22, 1864.

30. *Official Records*, Ser. III, V, 470-71.

31. Between Oct., 1864, and April, 1865, 1,680 feet of bridges was replaced on the Pacific Railroad of Missouri after rebel raids. *McCallum Report,* p. 27. According to the *American Railroad Journal,* 3,402 feet of main line was destroyed on this railroad by rebel raids, plus rolling stock and buildings (issue of Nov. 26, 1864 quoting the St. Louis *Republican*). This railroad, the North Missouri, and the Iron Mountain RR were under Parsons's control to supply troops in Missouri. See Memo of Transportation Dept., Feb. 9, 1862, in *Stanton Papers,* Vol. II.

32. *McCallum Report,* p. 28. Sherman destroyed the Macon and Western Railroad, and the line of the Central Railroad and Banking Co. of Georgia from Macon to Savannah.

33. *Ibid.*

34. *Official Records,* Ser. III, V, 29 (Wright's Report).

35. *Ibid.,* pp. 30, 970.

36. *Ibid.; McCallum Report,* p. 28; Jacob D. Cox, *The March to the Sea,* p. 147.

37. *Official Records,* Ser. III, V, 44.

38. *Ibid.,* p. 30.

39. *Ibid.,* p. 33; *McCallum Report,* p. 28.

40. *Official Records,* Ser. III, V, 540.

41. *Official Records,* Ser. III, V, 31, 44.

42. Schofield to Sherman, April 3, 1865, *Stanton Papers,* Vol. XXV.

43. *McCallum Report,* p. 28; Cox, *op. cit.,* p. 211.

44. The following material is taken from *Battles and Leaders,* pp. 685-86 (Henry W. Slocum, "Sherman's March from Savannah to Bentonville").

45. *Official Records,* Ser. III, V, 31-2, 970.

46. *Ibid.,* pp. 32, 966; *McCallum Report,* p. 28.

47. *Official Records,* Ser. III, V, 32.

48. *Ibid.,* pp. 23-4.

49. *Ibid.,* p. 541.

50. *Ibid.,* pp. 33, 36; *McCallum Report,* pp. 28-9. In addition to the lines mentioned, the North Carolina Railroad was used for a while as far as Hillsboro, 40 miles beyond Raleigh, to parole Johnston's army. From May 1 to July 17, 1,747 loaded cars were received at the front. *Official Records,* Ser. III, V, 541.

51. *Official Records,* Ser. I, XLVII, Part 2, 219.

52. *Ibid.,* p. 215. He hoped to get from 200 to 300 cars from the Illinois Central alone. *Ibid.,* pp. 239-40.

53. *Ibid.,* pp. 216, 239-41, 278.

54. *Ibid.,* p. 216.

55. *Ibid.,* p. 248.

56. *Ibid.,* p. 249.

57. *Ibid.,* p. 216.

58. *Ibid.,* p. 260.

59. *Ibid.,* p. 273.

60. *Ibid.,* pp. 261, 268-69.

61. *Ibid.,* p. 271.

62. *Ibid.,* pp. 216-17. The accident occurred 30 miles west of Baltimore.

63. *Ibid.,* p. 284.

64. *Ibid.,* pp. 218, 283.

65. *McCallum Report,* p. 38. The South also had important railroad movements. In Sept., 1863, 2 divisions of Longstreet's corps were transferred from Petersburg, Va., in 16 days to reinforce Bragg in Georgia, going by way of Wilmington, Augusta, Atlanta, and Ringgold. See *Battles and Leaders,* pp. 745-46 (E. P. Alexander, "Longstreet at Knoxville").

66. *McCallum Report,* p. 32.

67. *Ibid.,* pp. 32-33. Figures do not include rolling stock borrowed from northern railroads. Breakdown shows:

Locomotives (419)	*Cars* (6330)
72 Virginia	1733 Virginia
38 North Carolina	422 North Carolina
260 Mississippi	3383 Mississippi
14 Georgia	213 Georgia
35 unused	579 unused

Also, about 26 miles of bridges were built or rebuilt ($18\frac{1}{2}$ in Mississippi, $6\frac{1}{2}$ in Virginia, small amounts in North Carolina and Missouri), and 642 miles of track laid or relaid (433 in Mississippi, $177\frac{1}{2}$ in Virginia, 31 in North Carolina). *McCallum Report,* p. 37.

68. *McCallum Report,* pp. 37-38.

69. *Ibid.,* p. 30.

70. *Ibid.*, pp. 30-31.

71. *Ibid.; Official Records,* Ser. III, V, 962.

72. *McCallum Report,* p. 32. The mill's capacity was estimated at 50 tons a day, but since its production in six months was under 4,000 tons, it was not worked to capacity. *Official Records,* Ser. III, V, 537-38.

73. *Official Records,* Ser. III, V, 26-28.

74. *Ibid.*, pp. 40-42.

75. *Ibid.*, pp. 234-35.

76. *Ibid.*, pp. 355-56.

77. *Ibid.*, pp. 296, 298-99, 595.

78. *Ibid.*, pp. 596, 599.

79. *Ibid.*, p. 357.

80. *Ibid.*, p. 528.

81. *McCallum Report,* p. 26.

82. *Official Records,* Ser. III, V, 598.

83. *Ibid.*, pp. 47, 99-101.

84. *McCallum Report,* p. 35.

CHAPTER XIV

1. *19th Annual Report . . . of the Pennsylvania Railroad . . . Feb. 20, 1866,* p. 32.

2. See the various annual reports of the Illinois Central.

3. Unless otherwise noted, the figures in this section are taken from the annual reports. Other instances: Central Railroad of New Jersey, 1861, 27,000 troops, about 7 per cent of its 400,000 passengers; Philadelphia, Wilmington, and Baltimore, 1861, 154,303 troops, about 25 per cent of its 629,098 passengers; Chicago and Rock Island, 1861, 10,384 troops, about 7 per cent of its 150,000 passengers; in 1865, 52,749 troops, about 11 per cent of its 463,866 passengers.

4. Other increases in passenger business: Philadelphia, Wilmington, and Baltimore, 629,000 to 1,400,000; New Jersey Railroad, 2,300,000 to 3,700,000; Chicago, Burlington, and Quincy, 273,000 (1862) to 842,000; Boston and Maine, 1,800,000 to 2,600,000; Boston and Worcester, 1,400,000 to 2,100,000 (1864); New York and New Haven, 1,000,000 to 1,800,000.

5. Similarly, the Northern Central, 459,000 to 745,000 (1864); Chicago and Rock Island, 283,000 to 454,000; Chicago, Burlington, and Quincy, 539,000 to 800,000; Western Railroad (Massachusetts), 508,000 to 694,000; New York and New Haven, 55,000 to 168,000.

6. Similarly, the New York Central could increase its engines only from 215 to 258, the Illinois Central from 112 to 133 (1864), and the New York and New Haven from 32 to 33.

7. Of course the early part of this expanded business served merely to absorb the part of the railroad plant unused since the panic of 1857.

8. *American Railroad Journal*, March 8, 1862; *United States Railroad and Mining Register*, March 8, 1862.

9. Sir Morton Peto, traveling in the United States in 1865, found that through traffic on the New York Central, the Pennsylvania, and the Erie was about 65 per cent of their total business. Peto, *op. cit.*, p. 290. See Chapter I for the contrast at the beginning of the war.

10. This was part of Haupt's work in Virginia. See also Charles B. George, *Forty Years on the Rail*, p. 121.

11. *American Railway Review*, May 29, 1862.

12. Katherine P. Wormeley, *The Other Side of War with the Army of the Potomac*, p. 129.

13. Wormeley, *The United States Sanitary Commission*, p. 287.

14. U. S. Sanitary Commission, Bulletin 9, March 1, 1864, p. 260; Wormeley, *The U. S. Sanitary Commission*, p. 174.

15. Sanitary Commission, Bulletin 9, p. 259.

16. *Ibid.*, p. 260.

17. *Ibid.*, pp. 261-62; Wormeley, *The U. S. Sanitary Commission*, p. 288.

18. Sanitary Commission, Bulletin 9, 260, 262; Wormeley, *The U. S. Sanitary Commission*, p. 288. A U. S. Army hospital car exhibited at the Chicago Railroad Fair in 1948 had 36 bunks in the main ward, 18 on each side arranged in three tiers. Further bunks at the end of the car could accommodate hospital personnel or extra patients.

19. Sanitary Commission, Bulletin 9, p. 259.

20. *Ibid.*, Bulletin No. 19, Aug. 1, 1864, pp. 599-600.

21. *Ibid.*, Bulletin No. 9, p. 261; Pratt, *op. cit.*, p. 90.

22. Plum, *op. cit.*, II, 176-77.

23. Sanitary Commission, Bulletin 25, Nov. 1, 1864, p. 797. The L & N hospital train transported 11,880 cases through December, 1863. Bulletin 9, *op. cit.*, p. 261.

24. *Ibid.*, Bulletin 23, Oct. 1, 1864, p. 723. This was some improvement over the springless boxcars.

25. Wormeley, *The U. S. Sanitary Commission*, pp. 124-45.

26. *Ibid.*, p. 288; Pratt, *op cit.*, p. 89. The government met most of the expense in fitting out the hospital cars (Sanitary Commission, Bulletin 31, Feb. 1, 1865); The Sanitary Commission spent $9,-275.79 on them (New York *Times,* Nov. 23, 1865).

27. *American Railroad Journal,* Oct. 18, 1862.

28. Winnifred K. Mackay, "Philadelphia during the Civil War, 1861-1865," *Pennsylvania Magazine of History and Biography,* (Jan., 1946), p. 15; John T. Scharf and Thompson Westcott, *History of Philadelphia, 1609-1884,* p. 764.

29. R. R. Zell, in "The Raid into Pennsylvania," *Confederate Veteran,* XXVIII, no. 7, (July, 1920), 261, tells of a raid in which he took part.

30. *American Railway Review,* April 10, 1862.

31. *American Railway Review,* March 13, 1862 (from Chicago *Tribune*).

32. *American Railroad Journal,* May 9, 1863.

33. Clark E. Carr, *The Railway Mail Service,* p. 11.

34. *History of the Railway Mail Service,* pp. 81-83; William H. Stannett, comp., *Yesterday and Today, a History of the Chicago and North Western Railway System,* pp. 44-45, gives 1859 as the date.

35. *History of the Railway Mail Service,* p. 83. One of the originators was the assistant postmaster at Chicago, George B. Armstrong. Carr, *op. cit.,* pp. 12-14.

36. *History of the Railway Mail Service,* pp. 83, 86, 160. There was similar service from New York to Boston; see *New York and New Haven Railroad . . . Annual Report . . . May, 1865,* p. 10.

37. *History of the Railway Mail Service,* p. 154.

38. *Ibid.,* p. 205.

39. The name was suggested by A. N. Zevely; *ibid.,* p. 147.

40. Charles E. Fisher, "The Lehigh Valley Railroad," Rail-

way and Locomotive Historical Society, Bulletin 42, Feb., 1937, pp. 14, 53.

41. *American Railway Times,* Aug. 13, 1864.
42. May 24, 1865, was the date; *ibid.,* June 17, 1865.
43. *American Railway Review,* April 10, 1862.
44. *American Railroad Journal,* Feb. 23, 1861, March 8, 1862.
45. A. K. McClure, *Old Times Notes of Pennsylvania,* I, 152-53.

BIBLIOGRAPHY

PRIMARY SOURCES

Edwin W. Stanton Papers, Library of Congress.

1. GENERAL

Ashcroft's Railway Directory, 1862, 1864, 1865.
Barry, Joseph, The Strange Story of Harper's Ferry. Martinsburg, W. Va., 1903.
Barry, Patrick, Over the Atlantic and Great Western Railway. London, 1866.
Bates, David H., Lincoln in the Telegraph Office. New York, 1907.
Benjamin, Charles F., "Recollections of Secretary Stanton," Century Magazine, XXXIII, March, 1887.
Brown, George W., Baltimore and the 19th of April 1861. Baltimore, 1887. Johns Hopkins University Studies in History and Political Science, extra Vol. III.
Considerations upon the Question Whether Congress Should Authorize a New Railroad between Washington and New York. Washington, 1863.
Cox, Jacob D., The March to the Sea. New York, 1882.
A Defence of New Jersey in Relation to the Camden and Amboy Railroad and Its Privileges. Washington, 1864.
Dodge, Grenville M., How We Built the Union Pacific Railway. Council Bluffs, Iowa, no date.
"Effect of Secession upon the Commercial Relations between the North and South, and upon Each Section." New York Times. New York, 1861.
Felton, Samuel M., Impolicy of Building Another Railroad between Washington and New York. Philadelphia, 1864.
Flint, Henry M., The Railroads of the United States. Philadelphia, 1868.
Garrett, John W., Address to the Board of Directors of the Baltimore and Ohio Railroad, December, 1868. Baltimore, 1868.

George, Charles B., Forty Years on the Rail. Chicago, 1887.

Grant, U. S., Personal Memoirs. New York, 1866.

Haupt, Herman, Reminiscences. Milwaukee, 1901.

Johnson, Robert U., and Clarence C. Buel, eds., Battles and Leaders of the Civil War. New York, 1884, 1887, 1888.

Livermore, Mary A., My Story of the War. Hartford, 1889.

McClure, A. K., Old Time Notes of Pennsylvania. Philadelphia, 1905.

McPherson, Edward, The Political History of the United States of America during the Great Rebellion. Washington, 1864.

Moss, Lemuel, Annals of the United States Christian Commission. Philadelphia, 1868.

Nicolay, John G., and John Hay, Abraham Lincoln, a History. New York, 1890.

Ohio and Mississippi Railroad, Documents 3 and 4. Undated.

Palmer, William H., Letters, 1853-1868, comp. by Isaac H. Clothier. Philadelphia, 1906.

Parker, Joel, Governor of New Jersey, Message to the Legislature in Relation to the Bill Pending Before U. S. House of Representatives Concerning the Camden and Atlantic Railroad Company and the Raritan and Delaware Bay Railroad Company. Trenton, 1864.

Peto, Sir Samuel M., The Resources and Prospects of America Ascertained during a Visit to the States in the Autumn of 1865. London and New York, 1866.

Pittenger, William, Daring and Suffering: a History of the Andrews Raid into Georgia, 1862. 1887.

Plum, William R., The Military Telegraph during the Civil War in the United States. Chicago, 1882.

Poor, Henry V., Railroad Manual of the United States. 1868.

Porter, Fitz John, Narrative of the Services of the Fifth Army Corps in 1862 in Northern Virginia. Morristown, N. J., 1878.

Porter, W. E., "Keeping the B & O in Repair in War Time was a Task for Hercules," Book of the Royal Blue, June, 1907.

Richardson, James D., A Compilation of Messages and Papers of the Presidents, 1789-1907. Washington, 1908.

Shall the Extension or Recreating of the Camden and Amboy Railroad Monopoly Be Permitted by the People of New Jersey and Made Perpetual? 1864.

Sherman, William T., Memoirs. New York, 1891.

Statement Made by the Railroad Companies Owning the Lines between Washington and New York to the Postmaster General. Washington, 1863.

Stockton, Richard F., Defense of the System of Internal Improvements of the State of New Jersey. Philadelphia, 1864.

Sumner, Charles, Senator from Massachusetts, "Railroad Usurpation of New Jersey." Speech in the Senate, Feb. 14, 1865.

United States Christian Commission for the Army and Navy, 2nd Annual Report. Philadelphia, 1864.

United States Sanitary Commission, Bulletins. Vols. I-III, 1864-1865.

Wormeley, Katherine P., The Other Side of War with the Army of the Potomac. Boston, 1889.

—— The U. S. Sanitary Commission. Boston, 1863.

Zell, Robert R., "The Raid into Pennsylvania—the First Armored Train," *Confederate Veteran*, XXVIII, No. 7, July, 1920.

2. PERIODICALS AND NEWSPAPERS

American Railroad Journal, 1861-1865.

American Railway Review, January-June, 1861; January-June, 1862.

American Railway Times, 1861-1865.

Army and Navy Journal, June 11, 1864; April 15, 1865; March 3, 1866.

The Merchants' Magazine and Commercial Review, 1861-1865.

New York *Times*, 1861-1865; Dec. 28, 1878; Dec. 15, 1905.

United States Railroad and Mining Register, 1861-1865.

3. OFFICIAL GOVERNMENT DOCUMENTS

Census Board, Preliminary Report on the Eighth Census, 1860, Joseph C. G. Kennedy, superintendent. Washington, 1862.

—— Ninth Census of the United States, Statistics of Population. Washington, 1872.

Congressional Globe, 36th Congress, 1st Session; 36th Congress, 2nd Session; 37th Congress, 1st Session; 37th Congress, 2nd Session.

House of Representatives, Executive Document No. 1, 39th Congress, 1st Session (final report of D. C. McCallum).

—— Executive Document No. 79, 37th Congress, 2nd Session (letter of John W. Garrett, February 9, 1862).

—— Report No. 31, March 9, 1864, 38th Congress, 1st Session (Deming report on Raritan and Delaware Bay Railroad).

History of the Railway Mail Service. Washington, 1885.

United States Statutes at Large, XII.

U. S. War Department, Military Railroads, Order Book of General Orders, Instructions, and Reports. Cited as *Order Book.*

War of the Rebellion, The: a Compilation of the Official Records of the Union and Confederate Armies. Washington, 1899. Cited as *Official Records.*

4. RAILROAD REPORTS (DATES REFER TO FISCAL YEARS)

Atlantic and Great Western Railway, 1863-1864 (December 31).

Baltimore and Ohio Railroad, 1861-1865 (September 30).

Boston and Maine Railroad, 1861-1865 (May 31).

Boston and Worcester Railroad, 1861-1865 (April 30).

Central Railroad of New Jersey, 1861-1865 (December 31).

Chicago and North Western Railway, 1862-1863, 1865 (May 31).

Chicago and Rock Island Railroad, 1862, 1865, (March 31).

Cleveland and Pittsburgh Railroad, 1862, 1864-1865, (November 30).

Cleveland and Toledo Railroad, 1865 (April 30).

Erie Railway, 1862-1865 (December 31).

Illinois Central Railroad, 1861-1865 (December 31).

Little Miami Railroad and Columbus and Xenia Railroad, 1864 (November 30).

Louisville, New Albany, and Chicago Railroad, 1865 (October 1).

Michigan Central Railroad, 1861-1865 (May 31).

Michigan Southern and Northern Indiana Railroad, 1861-1865 (February 28).

Milwaukee and Prairie du Chien Railway, 1861-1862, 1864-1865 (December 31).

New Jersey, Annual Reports of the Railroad and Canal Companies of the State of, for the Year 1865.

New Jersey Railroad and Transportation Company, 1860-1861, 1863, 1865 (December 31).

New York and New Haven Railroad, 1862-1866 (March 31).

New York Central Railroad, 1861-1865 (September 30).
Northern Central Railway, 1861-1865 (December 31).
Pennsylvania, Reports of the Several Railroad Companies of, Communicated by the Auditor General to the Legislature, January 22, 1863.
Pennsylvania Railroad, 1860-1865 (December 31).
Philadelphia and Reading Railroad, 1861-1862 (November 30).
Philadelphia, Wilmington, and Baltimore Railroad, 1861-1865 (October 31).
Pittsburgh, Ft. Wayne, and Chicago Railroad, 1861 (December 31).
Pittsburgh, Ft. Wayne, and Chicago Railway, 1862-1865 (December 31).
Portland, Saco, and Portsmouth Railroad, 1863 (May 31).
Western Railroad, 1861-1863, 1865 (December 31).

SECONDARY SOURCES

Ambler, Charles H., A History of Transportation in the Ohio Valley. Glendale, Cal., 1932.
Bacon, E. L., "How Railroads Helped Save the Union," *The Railroad Man's Magazine*, IX, July, 1909.
Barringer, Graham A., "The Influence of Railroad Transportation on the Civil War," *Indiana University Studies in American History Dedicated to James Albert Woodburn*, Vol. XII, Nos. 66-68, 1925.
Barton, Roger A., "The Camden and Amboy Railroad Monopoly," *Proceedings of New Jersey Historical Society*, n.s., XII, No. 4, October, 1927.
Bradlee, F. B. C., Blockade Running during the Civil War. Vols. 61 and 62 of Historical Collection of the Essex Institute. Boston, 1925.
Brownson, Howard G., History of the Illinois Central Railroad to 1870. University of Illinois Studies in the Social Sciences, IV, September to December, 1915.
"Camden and Amboy Railroad, The," *North American Review*, April, 1867.
Campbell, E. G., "The United States Military Railroads, 1862-1865," *Journal of the American Military History Foundation*, Vol. II, spring, 1938.

Carr, Clark E., The Railway Mail Service, Its Origin and Development. Chicago, 1909.

Century of Progress, A: History of the Delaware and Hudson Co., 1823-1923. Albany, 1925.

Cotterill, Robert S., "The Louisville and Nashville Railroad," *American Historical Review,* Vol. XXIX, July, 1924.

Coulter, E. Merton, "Commercial Intercourse with the Confederacy in the Mississippi Valley, 1861-1865," *Mississippi Valley Historical Review,* Vol. V, March, 1919.

Derleth, August, The Milwaukee Road. New York, 1948.

Ennis, Riley F., "General Sherman on Supply vs. Mobility," *Infantry Journal,* Vol. XXXVII, September, 1930.

Fish, Carl R., The American Civil War. New York, 1937.

—— "The Northern Railroads, 1861," *American Historical Review,* Vol. XXII, July, 1917.

Fisher, Charles E., "The Chicago, Burlington, and Quincy Railroad," *Bulletin No. 24, Railway and Locomotive Historical Society,* March, 1931.

—— "The Galena and Chicago Union Railroad," *Bulletin No. 27, Railway and Locomotive Historical Society,* March, 1932.

—— "The Lehigh Valley Railroad," *Bulletin No. 42, Railway and Locomotive Historical Society,* February, 1937.

—— "The Michigan Central Railroad," *Bulletin No. 19, Railway and Locomotive Historical Society,* September, 1929.

—— "The Philadelphia, Wilmington, and Baltimore Railroad Co.," *Bulletin No. 21, Railway and Locomotive Historical Society,* March, 1930.

Fite, Emerson D., "The Agricultural Development of the West during the Civil War," in *Quarterly Journal of Economics,* Vol. XX, February, 1906.

—— "The Canal and the Railroad from 1861 to 1865," *Yale Review,* Vol. XV, August, 1906.

—— Social and Industrial Conditions in the North during the Civil War. New York, 1910.

Hall, Clayton C., ed., Baltimore, Its History and Its People. New York and Chicago, 1912.

Haney, Lewis H., A Congressional History of Railways in the United States, 1850-1877. Bulletin No. 342, University of Wisconsin, Economic and Political Science Series, VI, No. 1, 1-336, 1910.

Hargrave, Frank F., A Pioneer Indiana Railroad. Indianapolis, 1932.

Haydon, F. Stansbury, "Confederate Battery at Jacksonville, Florida, March 1863, Not the First Use of Railway Ordnance in the United States," *Journal of the American Military History Foundation*, Vol. II, spring, 1938.

Hendrick, Burton J., The Life of Andrew Carnegie. Garden City, 1932.

Henry, Robert S., "Railroads and the Confederacy," *Bulletin No. 40, Railway and Locomotive Historical Society*, May, 1936.

—— This Fascinating Railroad Business. New York and Indianapolis, 1942.

—— Trains. Indianapolis, 1943.

Herr, Kincaid A., The Louisville and Nashville Railroad, 1850-1942. Louisville, 1943.

Hulbert, Archer B., The Paths of Inland Commerce. New Haven, 1921.

Hungerford, Edward, Men and Iron, the History of the New York Central. New York, 1938.

—— Men of Erie. New York, 1946.

—— The Story of the Baltimore and Ohio Railroad, 1827-1927. New York and London, 1928.

—— Transport for War. New York, 1943.

In Memoriam—General Lewis Baldwin Parsons. 1908.

Johnson, Emory R., American Railway Transportation. New York and London, 1912.

Kamm, Samuel R., The Civil War Career of Thomas A. Scott. Philadelphia, 1940.

Kerr, John L., The Story of a Southern Carrier, the Louisville and Nashville. New York, 1933.

Killough, Edward M., History of the Western Maryland Railroad Company. Baltimore, 1940.

Kutz, Charles R., War on Wheels, the Evolution of an Idea. Harrisburg, 1940.

Mackay, Winnifred K., "Philadelphia during the Civil War, 1861-

1865," *Pennsylvania Magazine of History and Biography*, January, 1946.

McMaster, John B., A History of the People of the United States during Lincoln's Administration. New York and London, 1927.

Markham, Charles R., "The Illinois Central System," *Shipper and Carrier*, Vol. VI, January, 1925.

Moody, John, The Railroad Builders. New Haven, 1921.

Murphy, Hermon K., "The Northern Railroads and the Civil War," *Mississippi Valley Historical Review*, Vol. V, December, 1918.

Overton, Richard C., Burlington West. Cambridge, Mass., 1941.

Paris, Comte de, History of the Civil War in America. Philadelphia, 1875.

Pearson, Henry G., An American Railroad Builder, John Murray Forbes. Boston and New York, 1911.

Perkins, Jacob R., Trails, Rails, and War: the Life of General G. M. Dodge. Indianapolis, 1929.

Pratt, Edwin A., The Rise of Rail Power in War and Conquest, 1833-1914. London, 1915.

Quiett, G. C., They Built the West. New York, 1934.

Railroad Gazette, Dec. 22, 1905; Jan. 4, 1907; Jan. 11, 1907.

"Use of Railroads in War an American Development, The," *Railway Age Gazette*, June 22, 1917.

Ramsdell, Charles W., "The Confederate Government and the Railroads," *American Historical Review*, Vol. XXII, July, 1917.

Randall, James G., Constitutional Problems under Lincoln. New York, 1926.

Rhodes, James F., History of the Civil War, 1861-1865. New York, 1930.

Riegel, Robert E., "Federal Operation of Southern Railroads during the Civil War," *Mississippi Valley Historical Review*, Vol. IX, 1922.

—— "The Missouri Pacific Railroad to 1879," *Missouri Historical Review*, Vol. XVIII, 1923.

Ripley, William Z., ed., Railway Problems. Boston, 1907.

Roseboom, Eugene H., The Civil War Era, 1850-1873. Columbus, 1944. Vol. IV of *History of the State of Ohio*, ed. by Carl Wittke.

Scharf, John T., History of Baltimore City and County from the Earliest Period to the Present Day. Philadelphia, 1881.

Scharf, John T., and Thompson Westcott, History of Philadelphia, 1609-1884. Philadelphia, 1884.

Schotter, H. W., The Growth and Development of the Pennsylvania Railroad Company. Philadelphia, 1927.

Shannon, Frederick A., Organization and Administration of the Union Army, 1861-1865. Cleveland, 1928.

Shippee, Lester B., "The First Railroad between the Mississippi and Lake Superior," Mississippi Valley Historical Review, Vol. V, September, 1918.

Sillcox, Lewis K., Safety in Early American Railway Operation, 1853-1871. Princeton, 1936.

Stannett, William H., comp., Yesterday and Today, a History of the Chicago and North Western System. Chicago, 1910.

Starr, John W., Jr., Lincoln and the Railroads. New York, 1927.

Stearns, F. P., "Vanderbilt and Lincoln," New England Magazine, Vol. XL, March, 1909.

Stephens, George W., "Some Aspects of Early Intersectional Rivalry for the Commerce of the Upper Mississippi Valley," Washington University Studies, Vol. X, No. 2, Humanistic Series, April, 1923.

Summers, Festus P., The Baltimore and Ohio in the Civil War. New York, 1939.

Swantner, Eva, "Military Railroads during the Civil War," The Military Engineer, Vol. XXI, No. 118, July-August, 1929; No. 119, September-October, 1929; No. 120, November-December, 1929; No. 121, January-February, 1930.

Taylor, Frank H., Philadelphia in the Civil War, 1861-1865. Philadelphia, 1913.

Thompson, Slason, Short History of American Railways. Chicago, 1925.

Trottman, Nelson, History of the Union Pacific. New York, 1923.

Van Metre, T. W., Trains, Tracks, and Travel. New York, 1939.

Von den Steinen, Karl A., "Military Bridging in the American Civil War," The Mines Magazine, November-December, 1938.

Watkins, John E., The Camden and Amboy Railroad, Origin and Early History. Undated address delivered at Bordentown, N. J.

Wilson, William B., History of the Pennsylvania Railroad Company. Philadelphia, 1899.

INDEX